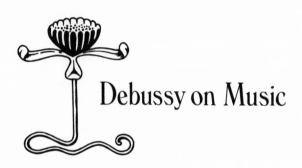

Debussy on Music

Debussy on Music

The critical writings of the great
French composer Claude Debussy
collected and introduced
by François Lesure,
translated and edited by
Richard Langham Smith

Alfred A. Knopf
New York   1977

THIS IS A BORZOI BOOK
PUBLISHED BY ALFRED A. KNOPF, INC.

English translation and translator's introduction Copyright © 1977
Martin Secker & Warburg Ltd and Alfred A. Knopf, Inc.

All rights reserved under International and Pan-American Copyright Conventions.
Published in the United States by Alfred A. Knopf, Inc., New York,
and simultaneously in Canada by Random House of Canada Limited, Toronto.
Distributed by Random House, Inc., New York. Originally published in France
as *Monsieur Croche et autres écrits* by Editions Gallimard, Paris.
Copyright © 1971 by Éditions Gallimard.

Library of Congress Cataloging in Publication Data

Debussy, Claude, 1862–1918. Debussy on music.

Translation of Monsieur Croche et autres écrits.
Bibliography: p.
Includes index.
1. Music—Addresses, essays, lectures. I. Title.
ML410.D28A333   780'.8   76–13717
ISBN 0–394–48120–8

Manufactured in the United States of America
First American Edition

Contents

Translator's Acknowledgments

With a translation of the nature of the present collection, assistance comes from many sources. A chance reference may illuminate an obscurity or the source of a quotation. First acknowledgments must be to François Lesure, not only for providing the splendid French edition of Debussy's writings on music, but also for answering my queries. I am deeply grateful to the late Edward Lockspeiser for our many conversations on the subject of Debussy, and for his guidance in the early stages of the book. Irreplaceable help was given by the late Dr. Lucy Ruinen of the University of Amsterdam, and by several colleagues in the French Department of the University of Lancaster, notably Dr. Susan Horrex. For his advice on Debussy's reference to the Futurists, I am indebted to Professor Michael Kirby. Most useful advice has been proffered all along by Sophia Macindoe of Secker & Warburg and by Mrs. Herta Ryder of Hughes Massie, and last, but in no way least, by my wife.

R.L.S.

Foreword

DEVOTEES of Debussy's music who have come across the more cavalier phrases of the composer's music criticism will no doubt have been taken aback at his seemingly inconsistent gaucherie, marring the widely held but oversimplified view of Debussy the refined sensualist, the lover of cats, luxurious wall hangings, Japanese prints, and women with green eyes. How could the composer of *Prélude à l'après-midi d'un faune,* a piece that startled the musical world of the nineties with its luminescent orchestral color and breathtaking sensuality, or the composer of *Pelléas,* that most moving opera of the half-lights, be so flippant, so casual and boorish when faced with the task of expressing his artistic ideas in words?

"There is more to be gained by seeing the sun rise than by hearing the *Pastoral* Symphony," he had written to complement his oft-quoted "Nothing is more musical than a sunset," and in 1914, writing of Gabriel Pierné's interpretation of the same symphony, he added that "one could almost smell the stables." To take one further example, the Opéra is scurrilously dismissed as a place "whose business is noise: those who have paid for it call it music. Don't believe them."

Such odd phrases, out of context, hardly approach the heart of Debussy's criticism. Was it all like this—a mixture of fashionable journalistic knifing with a degree of turn-of-the-century romanticism of the kind that calls sounds colors and colors smells? For the answer, the reader must judge for himself, but to do this he will need more than the two English editions previously available—the unchronological *Monsieur Croche, antidilettante* and Léon Vallas's *The Theories of Claude Debussy.* Until François Lesure's publication of the collected articles, *Monsieur Croche et autres écrits*—on which the present edition is based—the complete picture was available only to those with the time and patience to delve back into a number of now-forgotten periodicals.

Central to an understanding of Debussy's criticism is the character of M. Croche himself, the alter ego created by Debussy to voice some of his more extreme ideas, and the title under which, some years after his death, a selection of the composer's articles was printed. First introduced in the sixth article Debussy published during his spell on *La Revue blanche,* M. Croche cuts a striking figure:

> M. Croche was short and wizened. His gestures were visibly cultivated for the purpose of making points in metaphysical discussions, and you would best imagine his manner if you were to think of a jockey. . . . His overall manner was sharp as a razor and he spoke very softly and never laughed. Sometimes he would underline his meaning with a silent smile, which would begin at his nose and gradually spread out in wrinkles all over his face—as if someone had thrown a pebble into some calm pool. It would last for ages and was quite intolerable.

Several Debussy scholars have commented upon the similarity between Debussy's M. Croche and the character of M. Teste in Paul Valéry's *La Soirée avec Monsieur Teste,* dating from 1896.[1] In his preface François Lesure brings to light a letter of Valéry showing that the creator of M. Teste had himself noticed Debussy's reworking of his *Soirée avec Monsieur Teste* in the form of music criticism. From the form of a dialogue between a narrator and M. Teste, the similarities between the two pieces of writing are apparent. Even the names of the two characters, monosyllabic and having doubly significant meanings,

---

[1] Based on an intuitive recognition of the similarities between the two characters, Edward Lockspeiser noticed that Debussy was associated with Valéry just at the time when *Monsieur Teste* had been written, their names appearing together on the cover of a new literary review, *Le Centaure.* He also established that the root of Debussy's attraction to *Monsieur Teste* lay in its openly admitted debt to Poe, whose writings Debussy was already considering as the basis for a piece. See Chapter 3, "M. Croche and M. Teste," in E. Lockspeiser's *Debussy, His Life and Mind,* vol. 2 (London, 1965).

are similar. M. Croche is "Mr. Quaver," but *croche* also means "bent or hooked," and *avoir les mains croches* means "to be close-fisted." M. Teste was no doubt so named because of the dual meaning of Teste, which is the old French spelling of *tête,* "head," but also means "spectator": "He watches himself, he maneuvers, he is unwilling to be maneuvered," wrote Valéry. Physically, and in character, the two are strikingly similar; compare the following description of M. Teste with Debussy's M. Croche: ". . . perhaps forty years old. His speech was extraordinarily rapid and his voice quiet. Everything about him was fading, his eyes, his hands. . . . When he spoke, he never raised an arm or a finger: he had killed his marionette."

More important than external similarites, however, are the overlapping ideals of the two writers, for although M. Croche makes only a sporadic appearance, the ideals he symbolizes—drawn from Valéry's M. Teste—underlie Debussy's whole approach to criticism. What was it in M. Teste that fired Debussy's imagination? In Valéry's dialogue, as in Debussy's *Entretien avec Monsieur Croche,* there is really but one person, an alter ego: the process is one of self-discovery, a coming to terms with his own intellectual processes. A glance at Valéry's own preface to the second English translation of *Monsieur Teste* (1925) explains this quest for self-knowledge:

"I was affected with the acute malady of precision. I was straining toward the extreme of the reckless desire to understand, seeking in myself the critical limits of my powers of attention." Rejecting the limits imposed on intellectual processes by the "impure" forms of poetry, literature, and philosophy, Valéry goes on to explain how he had made himself "an inner island" and "spent his time exploring it and fortifying it."

From his very first article, long before the introduction of the character of M. Croche, Debussy explains his own search for a purified cricitism—"my own sincere impressions." Just as Valéry had in *Monsieur Teste* rejected other writings—"he had burned his books"—M. Croche no longer listened to the music of the past. Debussy desired an immunity from "parasite aesthetics." Another crucial issue on which both M. Teste and M. Croche feel alike is the one of glory (in the sense of public recognition) coming too easily. Genius, according to Teste, should be reclusive, and this is an idea many times reiterated by Debussy. It is only to oneself that one is ultimately responsible—a related idea shared by the two figures. "If I had gone on as most men do," says M. Teste, "not only would I have believed myself their superior, but would have seemed so. I have preferred myself." M. Croche is likewise obsessed with the conflict between success and the constant need to improve:

> All these question marks were posed, I fear, by a kind of childish egotism and the need to rid oneself at all costs of an idea which has been in one's head for too long. But all this served only as a thin disguise for that stupid obsession with trying to prove oneself superior to everyone else: a preoccupation which never needed much effort unless it was combined with a desire to better oneself. The alchemy of that is far more complex, for it requires the sacrifice of one's whole precious little personality. High ideals! and quite useless in the end. Moreover, trying to persuade everybody else that one really is superior means a considerable amount of time wasted in manifestation of the fact or endless self-propaganda.

Debussy's reworking of *Monsieur Teste* is little more than pastiche, and it was a pastiche his limited literary ability was unable to sustain. Nor did his job as a critic really require him to sustain such high ideals, and he was content to lapse into the altogether lighter journalistic style more usually to be found in music columns—in some ways a style in which he was more at home. Nonetheless, the character of M. Croche, and certainly his ideals of purity, remained in the back of Debussy's mind for many years, and long after Debussy had abandoned his mouthpiece character, echoes of M. Croche's stern aesthetics can be discerned in Debussy's columns. Purity was an ideal that shot through the whole of the Debussian aesthetic, not only of his ideals of criticism, but also in his approach to composition.

The present edition is arranged as a chronological sequence of all Debussy's own writings, with a selection of the more interesting journalistic interviews incorporated into the body of primary material. These secondary sources—rendered a little suspect by journalistic intervention—will need to be distinguished by the serious scholar, for whom the French Ur-text will of course be a necessity. In all cases the titles of these contain the word "interview," and so may be clearly distinguished. Three interviews not included in the French edition have been added here: an interview in *Harper's Weekly* of 1908; one from the Hungarian *Azest,* translated from the French translation unearthed by François Lesure and kindly sent to me by Mme G. Cobb of the Centre de Documentation Claude Debussy; and a third from the Philadelphia music magazine *The Etude.* For those wishing to collect the complete interviews (as far as they have been rediscovered), these three should be added to those indexed in the French edition.

More important, for the sake of completeness, is the inclusion of all the articles that have not before been rendered in English in any previous edition. Into this category come the important late series of articles from the monthly bulletin of the Société Internationale de Musique (the *SIM*) here translated for the first time. By providing an insight into the changing ideas of the composer, now aware of the powerful forces of both Stravinsky and Schönberg, they complete our perspective on Debussy's taste as shown through his criticism.

My text has followed that of *Monsieur Croche et autres écrits,* but in one or two minor details I have found the original text as printed in the magazines at slight variance with that of the Gallimard collection. For example, phrases are omitted from the *Revue blanche* articles of 1 and 15 May 1901. In translation these have silently been restored.

Some names, evidently celebrated in Debussy's own day, have long since passed out of circulation: rather than clutter the text with asterisks it has been decided to append a list of brief notes on some of the lesser-known figures. In the absence of a *Grove's* for the musicians, and a *Talvert et Place* for the literary figures, it is hoped that this may provide a serviceable *aide-mémoire.*

For the English reader the book should fulfill a very different function from the French scholar's Ur-text, and the text has been amplified with material that fills in the background to Debussy's life as a critic and certain of the ideas he touches upon. Those searching for a clear picture of the composer's artistic tastes will frequently be frustrated: so much frivolity to mask Debussy's true feelings; stylistically dense passages that border on obscurity. Yet, reading between the lines, some of the key ideas to a full understanding of Debussy's thought are to be found, and it is hoped that the chapter introductions and footnotes will enable the reader to focus upon these and participate in the then-prevalent climate of criticism that allowed caustic cruelty, light-hearted wordplay, and serious philosophical discussion to co-exist as contented bedfellows within the same paragraph. This done, the articles of Debussy form a unique document offering the reader a viewpoint on one of the most fascinating periods in the musical life of Paris—the viewpoint of one of her most important and radical composers.

RICHARD LANGHAM SMITH

Introduction

READERS of *Monsieur Croche, antidilettante*[1] have every reason to believe that they have before them an authoritative work, written by Debussy to expound his artistic ideas. There is no preface, no editor's note, no date to be found in the twenty-five chapters to explain that the book is a selection, a composite collection of articles that represents scarcely one half the composer's critical works. Before its publication, certain of those intimate with Debussy lamented his intervention in the makeup of the collection: G. Jean-Aubry estimated that the publication of the original articles, together with their dates, would give "a truer image of his ideas at the different stages of his life."[2] Shortly after the appearance of *Monsieur Croche*, Emile Vuillermoz expressed a similar idea: "Some modest editor, mindful of historic exactitude, faced with the same task would perhaps have given us a richer and more colorful collection than that which we owe to the author's own initiative."[3]

Fifty years later, there is no reason to prevent a restoration of every aspect of his thought. The important historical position of Debussy's work has been increasingly realized, and studies devoted to him have reached the point where a corpus of his complete writings has become a necessity.[4] To do this it has been necessary to dispense with the

[1] This earlier edition of a selection of Debussy's articles has been available in English since 1927 (*Three Classics in the Aesthetic of Music* [New York, 1962]).

[2] *Revue musicale*, Debussy, 1 December 1920 (pp. 191–2).

[3] *Le Temps*, 16 December 1921.

[4] The work of Léon Vallas, *Les Idées de Claude Debussy*, published in 1927 and translated into English in 1929, attempted to reconstruct the musical lean-

order of *Monsieur Croche.* In presenting Debussy's articles in strictly chronological order, without omissions or cuts, I have found myself leaving the composer responsible for certain repetitions and reproducing certain rather trite sections written in a careless way or in haste, but this is scarcely avoidable in a collection of this sort. As compared with the former publication, this presentation will certainly enrich our knowledge of the wide-ranging opinions he held, both on lesser-known pieces and minor figures, and help us to define his conception of music.

Briefly, let us go over his career as a critic. His first article appeared in *La Revue blanche* of 1 April 1901, a month before Albert Carré promised in writing that *Pelléas* would be performed at the Opéra-Comique. Among the circle of young contributors, Debussy was not lacking in friends: Ferdinand Hérold, Léon Blum, Pierre Quillard, and above all Pierre Louÿs, at whose home the Natansons, founders of *La Revue blanche,* had heard extracts from *Pelléas* performed at the piano by the composer himself. The music columns of *La Revue blanche* had not previously been noted for either continuity or originality—the Wagnerian music columnist Alfred Ernst and André Corneau, critic of *Le Matin* and *Le Français,* succeeded each other between 1892 and 1901—so the appearance of Debussy on the team was much more in line with the style of this dynamic and advanced review.

M. Croche does not make his appearance until the issue of 1 July. It is probable that few readers immediately recognized the

---

ings of the composer by juxtaposing random fragments of his articles without taking their chronology into account. Such a method does not facilitate a return to the original texts (still more difficult in translation) and it dangerously divorces them from their context. Apart from Vallas's book, certain other studies devoted to Debussy's critical work may be mentioned: M. D. Calvocoressi, "Claude Debussy critique" (*La Renaissance latine,* 15 December 1902); M. Pincherle, "Claude Debussy écrivain" (*L'Echo musical,* November 1919); G. Jean-Aubry, "L'Oeuvre critique de Debussy" (*Revue musicale,* 1 December 1920); John G. Palache, "Debussy as Critic" (*Musical Quarterly,* July 1924); L. Vallas, "Debussy critique musical" (*Nouvelle revue musicale,* January 1925); Jean Chantavoine, "Les Ecrits de Claude Debussy" (*Le Mênestrel,* 7 January 1927); F. Onnen, *Debussy als criticus en essayist* (in Dutch), The Hague, 1946; Edward Lockspeiser, *Debussy: His Life and Mind,* 1965 (vol. 2, chapter 3, "M. Croche and M. Teste").

model who had inspired this character. Certainly one of the first to react was Paul Valéry, who wrote at once to his friend Pierre Louÿs:

> I now have the pleasure of reading my old works in the form of music criticism. I must confess I'd never have foreseen this outcome. I don't know if you've read *Entretien avec Monsieur Croche,* but C.A.D. has certainly read *La Soirée avec Monsieur Teste.* I found it most comical after the precedent set by Leonardo himself, when he was of use to music, and I can only regret not having written more to keep these exercises in transposition going on. Most curious and in the end quite flattering, I suppose?[5]

But M. Croche's days were numbered, for the eighth column was also the last. At the end of December 1901, Debussy decided not to continue and wrote to Félix Fénéon giving his reasons: "I think that overwork and the nervous strain of the past few months are the reason why I have not been able to write as I should. I've tried all ways. . . . It's inexcusably stupid. . . ." The composition of the *Nocturnes* and then the completion of *Pelléas,* at last produced on the stage, suffice to explain his giving up.

It is difficult to estimate what repercussions this first group of articles caused in artistic circles, hardly accustomed to such freedom of speech in regard to music. The Sâr Péladan published a lengthy reproach which harped upon conservative reactions: "In *La Revue blanche* I have read blasphemies against masterpieces and the masters themselves and I have doubts about the merit of those who lack respect for our icons."[6] By the end of the following year, when Debussy was approached by the new directors of *Gil Blas,* Périvier and Ollendorf, he had, as the composer of *Pelléas,* become a public figure for the Paris cognoscenti. At the same time Binet-Valmer, director of the monthly *La Renaissance latine,* was hoping for a similar collaboration with his magazine, and even announced it in the issue of 15 Decem-

---

[5] This letter appeared for sale at the Hôtel Drouot on 26 February 1969 (cat. no. 146). Valéry and Debussy were for some time on close terms (about 1893-4).

[6] Published in *Le Cas Debussy,* by C. F. Caillard and José de Berys, 1910 (p. 92).

ber. Anxious to retain a platform for his ideas but not wishing to lose his freedom, Debussy appears to have hesitated. Calvocoressi served as intermediary and procured an article from him, "Thoughts on Music in the Open Air." Meanwhile, the director of *La Renaissance latine* was replaced. Glancing at the proofs, the new man declared "Ridiculous!" These proofs, marked with the direction "à détruire," are still in existence.[7] The text was simply transferred to Concerts Colonne and Lamoureux, the Schola Cantorum, and even a visit to Brussels to hear d'Indy and one to London to see Wagner! And in London, he claims to have attempted to interview Janos Richter. This was the period when he devoted most time to criticism. He appears to have composed little, except for putting the finishing touches to the *Images* for piano, and his correspondence is also sparse. But nowhere did he try to be the just critic, conscientious and attentive to all aspects of current musical events. Even when listening to the music of W. Chaumet or Edmond Missa he is at the very least offhand on several occasions, leaving before the end of the concert to have a beer, replying with a gentle irony to his readers "as diligent as they are faithful." Had he not anticipated from the beginning that he would not be discussing "great" music? However, six months was enough. Debussy abandoned journalism for almost ten years, with the exception of four short articles in honor of people dear to him: Massenet, Gounod, Mary Garden, and Jean Philippe Rameau.

Several of his friends pressed him, with varying degrees of insistence, to take up the pen again. In April 1905 Louis Laloy, consulting him in regard to a suitable title for a new music magazine, asked for his collaboration. "Reserve me," replied the composer, "on May 2nd, a corner under the title 'Conversations with M. Croche.' He's someone I used to see a lot of at one time. Let us hope I find him again." The *Mercure musical* hurried to announce this title on their cover, but Debussy had little sympathy with the tone of the first numbers and found none of the free atmosphere of *La Revue blanche*

---

[7] In fact, they are no longer to be found. They belonged to the late Edward Lockspeiser.

or *Gil Blas*. To be side by side with critics and musicologists frightened him; he wrote to Laloy on 13 September:

> Apart from yourself, the people on the *Mercure musical* are a dubious bunch; above all they are so terribly well-informed. I really don't see what poor M. Croche would do among such a hardy group of specialists. I'm thinking of informing you of his death in these terms: M. Croche, antidilettante, rightly disheartened by the musical standards of these times, has quietly passed away amidst general indifference. It is requested that no flowers or wreaths be sent and above all there is to be no music. . . .

Laloy repeated his request and obtained a fresh refusal from a Debussy somewhat disillusioned with the usefulness of criticism. "In these times, when we no longer know what to do or, still more, what to say, we improvise criticism of the arts. . . . There are certainly things to be said, but to whom? For whose benefit? For people who waver between Beethoven and Maurice Ravel?" (10 March 1906). Only in the following July issue did Laloy resign himself to withdrawing Debussy's name from the list of contributors.[8]

Six years later, all that remained of the *Mercure* was absorbed into the review *SIM* with Emile Vuillermoz as its chief editor. Debussy accepted the task of covering the Concerts Colonne each month while Vincent d'Indy did the Concerts Lamoureux. His collaboration lasted from November 1912 to March 1914. He gave his reasons for acceptance to his old friend Robert Godet: "One must loyally try to put things in their rightful place, to rediscover values from arbitrary judgments, for fanciful interpretations have distorted things so that it is no longer possible to distinguish a Bach fugue from the 'Marche lorraine' " (18 January 1913).[9] Anxious, as always, for a good typographical presentation, he congratulated Vuillermoz on the elegance of the layout of his magazine, but suggested ridding the cover of a "gentleman, who, in silly costume, seems to be playing the cello in the kitchen" (17 November 1912).

---

8 The Debussy–Laloy correspondence from which these extracts are taken appeared in the *Revue de musicologie*, 1962 (pp. 3–40).

9 *Lettres à deux amis*, 1942 (p. 134).

On several occasions Debussy had declined other requests for
articles: in 1904 from Paul Flat for *La Revue bleue,* and in 1910
from René Doire for the *Courrier musical.* "You ask me for some
lines on Chopin," Debussy replied. "I really don't see what place they
would have in a review whose conception of music seems to contra-
dict my own. Your subscribers might understand nothing any
longer." And on the eve of his departure for Russia on 24 November
1913, Debussy wrote to André Gide:

> *La Nouvelle Revue française* and its secretary, Monsieur Jacques
> Rivière, your amiable insistence is too kind for me not to excuse
> myself. . . . You know that I write articles of music criticism
> in the review *SIM.* Until now they have been sufficient to occupy
> all the time I can spare for the odd and fruitless task of express-
> ing my opinion. One would have to find something new to
> justify expressing it twice.

During the first stage of his critical activity, Debussy gives the
illusion of being able, in the future, to write something more substantial than mere reviews. A conversation with his young friend René
Peter indicates that he thought of founding a literary review with
contributors as celebrated as Jean Lorrain and Liane de Pougy. Other
projects appear to have been followed up more seriously. On 10 September 1893, at a time when he was virtually unknown to the general public, a review, *L'Idée libre,* announced the forthcoming publication of an article by Claude Debussy entitled "On the Uselessness
of Wagnerism." The same announcement was repeated in the five
subsequent issues, up to February 1894. Although printed in a review
with only a limited circulation, it did not pass unnoticed in certain
musical circles. Paul Dukas wrote to Vincent d'Indy on 1 October
1893: "I have no idea what that could be, but when it comes out, I'll
get it. It could be quite profound and it's rightly said that truth comes
from the mouths of children. The title is rather good, isn't it? and you
can tell its author a mile off!" The article never appeared, and no trace
of it has been discovered. It is possible that Debussy never wrote a
line of it.

Some time later, a comment made by Pierre Louÿs to Debussy in a
letter dated 23 January 1904 testifies to the composer's intention to

write a more extended work expounding his artistic ideas. In advising him not to publish any rejoinder to a pamphlet by Jean Lorrain, *Les Pelléastres,* Louÿs added:

> Reply to a music critic if he signs himself Reyer or d'Indy. But never discuss anything with a journalist. No artist does that. Even if you still had your column in *Gil Blas* I wouldn't advise you to put it to such a use. Your best reply will be your book. That will make your ideas known in circles they would otherwise not have reached and present them in such a way that people can no longer accuse you of intentions which were never yours.[10]

On this point, whatever regrets we may have, Debussy was wise to reserve for his own music the precious time he would have expended on this project.

His first ideas for a selection of articles seem to date back to 1906. On 25 December Debussy wrote to Laloy:

> I am thinking, for the future, of a collection of notes, opinions, etc., left by poor M. Croche, who decided to die. This most delicate of men considered that I couldn't very well continue these "conversations" where Mr. Nobody conducts a dialogue with Nothing at All [*où le Néant dialoguait avec le vague Rien-du-tout*]! He gave me the choice: to publish the papers? Or to burn them? Together we'll decide what's best.

Another friend, Robert Godet, without knowing of the project under way, had the same idea. On 30 April 1909 Debussy replied to him: "You are very kind, wanting me to revise my old articles, but for some time it has also been Laloy's concern: I should have let you know."

Things dragged on until the end of 1913, when the manuscript was deposited with the editor Dorbon, who at the beginning of 1914 asked Debussy for permission to publish it. In little hurry, it seems, to see the work appear, the composer once more asked Laloy, on 11 February, for an hour's meeting to help him to put the final touches

---

[10] *Correspondance de Claude Debussy et Pierre Louÿs,* 1945 (p. 177). This passage does not seem to apply to a previous project for *Monsieur Croche,* as the editor suggests.

to the manuscript. G. Jean-Aubry has confirmed for his part that "only a short while before his death," Debussy gave him these proofs,[11] and some pages carrying autograph corrections were preserved by him.[12] The rest we know. The war intervened while the book was on press in Belgium. *Monsieur Croche* did not appear until 1921, when it was published in the series Bibliophiles Fantaisistes, in an edition limited to five hundred copies.

Almost the entire collection had been taken from *La Revue blanche* and *Gil Blas*. Certain fragments had been excerpted and combined from other articles (for example, "Massenet," "Music in the Open Air," "The Prix de Rome"). Few revisions or corrections had been made on the originals, although those that we can point out are significant. Debussy omitted certain eulogies to Camille Chevillard, who conducted the première performances of the *Nocturnes* and *La Mer*. Having become more and more dissatisfied with Chevillard's interpretation of his music, Debussy deletes, for example, a passage ranking the conductor "among the very greatest." His few words on *Thamara,* the opera by Bourgault-Ducoudray, were heavily crossed out. On the other hand, certain adverse criticisms regarding Strauss's orchestration of *Till Eulenspiegel* are retracted. Further, a particularly virulent passage on realist operas is suppressed and the name of an insufficiently important person is replaced by "one." The apologies in *Monsieur Croche* are, however, very few.

The anti-Wagnerian diatribes, the blasphemous passages on the Prix de Rome, and the prejudices against Gluck and in favor of Rameau are well-known. But in several articles added to those which *Monsieur Croche* made famous, Debussy deals with more topical subjects: the administration of the state opera houses, child prodigies (the Mozart of Saint-Maur), musical polemics (the case of Fanelli), and quasi-musicological matters (the case of Rust). One also finds several allusions to the music used in the early days of the cinema. His opinion of mass culture he put in a nutshell: "Too much diffusion of art can lead only to a great mediocrity" (15 March 1903).

---

[11] *Revue musicale,* 1 December 1920, pp. 191–2.

[12] These were displayed in 1962 at the Bibliothèque Nationale "Exposition Debussy" (cat. no. 315).

His opinions on the works of his contemporaries are uncompromising, above all with regard to Saint-Saëns and Alfred Bruneau. Sometimes, as with Ropartz and Bordes, he so clearly slants his praise toward their personal or professional qualities that no sensitive reader can have any doubt about his real opinions. And in the special case of Vincent d'Indy, on which much has been written, he uses hardly less apparently polite expressions, writing of his integrity, respect, and "expression of Christian charity." Everywhere else the tone is caustic and ironic, even in the obituaries (see that on R. Planquette). More than that of M. Teste or Jules Laforgue, Debussy's style of criticism makes one think of Willy (H. Gauthier-Villars). His levity in treating serious matters, the twists of imagination that cause him to compare Schubert to Paul Delmet, or associate Fauré's art with Mme Hasselmans's shoulder straps, are largely a compensation for an undeniable looseness of style.

After a complete reading, the whole appears remarkably lively and coherent except on one point: the chauvinist tone he shows when discussing the musical tradition of his own country. Having to pass judgment on the works of his young compatriots, whom he advises to learn from the plight of Rameau, he has scarcely any models to propose—Couperin, Lalo's *Namouna,* a little Massenet, and Offenbach, a somewhat narrow musical tradition. In all, his chauvinism appears to be a pose based on matters of principle, and when, in 1915, he writes "Alone, at last," one wonders if it is not Debussy alone with himself.

In addition, the text of this final article contains a phrase that commands particular attention, coming as it does after an enumeration of all the "contaminations" suffered, according to him, by the French tradition: "We have tolerated overblown orchestras, tortuous forms, cheap luxury, and clashing colors, and we were about to give the seal of approval to even more suspect naturalizations when the sound of gunfire put a sudden stop to it all. . . ." There is scarcely any doubt that this last allusion refers to the music of Schönberg, which we know Debussy knew, and which he reprimanded Stravinsky for "leaning dangerously toward."

The material has been arranged chronologically. The written replies and inquiries should be distinguished from the interviews put together from notes made by journalists, who in any case did not go knocking at the composer's door before *Pelléas* had caught their attention. No less than a score of such interviews has been counted between 1902 and 1914. The bulk are after 1910, the date of publication by Caillard and Bérys of *Le Cas Debussy,* a pamphlet that annoyed the composer and made him recognize the necessity of keeping in contact with the public. Opinions attributed to him were often far from his own somewhat individual ideas, so it is no surprise to find him to some degree taking the opportunity of denying them. One of the catch phrases so often given as typical of his aesthetic, "Music must humbly seek to give pleasure," was included in just these words in an interview published by P. Landormy of which Debussy complained to Laloy: "It is extraordinary how badly this so-called musician can hear." Some time later, in regard to an article on the Italian realist school, he sent *Comœdia* a letter to set things straight. It has seemed to me that several judgments expressed in these texts, slightly suspect as they are, usefully complement the opinions gathered from his articles. The very fact that Debussy opened his door to journalists no less than fifteen times implies, after all, some degree of acceptance on his part.

Two short interviews have not been included here. One was in connection with a decoration "for merit" which the Emperor William II refused to award Debussy and Rodin at the same time (*Paris-Journal,* 2 February 1911). "You can say that I expect nothing from Germany," said Debussy, "nor anything official in my own country. I am working like a slave. Isn't that enough from my conscience?" The other interview was part of an inquiry conducted by Henry Malherbe on "Russian music and French composers" (*Excelsior,* 9 March 1911). "Russian music," Debussy was reported to have said, "interests me in the extreme. . . . Last year, a young man composed for his debut a ballet, *The Firebird,* which was performed in Paris. Well, this first work was an exquisite and original piece." Many parts of Debussy's writings call for annotations on forgotten, or largely forgotten, events and people, but an accumulation of critical notes has been avoided. It was not so much to inform his readers that Debussy wrote, more to guide them through less conventional forms and oblige them to discard their routine opinions. The present edition overlaps in part with the previous edition of *Monsieur Croche.* Perhaps some people will miss that now familiar collection. Its unity was built on the character of a person whose habits Debussy never fully understood, but it is hoped that the ideas of the composer will appear in a more true and complete light by being set in their original form.

FRANÇOIS LESURE

Part One

La Revue
blanche:
1901

IT was no accident that the first paper to engage Debussy as a regular critic was *La Revue blanche;* no other journal could have been better suited to the composer's writings. A magazine of ideas vitally interested in all that was new in the arts, *La Revue blanche* cast its net wide, publishing poems and novels in serial form and articles on literary subjects and current affairs; it employed critics to cover all the arts. As Julien Benda later recalled, it was a magazine "systématiquement avancé dans tous les ordres."[1] One step ahead on all fronts, the editors of the review had secured the services of Debussy at a time—May 1901—when the composer, aged thirty-seven, was on the eve of his grand entry into the public limelight. His opera *Pelléas et Mélisande* was about to be accepted for performance at the Opéra-Comique. Begun in 1893, this, his only large-scale dramatic work, had preoccupied the composer more than any other; several abortive attempts preceded its final staging. To *La Revue blanche,* then, Debussy was something of a scoop—more than they realized, for when the opera received its première the following year, the composer was to become the focus of both admiration and controversy. *Pelléas* was recognized as a truly advanced work, a piece that might be derided in certain quarters but could not be ignored. The music column of *La Revue blanche* had not previously included many notable figures among its contributors, Alfred Ernst and André Corneau being the now-forgotten names of Debussy's predecessors. Compared with the other columns, the magazine's music criticism lagged far behind, hardly living up to its otherwise progressive outlook. Thus the composer Debussy merited the bold type accorded him on the cover of the first issue containing his column.

The idea of writing about music had apparently been in Debussy's mind for some time. He had once thought of founding a literary review himself; and in 1893, just when he was beginning work on *Pelléas,* he had intended to publish an exposition of his then-revolutionary ideas on "the uselessness of Wagnerism." (Indeed, by 1904, with both his *Revue blanche* and *Gil Blas* columns behind him, Debussy was considering writing a book.)

What better place to begin than *La Revue blanche?* It was a paper where Debussy could let his ideas breathe, be himself. There were also financial considerations to be taken into account, for since 1899 Debussy had been unable to make ends meet and been forced to rely upon heavy loans. In 1902, unable to repay debts to the executors of the publisher Victor Hartmann, he was actually prosecuted. It may well have been these mounting debts that precipitated his appearance in print, but the circumstances surrounding his engagement as regular columnist in *La Revue blanche* remain something of a mystery: did the composer offer himself to the review, or was he invited to contribute? Either way, it would seem that the arrangement was attractive to the composer, at least at first; for not only was financial gain important to him, particularly at this time, but the position on the review also provided an outlet for his long-fostered wish to set down his ideas in writing.

There were several reasons why *La Revue blanche* was so eminently suited to carry Debussy's column. The composer was well-connected among established contributors to the review, and it is illuminating to focus on some of the literary figures among Debussy's circle who contributed to the dynamic tone of the magazine. Earlier in the nineties, the poets Verlaine, Mallarmé, and Jules Laforgue had all published in *La Revue blanche,* setting a precedent for the strongly symbolist bias of the magazine's first issues. It was primarily these poets who had left an indelible imprint on Debussy's mind. Verlaine's verses were of great importance to Debussy for many years. His youthful settings of the late *Fêtes galantes* precisely capture the Watteauesque landscapes and commedia dell'arte grotesques of Verlaine's poems. With his prelude to Mallarmé's *L'Après-midi d'un faune,* Debussy cemented his association with the symbolist movement, and much later in his life, in 1913, he returned to Mallarmé to compose three songs for voice and piano. Debussy never set Laforgue to music, but this poet made a deep impression on the composer's mind, and his letters and passages in his writing frequently allude to his imagery. G. Jean-Aubry, an intimate friend of Debussy, recalled, "Those of us who mentioned Laforgue to Debussy remember how attached he remained to him, frequently expressing affinities in his writings and conversations with the poet of *Pan et la Syrinx* and *Lohengrin, fils de Parsifal.*"[2]

Lesser-known poets and writers associated with Debussy also contributed to *La Revue blanche,* including Catulle Mendès, whose *Rodrigue et Chimène* was among the composer's many unfinished projects; another was the poet Henri de Régnier, a close friend of Debussy's at one time and author of the *Scènes au crépuscule,* upon which the composer drew in an early version of the orchestral *Nocturnes.* André Gide had a short term as prose critic of the magazine immediately preceding Debussy's engagement as columnist; in the mid-nineties he, too, through Pierre Louÿs, had been on close terms with Debussy. Others, now largely forgotten, were Pierre Quillard and Ferdinand Hérold. For the most part, these writers were symbolists, but *La Revue blanche* never stultified into an *école,* and those who have dismissed the magazine as just another symbolist periodical are mistaken. Indeed, at the time Debussy joined *La Revue blanche* its climate was changing: no longer were the symbolists dominant, for the review was already looking well ahead into the twentieth century, publishing works by Alfred Jarry, author of the *Ubu* cycle, and manifestos by Marinetti, leader of the Italian Futurists, mentioned in passing by Debussy in one of his articles.

Although it was not one of the more sumptuously produced reviews, *La Revue blanche* was also important for its art criticism, and it printed woodcuts and engravings by Manet, Bonnard, and Maurice Denis among other artists. (It also published some drawings by Verlaine and Laforgue.) Debussy was strongly attracted to Manet, and he was closely associated with Maurice Denis. This artist was to have illustrated an edition of the composer's *Prélude à l'après-midi d'un faune,* and he designed the elaborate cover for the composer's Pre-Raphaelite cantata *La Damoiselle élue.* Bonnard, too, was linked with the composer; at one time he expressed the desire to design the scenery for Debussy's *Pelléas.* The visual as well as the literary aspects of the review were more than likely to have excited Debussy's enthusiasm.

Several reminiscences by turn-of-the-century figures connected with the paper refer to an *ésprit Revue blanche*. The magazine and its contributors shared a corporate spirit that give it its decisive tone. What was this *ésprit Revue blanche?* Why, amid so many *revues,* did *La Revue blanche* stand out? Rémy de Gourmont commented on the host of reviews the nineties had produced: "At that time the only way to publish one's ideas freely was to establish oneself a *petite revue.* . . . A few people got together, collected a little money, and sought out a printer."[3] That was how *La Revue blanche* began, and that was how Debussy and René Peter tried to begin when they decided to found a review. Theirs soon collapsed, and so did countless others. But, along with the *Mercure de France, La Revue blanche* lived on. It is quite wrong to think of *La Revue blanche* as merely one of many symbolist reviews. It was never esoteric, nor did it ever allow itself to stagnate in a mire of self-perpetuating symbolist clichés. The fact that the review was not a specialized luxury magazine accounted in part for its success. It was above all a magazine of the streets. With its offices in the Fleet Street of Paris, at the center of the literary press—first in the rue Laffitte and later in the boulevard des Italiens—its contributors met in the literary cafés surrounding the offices. Thadée Natanson (one of the three brothers who had founded the review) and his teenage wife, Misia, kept open house at their apartment in the rue Saint-Florentin, where the writers might congregate, and they also gave banquets in their country home. In her fascinating memoirs[4] Natanson's wife recalls how Debussy was a frequent visitor during his year on *La Revue blanche*. With its center at the hub of business Paris, the magazine, hawked on street corners, reflected the life of the great city.

The review's popularity was no doubt heightened by the employment of Toulouse-Lautrec as publicity designer. He produced no less than thirty-three posters advertising the magazine and its publications, and he was a well-known figure in the nearby cafés, where he would earn his living sketching. One such sketch was of Footitt and Chocolat, the two famous clowns, whom Debussy was to meet in the Bar Reynolds. Others included drawings of the Natansons, and on several occasions sketches executed in the cafés were turned into posters, simply by overprinting them with advertisements. Lautrec's presence on the review's staff was another example of the editors' remarkable ability to utilize available talent.

Thadée Natanson played his part in this talent-spotting; his art criticism helped many a young artist to fame. But of more value than any of the Natanson brothers was the editor-in-chief of *La Revue blanche,* whose ability to recognize potential talent in young writers amounted almost to clairvoyance. This man was Félix Fénéon. His name seldom appeared on the cover of the magazine, but it was Fénéon above all who controlled the editorial policies of *La Revue blanche;* he was the power behind the throne. According to André Gide, it was Fénéon who was the "real director" of the magazine.[5]

Fénéon had several claims to fame. First and foremost, he was a writer who employed his critical faculties not only in his championing of the neo-impressionist painters—Seurat in particular—but also in his role as editor. Mallarmé pronounced him "one of the most subtle and astute critics that we have,"[6] and Rémy de Gourmont, looking back over the nineties, wrote "we have had, perhaps, one critic in a hundred years—and that is Félix Fénéon."[7] Fénéon wrote little, but what he wrote was of the highest order. Not only did he write intelligently of the pointillists at a time when they were little understood, but he produced impeccable translations of both Poe and Jane Austen for *La Revue blanche.* As far as the review was concerned, however, his main function was as editor. A quiet, withdrawn man, Fénéon was reprimanded by Rémy de Gourmont for not writing more: "Je préfère travailler indirectement," was Fénéon's reply. He was a specialist critic in the highest sense of the word, as well as a first-rate "talent spotter."

Apart from his impeccable criticism, Fénéon was a celebrated figure for other reasons. The years following the Commune saw an upsurge of anarchism in France—bombs were thrown in Paris and anarchists guillotined. Many of the *petites revues* were openly anarchist organs, and one police chief even went so far as to found an anarchist journal in order to have a reliable source of information. In 1894 a law was passed that allowed the police to arrest anyone suspected of anarchist leanings, and many of those who had been jour-

nalists on the free-thinking *petites revues* were rounded up. Fénéon
was one of these. He was tried and acquitted, though it seems that
explosive materials were planted in his flat. His witty answers at the
trial remain legendary.[8]

Any account of the forces of change in the arts—crystallized in the
music of Debussy—must take the anarchist movement into account.
Fénéon's trial was more than an amusing diversion: silent explosives
were shaking the foundations of the arts. In fact, the anarchist movement had a powerful nonmilitant "second rank" behind its violent
front that included artist sympathizers and a backing from the press.
Debussy himself was associated with the anarchists—an aspect
of the composer's personality that has been little explored. To some
extent—especially with its strong support of Dreyfus—*La Revue
blanche* was an anarchist paper. Other artists connected with the
movement were Camille Pissarro and his son Lucien, both friends of
Fénéon, and Octave Mirbeau. At Fénéon's trial, Mallarmé testified to
his nonviolent participation, an attitude common among the intellectual supporters of the movement. He characterized Fénéon as being
"above the use of anything else but literature to express his ideas."[9]

Debussy's associations with literary figures brought him into close
contact with this intellectual "second rank" of the anarchist movement: in his letters (particularly those to Louÿs) there are several
references to anarchism. Anarchist ideas also underlie Debussy's unpublished play *Frères en Art*,[10] which was written in collaboration
with René Peter. This curious work is in the form of a *pièce à clef,* in
which key figures of the time appear under pseudonyms, and it
includes the composer's plan for a "brotherhood" of artists in all
the arts, an association that would promote unity rather than intense competition, and through a sharing of income, produce a more
stable income for the individual artist. This pipe dream is interesting not only as a curious echo of the Pre-Raphaelite brotherhood,
which was becoming widely publicized in France during the nineties,
but also as an artistic counterpart to the militant anarchist unions.[11]
Characters in the play are described as "presque les anarchistes," and
they discuss the problems of fostering a taste for their seemingly
revolutionary arts among the uncomprehending masses. A similar
movement had been dreamed of by the painter Pissarro, and the writ-

ings of this remarkably lucid artist give us considerable insight into
the roots of intellectual ferment in the arts at this time.

Pissarro's letters are the clearest exposition of the ideas prevalent
among the intellectual second rank of anarchism. One primary aim
in his mind: to rid the arts of bourgeois standards. As early as 1883
Pissarro had lent his nephew "two little books on socialism." He
wrote to his son Lucien, encouraging him to explain their relevance as
far as the arts were concerned:

> He will begin to understand the movement, which will change
> everything. There is no more time for amusements; you are
> right, education is what is necessary. See how stupid the bour-
> geoisie—the real bourgeoisie—have become! Step by step they
> stoop lower and lower—in a word they are losing all notion of
> beauty: they are mistaken about everything. Where there is
> something to admire they shout it down, they disapprove!
> Where there are stupid sentimentalities from which you want to
> turn with disgust, they jump for joy or swoon. Everything they
> have admired for the last fifty years is now forgotten, old-
> fashioned, ridiculous.[12]

The struggle to educate the public against such bourgeois standards
was an ideal Debussy shared with Pissarro. The writings of both men
are shot through with a similar spirit of intellectual anarchism.
Fénéon's intense sympathy with such ideas helped to unite those of
both artist and composer. Debussy's writings were the first major
outpourings of anarchist ideas in music.

To achieve their aim to rid art of bourgeois standards—whether it
was the academic painting of Meissonier, the music of Saint-Saëns, or
the host of French imitations of Wagner—the intellectual wing of
anarchism developed an extreme cult of individualism, a cult of
novelty. "Schools" were out. Each artist had to find his own path, to
forge his own road. Pissarro advised his son against taking lessons—
"I continue to believe that it is better to perfect oneself little by little
but by one's own efforts"—and Debussy advised composers along the
same lines, rejecting his formal education at the Conservatoire. *La
Revue blanche* gave young men of ideas the chance to develop their
individualism—which was the essence of the review, stated in the

first issue. Julien Benda recalled how well the magazine succeeded in its aims in this respect:

> My entry into *La Revue blanche* was my first encounter with any circle of men of letters. I at once had an impression which was to return to me throughout my life in such situations: that of an absolute solitude such as is natural among the blind followers of logic and ideas, men whose only ideal is the experience of their own sensibilities. . . .

Here we find not only the idea of individualism crystallized, but also an expression of sentiments very close to those of M. Croche, Debussy's alter ego.[13]

Debussy was undoubtedly the first composer or critic of the period to stand up for his individual ideas about music. Advising a young composer, he displays an approach that would have been shared by Pissarro: "Gather impressions," he writes to Raoul Bardac, "but do not hurry to note them down."[14] Sometimes his ideas were extremely radical, not to say anarchic. No doubt he delighted in being bold in *La Revue blanche,* where he could be as fearlessly provocative as he liked. At times his daring strokes must be taken with a pinch of salt, but it should be remembered that, from his early days, Debussy had been a composer with the idea of revolution at the heart of his musical technique. Scorning his harmony teacher's so-called rules, Debussy provocatively declared that the only rules were "mon plaisir." And he meant it. Here in the columns of *La Revue blanche* was an opportunity for Debussy to clarify these ideas—to select and reject the premise on which the arts were built.

If so well-suited to the magazine, why did Debussy feel obliged to retire after writing only nine articles? In his letter of resignation to Fénéon, the composer gave his reasons as overwork and nervous strain. Debussy's efforts were concentrated elsewhere: there was *Pelléas* to be polished, and the *Nocturnes* were to receive their first complete performance in the autumn of 1901. Writing to René Peter he had complained of that side of the *Revue blanche* work which was odious to him: "Today, a full rehearsal of *Grisélidis:* doubly annoying. I *have* to go. . . ." Uninterested in reviewing works for which he has little sympathy, Debussy makes it clear that the reasons he took pleasure in writing lay elsewhere. The composer had thrown himself headlong into the *Revue blanche* circle; to be able to contribute to a magazine of ideas was stimulating. Natanson's wife, Misia, described the clublike atmosphere of the youthful staff, without exception creative artists rather than professional journalists:

> . . . I found myself quite at home, surrounded by Mallarmé, Paul Valéry, Lautrec, Vuillard, Bonnard (these last three still mocked by the world at large, who misunderstood their pictures), Léon Blum, Félix Fénéon, Ghéion, who exasperated me with his *javions,* Tristan Bernard, Jules Renard (whose wife managed the house), Henri de Régnier, the charming Mirbeau with his wife—the heroine of *Calvaire,* Jarry, La Jeunesse, Coolus, Debussy (married to a thin, dark little nanny goat), Vollard, the ravishing Colette with her triangular face and wasp waist drawn in so tightly that she had the silhouette of a schoolgirl, and her husband Willy, who called her *professeur* and whose crude stories I hardly understood. With few exceptions we were all under thirty, and I was but sixteen. . . .

On one occasion, Misia recalled, Debussy paid a select group of the *Revue blanche* circle the ultimate compliment: a preview of Debussy's opera at Louÿs's apartment.

> Pierre Louÿs, who lived in the rue Gluck, brought several friends home one day to hear this masterpiece—*Pelléas*—played on an upright piano by Debussy himself, who also sang all the parts. I was the only woman. A servant dressed in a white shirt served us cocktails. I had never drunk in my life. On this occasion they concocted a series of liqueurs—yellow, green, red,—which stayed in layers in the glass. I partook of several, stretched out on a chaise longue, transfixed by a larger-than-life Japanese doll, which was facing me. I hardly listened to the words of Maeterlinck. Distracted, only the playing of Debussy touched my heart, and intoxicated by the colors of the cocktails Mélisande became the Japanese doll: I invented a story that had no connection with the miracles that were taking place in the salon that evening.[15]

᭾NOTES

[1] Julien Benda, *La Jeunesse d'un clerc* (Paris, 1936).

[2] G. Jean-Aubry, "Jules Laforgue et la musique," *Revue de Genève,* October 1921.

[3] Rémy de Gourmont, *Promenades littéraires* (Paris, 1919).

[4] Misia Sert, *Misia* (Paris, 1952).

[5] A. B. Jackson, *La Revue blanche* (Paris, 1960). This book is a fascinating history of the magazine and its contributors.

[6] Henri Mondor, *Vie de Mallarmé* (Paris, 1941).

[7] Jean Paulhan, *Introduction aux oeuvres de Félix Fénéon* (Paris, 1948).

[8] The climax of the trial came when the presiding magistrate was sent an envelope said to contain an important piece of evidence. On opening it, he found to his dismay that its only contents were *de la matière fécale.* The judge called for a recess to wash his soiled hands. "Not since Pontius Pilate," said Fénéon, "has a judge washed his hands with such ostentation."

[9] Mondor, *Vie de Mallarmé.*

[10] Extracts published in "Frères en Art" by Edward Lockspeiser, *Revue de musicologie,* 1970, no. 2.

[11] See Maitron, *Histoire du mouvement anarchiste en France* (Paris, 1955).

[12] Camille Pissarro, *Lettres à son fils Lucien* (Paris, 1950).

[13] Benda, *La Jeunesse d'un clerc.*

[14] Debussy to Raoul Bardac, 25 February 1906. Quoted in Edward Lockspeiser's *Debussy,* rev. ed., 1963.

[15] Sert, *Misia.*

LA REVUE BLANCHE
1 April 1901

F I N D I N G myself called upon to discuss music in this review, perhaps I might be allowed a few words to explain how I intend to set about this task. What you will be finding here are my own sincere impressions, exactly as I felt them—more that than "criticism," which is all too often no more than a brilliant set of variations on the theme of "you didn't do it as I would, that's your mistake," or even "you have talent, I have none, and that certainly cannot go on." I shall try to see the works I discuss in perspective, to discover the various seeds from which they sprang, and what they contain of inner life. Isn't that quite as interesting as that game which consists of taking them to pieces, as though they were curious old watches?

Grownups tend to forget that as children they were forbidden to open the insides of their dolls—a crime of high treason against the cause of mystery. . . . And yet they still insist on poking their aesthetic noses into things that don't concern them! Without their dolls to break open, they still try to explain things, dismantle them and quite heartlessly kill all their mystery. I suppose it *is* more convenient to know how things work: at least it gives us something to chat about. But, my God! Some of them we can excuse because of their complete ignorance, but others—the more spiteful of them—give rein to their malice: they have to cling frantically to their own pitiful mediocrity. And these latter have a faithful flock of followers.

I shall be discussing "established classics" very little, no matter if they are popular or traditionally famous. Once and for all: Meyerbeer, Thalberg, and Reyer—they are men of genius. But that's as far as their importance goes.

On Sundays when the good Lord is kind, I shall not be listening to any music at all. For this I apologize in advance. Finally, let me add that I prefer to keep to "impressions," for only these can give me the freedom to keep my feelings immune from parasitic aesthetics.[1]

At the Concert Colonne: Schumann's Faust

I T would be possible to compare this *Faust* with several others. But we would only end up by saying some unfortunate things, and that wouldn't do anybody any good. Least of all Goethe.

As regards Schumann, it was always difficult to understand how he could let his own pure genius be influenced by Mendelssohn, that elegant and facile notary. Particularly in *Faust,* one is always stumbling over fragments of Mendelssohn. I prefer my Mendelssohn by itself. At least you know what to expect!

At the Concert Lamoureux: Overture to King Lear by Albert Savard (First Performance) and the Third Act of Siegfried

T H E overture to *King Lear* by Albert Savard has a ring that is rather too Wagnerian for my taste. Eternal cymbal clashing snuffing out the flutes—a typically Wagnerian impertinence! The main theme of *King Lear* has that kind of majestic chic which is found only in Götter-burg.[2] It testifies to a fine sense of musicianship (especially in the part where the gentle character of Cordelia is drawn), but it does rather end with a bump. Perhaps there is some music behind this overture? . . . I certainly hope so.[3]

There have been varied reactions to M. C. Chevillard's fragmentary presentation of excerpts from the *Ring*. For my own part, I must confess that I found them quite tasteful. Those people who assume all the customary affectations when talking of the *Ring* would obviously consider only a complete performance of this musical "Who's Who." Besides, M. C. Chevillard has an almost unique gift with an orchestra. Those costumes of scrap metal covered in animal hair (worn by all the characters in *Siegfried*) found an echo in the orchestra with him in command. With his prodigious imagination replacing the usual realistic scenery (which always fails to be sufficiently evocative), the characters appeared all the more human.[4]

Thanks also to M. C. Chevillard for abstaining from the "bull-fight" technique so common among international conductors these days. It is most disconcerting to watch banderillas being implanted in the mouth of cor anglais, or the poor trombones petrified by the gestures of a matador![5] M. Chevillard is quite content to give the orchestra the assurance that he understands the music completely—a simple enough ambition but very difficult to achieve in practice. Oh, and I almost forgot . . . M. A. de Greef gave a marvelous performance of a piano concerto by Saint-Saëns. But then, that's an "established classic."

At the Société Nationale: Orchestral Concert on 16 March

A SYMPHONY by M. G. M. Witkowski was greeted with much enthusiasm. But it seemed to me to be only further proof of the uselessness of the symphony since Beethoven. Certainly in Schumann and Mendelssohn it is merely a respectful reworking of the same old forms with a good deal less conviction. The Ninth is a landmark and a work of genius: it has a magnificent desire to grow, to liberate itself from the customary forms and at the same time to imbue them with the harmonious proportions of a fresco.*

Beethoven's real lesson to us was not that we should preserve age-old forms, nor even that we should plant our footsteps where he first trod. We should look out through open windows into clear skies. Many people appear to have closed them, seemingly for good; those successful so-called geniuses should have no excuse for their academic

---

* It has been stated elsewhere that Beethoven made the spoken word the "apotheosis and crowning glory" of this edifice in sound, and that the finale of the Ninth thus prepared the way for music drama. Isn't that just a convenient theory for the Wagnerians to hold? The intervention of the thousand voices is really to salute the art of music above all else.

contrapuntal exercises, which are called (out of habit) "symphonies."

The young Russian school attempted to rejuvenate the symphony by borrowing ideas from folk music. They succeeded in unearthing some real gems, but was there not always an irreconcilable conflict between the folk tunes themselves and the variations the composers felt they had to add? It wasn't long, however, before the fashion for the folk tune had spread throughout the world of music: you find it cropping up in the tiniest provinces, from east to west. You would hear a snatch of the most ingenuous refrain from some old peasant woman, quite embarrassed to be entwined in so much harmonic lace. These versions somehow seemed sadly constricted: the addition of all those weighty counterpoints had divorced the folk tunes from their rural origins.[6]

Must we conclude that despite so many attempts at transformation, the symphony—in all its elegance and formal order, and despite its serious-minded bejeweled public—is a thing of the past? Has not its worn-out gilt merely been replaced by a plating of shining copper, the shoddy finish of present-day orchestration?

Witkowski's symphony is based on a Breton chant. The first part consists of the usual presentation of the theme: the foundation on which the composer is going to build. Then comes the obligatory breakdown. The second part is rather like a laboratory devoted to the study of vacuums. The third unwinds with characteristic Breton gaiety, interspersed with strongly sentimental sections. In this part the Breton chant tactfully retires, but it soon reappears and the demolition continues, much to the delight of the connoisseurs, who visibly mop their brows while the public yells for the composer. . . . All the same that is the best part, the part where Witkowski's musical language is at its most spontaneous and persuasive. He undeniably has great experience and suffers from no lack of technique, even in the more extended sections. But he does pay too much attention to the voices of the "authorities." It seems to me they stifle a more individual voice within.

The only other thing I need mention after that are some *Poèmes danois* for voice and orchestra by Frederick Delius. They are very sweet, very pale—music to soothe convalescents in well-to-do neighborhoods. There always seems to be one note that drags on over a chord, like a water lily on a lake. Or a tiny balloon obscured by the clouds.[7]

It is ineffable, this music! It was sung by Mlle C. Andray-Fairfax with a dreamy voice full of remarkable melancholy. While the music flowed sadly on, Mademoiselle seemed to be amusing herself by singing alternately to the public and then to the chandeliers. In the end, I must add, it was the chandeliers who won. This charming game seemed to protect these delicate songs from the raucous noise of any bravos. Is it not strange, this instinctive need to clap our hands one against the other, shrieking with warlike cries, when we want to show enthusiasm? I am sure it goes back to the Stone Age. But you should not see this remark as a reproach nor as any attempt to criticize human nature. It is just a convenient way of rounding off these "impressions."

~*NOTES*

[1] Coming in the wake of impressionism, Debussy's stressed use of the word "impressions" requires some clarification. Since 1874, when the word "impressionism" had been coined as a term of abuse, the term had been freely bandied about in connection with all the arts, imbued with countless overtones. Debussy despised the use of the word as an umbrella: *"de symbolistes ou d'impressionistes:* useful terms of abuse." And elsewhere he expresses a similar scorn for the term "impressionism" in conjunction with the paintings of Turner. Here Debussy means something rather more precise. His emphasis on "impressions" was in line with much other *Revue blanche* criticism. New works—in all the arts—provided the critic with his most important task: to respond, and to keep his responses untainted by "parasite aesthetics." Thus Debussy rejects "established classics" and admits that "it is composers like Moussorgsky, Dukas, and only a few others" that make his column worthwhile. Valéry's Monsieur Teste had a similar desire to keep his impressions pure, and burned his books. For Monet, back in 1884, the idea of "impressions" implied a similar purity as an ideal: "I have always worked better alone, guided solely by my own impressions." The critic, like the artist, must be alone to keep his responses pure.

2 A word apparently coined by Debussy, meaning "the domain of the Gods" (compare *Götterdämmerung*).

3 A double meaning with a sting in its tail: *Peut-être y a-t-il de la musique* derrière *cette ouverture*. Perhaps there is some music *to follow,* or *underlying,* this overture.

4 In lamenting the inadequacy of the realistic scenery as compared with the music itself, Debussy was probably thinking of the passage in *Siegfried* known as "Forest Murmurs." There is no action, but the curtain is open: the music and the stage scenery have to convey the multitudinous voices of the forest at dawn. This was one of Wagner's most "impressionistic" works, and the French saw it as such. Jules Laforgue, writing of an exhibition in Berlin, wrote:

> The principle of colored vibrations is particularly obvious in the works of Monet and Pissarro . . . tiny, dancing touches of color that spread out in all directions, each struggling for supremacy. There is no single melody in these works: the canvas itself is a living, varied symphony, like the "Voices of the Forest" in the theories of Wagner, which similarly compete for an overall impression. (*Oeuvres complètes: Mélanges posthumes* [Paris, 1903].)

With its slow, static chords and trilling bird noises, "Forest Murmurs" was strongly hinted at in the central section of Debussy's own *Prélude à l'après-midi d'un faune.*

5 Colette later vied with Debussy for an amusing description of the new extrovert style of conducting (see p. 121).

6 Debussy was among the first composers to realize the essential incompatibility of folk song and symphonic technique: a cul de sac experienced not only by the Russians to whom Debussy refers but also by d'Indy, and later on Vaughan Williams. It was Constant Lambert who clinched the dilemma in his *Music Ho!:* "To put it vulgarly, the whole trouble with a folk song is that once you have played it through there is nothing much you can do except play it over again and play it rather louder."

7 Debussy's comments on Delius are repeated word for word in a later article, this time with regard to Grieg's "The Swan" (see p. 178). The image is strongly reminiscent of the poet Laforgue—"notre Jules," as Debussy referred to him on several occasions in his correspondence. Laforgue made considerable use of musical imagery: his poetry constantly evoked music in the background, in particular the sound of the piano being prac-

ticed—interminable scales and arpeggios become related to the poet's ennui. Certain elements in Debussy's own music seem to translate Laforgue's images back to the keyboard: the endless arpeggios of "Le Vent dans la plaine" and "Jardins sous la pluie," or the first piece in the *Children's Corner Suite*, "Dr. Gradus ad Parnassum," which creates a poetic image out of the routine boredom of practicing a technical exercise. Debussy's "music to soothe convalescents in well-to-do neighborhoods" is reminiscent of Laforgue's poem "Complainte des pianos dans les quartiers aisés."

LA REVUE BLANCHE
15 April 1901

O N the last Sunday in March (Palm Sunday) the two Sunday concerts were in competition . . . each played us Wagner! The result? No score on either side! At Colonne's it was a varied menu, at Chevillard's only one dish—a slice of the *Ring*. The heavens avenged themselves by causing all their reserves to come pouring down on the unhappy dilettanti beneath. "He who reigns in the skies"—is he or is he not a Wagnerian? (You know whom I mean, I take it.)

The Nursery, *Poem and Music by M. Moussorgsky*

T H I S is the title of a cycle of seven songs of which each one is a scene from childhood, and it's a masterpiece. Moussorgsky is little known in France and for this we can excuse ourselves, it is true, by remarking that he is no better known in Russia.[1] He was born in Karevo (central Russia) in 1839, and he died in 1881 in a bed in the Nicolas military hospital at Saint Petersburg. So you can see from these two dates that he had no time to lose if he was to become a genius. He did not lose a moment and he will leave an indelible imprint on the memories of those who love his music. Nobody has spoken to that which is best in us with such tenderness and depth; he is quite unique, and will be renowned for an art that suffers from no stultifying rules or artificialities. Never before has such a refined sensibility expressed itself with such simple means: it is almost as if he were an inquisitive savage discovering music for the first time, guided in each step forward by his own emotions. There is no question of any such thing as "form," or, at least, any forms there are have such complexity that they are impossible to relate to the accepted forms—the "official" ones. He composes in a series of bold strokes, but his incredible gift of foresight means that each stroke is bound to the next by a mysterious thread. Sometimes he can conjure up a disquieting impression of darkness so powerful that it wrings tears from one's heart. In the first piece, "The Nursery," we can hear the prayer of a little girl before she goes to sleep. Here the gestures themselves, the delicate, troubled soul of the child, even the wonderful way in which little girls pretend to be grown up—all these are captured with a truthfulness that is to be found nowhere else. "The Doll's Lullaby" seems to have been taken down word for word, thanks to enormous powers of assimilation and an ability to inhabit those magic landscapes so special to a child's mind. The end of this lullaby is so beautifully restful that even the little girl who is telling the story falls gently to sleep at the sound of her own voice. There is also a horrible little boy! He transforms the playroom into a battlefield by riding a toy truncheon like a horse, breaking the arms and legs of the poor defenseless chairs as he careens around, not to mention the more personal wounds he inflicts. Of course he soon hurts himself as well, and all the playful exuberance dissolves into screams and tears. But it is not too serious: a couple of minutes on his mommy's knee, a kiss to make him better, and he is off again and the battle begins once more. The chairs don't know where to hide themselves.

As I said, all these little happenings are noted with an extreme simplicity: for Moussorgsky, one chord is often sufficient (although it would have seemed poor to M. What's-his-name). Or else he uses a modulation so individual that it wouldn't even have been in the books of M. So-and-so. (Need I add that they are the same monsieur?)[2] We'll be returning to Moussorgsky later, for he's well worth our attention in many respects. Mme Marie Olénine sang these songs at a recent concert of the Société Nationale, so well that Moussorgsky himself would have been pleased—if I may dare to speak on his behalf.

A Piano Sonata by Paul Dukas

M O N S I E U R Paul Dukas has just published a piano sonata.[3] If this news isn't exactly going to alter the course of the world it's nonetheless an event worthy of note, displaying an impartiality rare in our times. Nowadays, when music is employed more and more as a mere accompaniment for sentimental or melodramatic tales, it begins to assume the somewhat shady role of a barker outside a fairground stall, enticing the crowds to share the mysteries of the sinister Mr. Nobody within.

Real music lovers have little time for the fairground: their concern is simply to play their few selected pages of favorite music over and over again at the piano—as intoxicating a way of conjuring up dreams as that "powerful yet subtle opium," but less debilitating. Paul Dukas seems to have had such people in mind when he wrote his sonata. The remoteness of its emotional appeal and the rigorous logic in its sequence of ideas inevitably demands an intimate communion with the work (and Dukas's work is noted for being demanding, even when it's only incidental music). It is the result of painstaking care as regards the arrangement of the various movements, but I fear that the sequence might not be very easily followed in a concert performance. Not that this detracts from its beauty in any way, nor from its overall conception. If only the mind that conceived this sonata would try to combine imagination with construction: the result need not be complication. Why should it? Monsieur Dukas understands the potentialities of music: he doesn't consider it merely for its brilliance—something to titillate our ears until they can't stand any more. He has a clear understanding of how various kinds of music one would have thought irreconcilable are blended without too much jarring against each other. For him, music is an inexhaustible treasure-trove of forms, of possibilities that enable him to mold his ideas into a musical kingdom drawn from his own imagination. He is master of his own emotions and knows how to avoid unnecessary outbursts; consequently he never lets himself be led into those unnecessary developments that often spoil otherwise very beautiful pieces. If you look at the third part of this sonata, you'll find, underneath the apparently picturesque exterior, a powerful force that controls, almost imperceptibly, the rhythmic tension as if by a steel spring. A similar force is to be found in the last movement, which shows the art of controlling the emotional content at its best. You could even say that the emotions themselves are a structural force, for the piece evokes a beauty comparable to the most perfect lines found in architecture—lines based on natural forms that blend so well with the open spaces of the air and of the sky that all is a perfect and total harmony.

I felt it necessary to write about this rather special piece. We all know of Dukas's reputation as a contemporary musician, but this latest work rises above all preconceptions. It has been composed with the utmost care. It's music as Moussorgsky felt it, or Dukas understands it, and only a few others that makes my column worthwhile.

The Vaudeville Symphony Concerts

T H E S E last few weeks have seen the arrival of a host of German conductors. It hasn't exactly been an epidemic, but it has caused at least as much stir, what with a conductor being worth ninety times as much as an ordinary person. Now if Weingartner or Richard Strauss or Mottl (so excitable) or even the great Richter wished to come and reinstate the Masters in their true beauty, I wouldn't deny them the opportunity. But you can have too much of it: we must not allow them to overrun Paris and use us for their trial runs. And if only these gentlemen would give us something of novelty in their programs, it would make life a bit more interesting. But not a bit of it! They draw their funds from the same old symphonic bank and we have to sit through the usual parade of all the different ways of conducting Beethoven symphonies. This one hurries, that one takes his time, but it's always poor old Beethoven who comes off worse in the end. The informed will declare that so-and-so conductor's got the "correct" tempo. But who are they to know! Are they in receipt of communications from Above? It's nothing more than posthumous chitchat—astonishing coming from Beethoven. If his errant spirit were to wander into a concert hall, I'm sure he would fly back as quickly as he could to the place where the only music is that of the spheres! And old Father Bach could say to him, with the hint of a reprimand, "But my dear Ludwig, I can see from your wilting soul that you've been down to that dreadful place again." Perhaps that would be the last time they'd speak to each other.

P.S. I heard too much music on Good Friday to add any more to this miscellany of jottings: Chevillard conducted the whole of the Ninth Symphony by heart. And with such a sure hand. So there, you Germans! Your visit hasn't been entirely in vain!

᏶NOTES

[1] Debussy's admiration for Moussorgsky dated from his twenties. Robert Godet, one of the composer's lifelong friends, had acquired a copy of Moussorgsky's *Boris Godunov* in 1889, nineteen years before the Diaghilev company was to stage the opera in Paris for the first time. Godet placed the score open on Debussy's piano. For weeks, when Godet visited Debussy, the score would be on the piano, always open at the same page. It seemed a gesture of courtesy rather than interest. But *Boris* made a deep impression on Debussy in the years preceding *Pelléas,* and again after the 1908 performances of *Boris* in Paris. In between came the publication of Moussorgsky's *The Nursery.* A memoir of G. Jean-Aubry testifies to the influence the music of *Boris* had on *Pelléas*—quite apart from the stylistic evidence that the music of Debussy's opera provides. "One evening," writes Jean-Aubry,

> I had to leave Debussy with unexpected haste, and I explained to him that I was going to one of the first performances of *Boris Godunov* being given at the Opéra by the Diaghilev company. Debussy, on the doorstep, took me by the arm, and looking at me with a feigned seriousness, said, "Ah! You are going to *Boris.* You will find all of *Pelléas* is there!"

A detailed study of the impact of Russian music on Debussy has been made by André Schaeffner (in Souvtchinsky, *Musique Russe* [Paris, 1953]).

On one other occasion in his life, Debussy put pen to paper with regard to *The Nursery.* Louis Laloy (later to be Debussy's biographer) had compared the *Histoires naturelles* of Ravel to Moussorgsky's song cycle in an article in the review *SIM*. Debussy took Laloy to task: "I have received your second number of the *SIM* and am dismayed to find that a man of your taste deliberately sacrifices such a pure, instinctive masterpiece as *The Nursery* to the artificial Americanism of the *Histoires naturelles* of M. Ravel." Debussy still regarded *The Nursery* as something of a land-mark. (See "Correspondance de Claude Debussy et de Louis Laloy" in the Debussy number of the *Revue de musicologie,* 1962.)

2 Probably an allusion to the harmony treatise of Emile Durand, Debussy's harmony teacher at the Conservatoire (1877–80). Debussy had rebelled against the teaching of this amiable but dry pedagogue, whose harmony treatise was admired and recommended by Saint-Saëns.

3 Dukas's Piano Sonata is a massive, four-movement work lasting over an hour. It is dense in style and uses three staves. In its constantly roving chromaticism it strongly recalls Franck and d'Indy, as well as referring to the sonatas of Beethoven.

Good Friday

T H I S is the day the symphony concerts became the *concerts spirituels.*
One never quite knew how the same old things could suddenly be
played "spiritually."

This year, Monsieur Colonne certainly showed great "spirit" in
livening up his programs with a handsome bunch of virtuosi, so one
could let oneself be overwhelmed by a feeling of the international.
Even so, I think I can safely say that our devoted music lovers still
had to put up with neighbors more interested in the orchestral pantomime than in anything really artistic.

The attraction that binds the virtuoso to his public seems much the
same as that which draws the crowds to the circus: we always hope
that something dangerous is going to happen.[1] M. Ysaÿe is going to
play the violin with M. Colonne on his shoulders. Or M. Pugno will
finish by seizing the piano between his teeth. . . . None of these
acrobatics materialized. . . .

Ysaÿe played Bach's Violin Concerto in G as only he is capable of
doing. Without any sense of having intruded on the music, he has a
freedom of expression and a spontaneous, natural beauty of tone—
essential gifts for the interpretation of this music.

He was as lucid as the rest of the performance was nauseatingly
pedestrian. The stolid way it was played made Bach seem to be bearing
the weight of many subsequent centuries.

However, this is a marvelous concerto—like so many others inscribed in the notebooks of the grand old Bach. Once again one finds

that almost the entire piece is pure "musical arabesque," or rather it is based on the principle of the "ornament," which is at the root of all kinds of art. (And the word "ornament" here has nothing to do with the ornaments one finds in musical dictionaries.)

The primitives—Palestrina, Vittoria, Orlando di Lasso, etc.—had this divine sense of the arabesque. They found the basis of it in Gregorian chant, whose delicate tracery they supported with twining counterpoints. In reworking the arabesque, Bach made it more flexible, more fluid, and despite the fact that the Great Master always imposed a rigorous discipline on beauty, he imbued it with a wealth of free fantasy so limitless that it still astonishes us today.[2]

In Bach's music it is not the character of the melody that affects us but rather the curve. More often still it is the parallel movement of several lines whose fusion stirs our emotions—whether fortuitous or contrived. Based on this conception of the ornamental, the music will impress the public as regularly as clockwork, and it will fill their imaginations with pictures.

Perhaps we find it difficult to believe in anything so unnatural and artificial. Well, it is a good deal more "natural" than all that silly wailing you find in opera. Above all, such music preserves a sense of nobility: it never lowers itself to the taste of those affected listeners who want only "sensibility"—the ones who say, "We like music *so* much." Still more to its favor, it forces one to respect if not to adore.

I expect you have noticed how you never hear Bach being whistled . . . an honor that is not denied Wagner: when the "prisoners de luxe" are released from their musical detention centers, you often hear the "Spring Song" or the opening phrase of *Die Meistersinger* being whistled gleefully in the street. I am sure that for a lot of people a piece achieves fame only by being whistled in the street, though one could hold the opposite view without seeming too extreme.

I must add that this ornamental conception of music has now completely disappeared: we have succeeded in domesticating music, for it has become the business of families who, not knowing what to do with one of their children—the engineering profession is so crowded these days—teach him music instead. And so more mediocre amateurs are born. If by chance some real genius tries to shake off traditional constraints, it's somehow arranged that he should drown in ridicule, so the poor geniuses often take it upon themselves to die young, and it's only for this gesture that they receive any encouragement at all.

But back to M. Ysaÿe, who next played his own transcription of a study in the form of a waltz by Saint-Saëns, originally for piano. In this piece Ysaÿe showed more virtuosity than art, and it seemed to trouble the more serious-minded members of the audience, for they made it quite plain that they had no time for "such a lot of virtuosity about nothing." Some people will never understand a joke. Why can't Saint-Saëns be humorous if he wants?

Next M. Pugno played a concerto by Mozart; it couldn't be played badly because it is so well written for the piano. He played it impeccably, as he always does.

In between, M. A. van Rooy from Bayreuth sang Wolfram's aria from the singers' competition in the second act of Tannhäuser—with such charm that you could almost excuse the dreadful setting. My God, it certainly is a competition! In fact it's so much of a contest that in the end we can almost accept that military two-step with which Tannhäuser stifles the heavy eloquence of suave old Wolfram—not that this same Wolfram isn't able to sing his song to the evening star a quarter of an hour later. An incorrigible fellow, this Wolfram! Next M. van Rooy sang three songs by Schubert. Harmless songs, these: they seem to have been found in the bottom drawers of some pretty but rather aging provincial girls—pieces of faded ribbon, pressed flowers and photographs of long since forgotten people. We find the same effects lasting for an interminable number of couplets. By the third we are asking ourselves if it isn't really Paul Delmet who is on stage![3] In order to show off the variety of his finely engineered throat, M. van Rooy ended his program with "Wotan's Farewell," a piece whose fireworks never fail to work on any audience. His voice fought arduously with the orchestra, and as the tumultuous applause assured us, he won the day without a shadow of doubt.

The Ninth Symphony

T H E Ninth has long been surrounded by a haze of adjectives. To-gether with the Mona Lisa's smile—which for some strange reason has always been labeled "mysterious"—it is a masterpiece about which the most stupid comments have been made. It's a wonder it hasn't been submerged entirely beneath the mass of words it has excited. Wagner intended completing the orchestration; others imagined an explanation of its development in terms of illuminated pictures. In the end, this fine, intelligible work is turned into something unapproachable by the general public. I suppose some light is thrown upon the subject by admitting that it does contain a mystery, but does that really help?

You know Beethoven's literary side wasn't worth twopence—at least not in the present-day sense of the word. He loved music and was proud of her; for him she contained all the passion and joy that were so noticeably missing from his private life. Perhaps we should see the *Choral* Symphony as simply an overblown gesture of musical pride. A notebook containing over two hundred different versions of the main theme of the coda to this symphony tells us of the pains-taking care and the purely musical vision that was guiding him; Schil-ler's verses are included only for their value as sounds. His wish was that the initial theme should contain all the potential for development. As well as being of prodigious beauty in itself, it is also magnificent because of the other elements it throws into relief. There is no more triumphant example of how flexible an idea can become within the mold imposed upon it. At each leap forward a new joy is discovered, and it never seems tired or repetitious. You could say it was like the magical growth of a tree that was sprouting fresh leaves and blossom-ing at the same time. There is nothing redundant in this work of such giant proportions, not even the Andante, which some recent aesthetes have accused of being too long. Is this not just a finely judged mo-ment of repose to offset the rhythmic insistence of the Scherzo and the instrumental torrent that carries, invincibly, the voices toward the glory of the Finale? Beethoven had already written eight symphonies; the Ninth seemed almost to signify a fight against destiny. He had tried to excel himself, and I hardly see how anyone could deny that he succeeded. As for the excesses of humanity that burst the customary seams of this symphony: they sprang out of his own soul, which, drunk with the idea of freedom, was gradually destroying itself. Ironically, he was already destined for the golden gates that would force him to be numbered among the unlucky company of many other great men. Beethoven suffered with all his heart; he ardently desired humanity to find communion in him, and from that desire was born his cry "to the humblest and poorest of his brothers," uttered by the thousand voices of his genius. But did they hear him? A vexed question. The *Choral* Symphony was conducted on Good Friday by Chevillard, with an understanding that ranks this conductor among the very greatest. It found itself in the company of several festering pieces by Richard Wagner. Tannhäuser, Siegmund, Lohengrin—everybody once again staked his claim to a leitmotiv. But the severe and loyal mastery of old Beethoven easily won the day from such meandering, high-hatted humbugs!

☙ NOTES

1 Debussy's comparison of the virtuoso to the circus artist is not as flippant as it appears at first sight, for the art of the circus was held in the highest esteem by poets and artists at the turn of the century: the clown, the circus parade, and the precariousness of the trapeze were to provide nourishment for all the arts. Baudelaire and Laforgue in particular drew upon the art—for an art it was—and Lautrec, Renoir, and Degas all painted its various aspects. In his use of the cakewalk and other features of the music of circus and music hall, Debussy both complemented the writers and painters of a previous generation and anticipated the music of Les Six in the Cocteau era of the twenties. In the host of reviews of the day, many articles appeared in appraisal of the circuses, of which Paris could boast a half a dozen. "Do you enjoy fear?" wrote one commentator on the spectacles of Paris. "Evidently you do, and so does everyone, for the circuses continue to present us with acrobatics whose sole purpose is to send shivers of fear down our spines" (Pierre Bost, *Petit Plan cavalier des divertissements parisiens*). Debussy's statements about the virtuoso must thus be seen as belonging to an era in which the circus was considered to be one of the fine arts.

[2] It was in Rome that Debussy first heard the music of the "primitives"—Palestrina, Vittoria, and Lasso—apparently at the suggestion of Liszt. Hearing this music was one of the few consolations during the composer's unhappy Prix de Rome sojourn. That was in 1885. Eight years later, writing to Prince Poniatowski, he mentions Renaissance church music once more:

> It was at Saint-Gervais, a church where some intelligent priest took it into his head to revive some of that extremely beautiful sacred music of olden times. They sang an *a cappella* mass by Palestrina—marvelously fine. This music, although written in a very strict style, appears entirely white. The feelings are not conveyed by screaming (as has happened since) but by melodic "arabesques." It is achieved by the contours and by these arabesques intertwining to produce *melodic harmony:* something that now seems to be unique. I also heard a mass by Vittoria—a Spanish primitive. With him it seems to achieve an ascetic and powerful mysticism with a similar simplicity of means. (Prince Poniatowski, *D'un siècle à l'autre* [Paris, 1948].)

Debussy's notion of "arabesque"—he had written two piano "arabesques"—is crucial to an understanding of his art, for it meant something quite different from the concept of melody. It was an ornamental line "based on natural curves." His ideas on the nature of such lines had been fertilized by writings on visual art, probably by Ruskin, whose ideas were echoed by many painters at the turn of the century. The so-called art nouveau movement, with which Maurice Denis was associated, inherited Ruskinian and Pre-Raphaelite ideals of natural line. Ruskin's ideas were newly translated into French and received considerable attention, particularly through the efforts of the Anglophile Robert de la Sizeranne, who published a book, *Ruskin et la Religion de la Beauté,* in which he summarized Ruskin's theories. "Ruskin," he writes,

> praises the artists of the ducal palace [in Florence] for having discovered the grandeur of foliage and for incorporating it into the huge surfaces of their powerful murals, just as Nature takes pride in the sorrel leaf or water lily. He requires one to give the vegetable ornament the same value as nature herself.

Such phrases are remarkably similar to what Debussy expressed in his several expositions of his theory of musical "arabesque"—a word that was used to describe these "vegetable ornaments." Denis himself stresses the sinuous arabesque based on natural forms. "I dream of ancient missals with rhythmical borders . . . an embroidery of arabesques on the pages, an accompaniment of expressive contours" (*Art et Critique,* 30 August 1890).

[3] Debussy's admiration for the music-hall singer Paul Delmet was made evident on several occasions. In a letter to Louÿs of 1897 he wrote: "We have only one musician who is really French, and that's Paul Delmet."

L'Opéra

E V E R Y B O D Y knows the Paris Opéra, at least by reputation. It is with regret that I assure you it hasn't changed at all: for the sake of the passer-by who hasn't been warned, let me say that it looks like a railway station. But once you're inside you'll be more likely to mistake it for a Turkish bath.

The Opéra's business is noise: those who have paid for it call it "music." Don't believe them.

By special favor and a subsidy from the state, this theater is able to put on anything at all, though it hardly matters what is on, as they have most extravagantly fitted *loges à salons*—tiny antechambers behind the boxes—so called because they are especially placed so you can't hear any of the music: the last remaining salons where one can chat.

With regard to all this, I am not challenging the wisdom of the directors, for I'm sure the best good will in the world would be shattered there, coming up against that solid wall of red tape that lets in no light at all. It won't be changed by anything short of a revolution, and revolutionaries don't often bother with such establishments as opera houses. One would wish for a fire, except that too many innocent people might be hurt. If only the resigned apathy of the place could be given a thorough shake-up, perhaps some really beautiful things could be done. Should we not have had the complete *Ring* by now? Something long overdue. It would at least have got it out of the way, and the Bayreuth pilgrims wouldn't have been able to bore us with their stories any more. . . . It would have been good to have *Die*

Meistersinger, too, but *Tristan und Isolde* would be even better (for there the charming ghost of Chopin appears, keeping the passion in check). That would leave us only *Parsifal* to fear, though for family reasons and because of pressure of work, Cosima Wagner has reserved rights on the enterprise.

To continue our complaining, let us see how important the Opéra has been in forwarding the development of dramatic music in France.

Well, a lot of Reyer is performed. I think the reasons for this are most bizarre. There are people who look at landscapes with the disinterest of a cow; those same people listen to music with cotton wool in their ears.

Old Saint-Saëns wrote operas in the spirit of an impenitent symphonist. Will that be a good enough reason for him to be admired in the future?

Massenet seems to have been the victim of some devoted fan-waving on the part of his lady listeners; for some time now they have been idolizing him, and he desperately wanted the beating of those perfumed wings to continue to adorn his name. Unfortunately, he might just as well try to tame a swarm of butterflies! Perhaps it was just that he lacked patience and underestimated the value of silence. . . . His influence on contemporary music is clear enough, although it is not acknowledged by some who owe him a great deal—ungrateful hypocrites!

There are many more operas that could be mentioned, but the complete list would be too tedious. We might mention *Thamara* by M. Bourgault-Ducoudray, who, undeterred by his lukewarm reception, hasn't yet said all that he has to.

Among too many stupid ballets there's one that stands out as something of a masterpiece: Edouard Lalo's *Namouna.* But some sort of blind malice has caused this music to be buried so deep that nobody ever mentions it nowadays—a sad thing for the cause of music.

Of all these there is not a thing that is really new. Nothing but the churning of a factory, the same old things over and over again. You'd think that music had to put on an obligatory uniform as it entered the opera house, as if it were a convict. It assumes all the false grandeur of the place, competing with the celebrated Grand Staircase that an

error in perspective and too many details made . . . well . . . not
so grand.

Le Roi de Paris

Opera in three acts;
lyrics by Henri Bouchut, music by Georges Hüe

O N E more opera to add to the rest. . . . Its subject matter is historical: about the assassination of the duc de Guise—not one of the better moments in French history, and it doesn't seem to me to do much
good to aggravate the situation by setting it to music. And they dressed
so badly in those days! The men seemed to wear the most inelegant life
jackets, and the women had their waistlines in a region where
one would least expect to find them! If we really must turn the
opera into a history lesson, why not try to find events free from such
ridiculous political intrigues? I would suggest the time of Louis
Philippe, an unexplored field and a fertile one. Monsieur Georges
Hüe has set this little episode to too much music: it prevents one
from hearing the words of the poem, which itself seems to have been
inspired by Flaubert's great and unforgettable twins Bouvard and
Pécuchet.

It would be most untimely to express the wish that M. Georges
Hüe had refrained from composing this piece. I must say that it was
a fine piece of historical interpretation to give the somewhat dubious
character of Henry III to a tenor.

L'Ouragan

Opera in four acts;
poem by Emile Zola, music by Alfred Bruneau[1]

W A G N E R has set us a number of precedents in how to fashion
music for the theater. One day we shall see how useless they all are.
For his own benefit he invented the "leitmotiv guide" to aid those who

cannot read a score. It's perfect: it enables the listener to get through all the more quickly. . . . But what is more serious, he has accustomed us to making the music servile, in being responsible for the development of the characters. I feel I should try to explain this, for it seems to me to be the main trouble with dramatic music these days. Music has a rhythm whose secret force shapes the development. The rhythm of the soul, however, is quite different—more instinctive, more general, and controlled by many events. From the incompatibility of these two rhythms a perpetual conflict arises, for the two do not move at the same speed. Either the music stifles itself by chasing after a character, or the character has to sit on a note to allow the music to catch up with him. Nonetheless, there are miraculous moments where the two are in harmony, and Wagner has the honor of being responsible for some of these. But they are for the most part due to chance, and more often than not awkward and deceptive. All in all, the application of symphonic form to dramatic action succeeds in killing dramatic music rather than saving it, as was proclaimed when Wagner was crowned king of opera.

This work by Zola and Bruneau is full of symbols. I must say I don't understand this excessive need for symbols. They seem to have forgotten that it is still music that is supreme in its beauty. As you would expect, each symbol takes the form of a leitmotiv; once again music is weighed down by these obstinate little phrases, which insist on having their say no matter what else is going on. Really, to pretend that such-and-such a succession of chords represents this or that sentiment, and that so-and-so phrase is one or another character—it is nothing but an anthropometrical game.

Are there not other approaches? Here I address myself to Monsieur Bruneau himself, for he would seem to me to have enough imagination to find some interesting alternatives. Of all musicians he has an admirable contempt for set forms: he uses successions of harmonies without ever worrying about their grammatical "correctness," and he finds melodic links that others would too readily class as monstrous, when in fact they are merely unusual. The third act of this work seems to me to be the most securely successful: the music is furious and poignant. It goes much deeper than the facile tragedy of the plot, which ought to move far more quickly and not waste time holding psychological discussions about the jealousy experienced by two of the characters in this act. For the rest of it, the music carelessly bullies the words, seeming to say to them, "Out of my way! You know full well that I'm the strongest." And so everything falls into line. . . . I don't so much like the way in which the character Lulu is handled either, or what she symbolizes. Should we not have had something rather more special? A magic touch different from all the rest of the music? I can see the charm of it all but not the depth, nor the attraction of the constantly changing scenery.

I might seem as if I am imposing restrictions, something that isn't really relevant to this piece. You must either take it or leave it. If you accept it, you must love its faults as attractions; otherwise it becomes intolerable. Nonetheless, it flowed from the pen of a man who is enduring much suffering for the cause of truth—something rare in these times when many of the self-styled masters are merely trying to score points in a tradition that they do not share, a tradition handed down by a man who is greater than them all.

I am not qualified to write of Zola's poem, but he would seem to me to be better at "situations" than at such wordy lyricism.

I do not see why one should congratulate M. Albert Carré for his marvelous scenery. Has he ever thought of sending his card to the Almighty to congratulate Him for having made the sunset so wonderful?

Mlle Delna was as tragic as one could have wished. Mlle Raunay was as beautiful as ever, and Mlle Guiradon was like an exotic bird. MM. Bourbon, Dufrane, and Maréchal completed the group.

☙ *NOTE*

[1] Some years earlier, in 1897, Debussy had expressed strong views on Bruneau and Zola. With regard to their collaboration on *Messidor* he wrote to Louÿs:

I got no further than you with *Messidor*—life being so short and it being preferable to go to the café or look at pictures. How can dreadful people such as Zola and Bruneau be capable of nothing else but mediocre efforts? Have you noticed the deplorable use of patriotism in their articles? It's no more than an opportunity to say, "It may be bad but at least it's French!"

LA REVUE BLANCHE
1 June 1901

The Nikisch Concerts

ON Sunday, 19 May, there was an overpowering but quite irresistible spell of sunshine that seemed to thwart all attempts at listening to music. The Berlin Philharmonic Orchestra, with Nikisch as conductor, chose this day to give its first concert. I hope the good Lord will pardon me for having broken my vow never to hear music on a Sunday and that some other people, luckier than I, will have paid homage to the green grass He litters with sausage skins on such days, given over to the creation of lovers' idylls.

All the famous ears of Paris were there! Especially those strange old ladies. It was the very best of "good audiences"—ripe for someone to take advantage of. All you need is an elegant stance and a romantically curling lock of hair and you'll be assured of their enthusiasm.

Nikisch has both. Luckily, he also has some more worthwhile talents. Moreover, his orchestra is marvelously disciplined, and one feels that one is in the presence of people whose only concern is serious music-making. They are both grave and unassuming, like the figures in a primitive fresco. It is most rare and quite touching.

M. Nikisch is an incomparable virtuoso: it even seems that his virtuosity makes him forget that one also needs good taste! I would take as an example of this his performance of the Overture to *Tannhäuser,* where he makes the trombones play with portamenti more suited to that lady in charge of the sentimental songs at the Casino de Suresnes. He also takes the horns up to a climax for which there is no apparent reason. These are "effects" without any appreciable justification, and they are quite astonishing coming from such an otherwise

well-informed musician as Monsieur Nikisch. Before that, he proved
the rarity of his gifts in Richard Strauss's *Till Eulenspiegel*. That
piece ought to be called "An Hour of Music with the Clowns," for
clarinets soar like rockets into the sky; the trumpets all but choke; the
horns, feeling a sneezing fit coming on, hurriedly put in a "Bless
you!" and the big bass drum goes "boum-boum," marking time for
this parade of clowns.[1] One either dies laughing or cries one's eyes
out. Amazingly, the musicians play in their normal way: one
wouldn't have been surprised to see the double basses blowing down
their bows, or the trombones bowing their crooks with imaginary
bows. And even if M. Nikisch had conducted while being seated on
an usherette's lap, one wouldn't have been too shocked. All this
doesn't prevent the piece from having a few strokes of genius: its
orchestral assurance, for example, and the way in which the frenzied
movement is upheld from beginning to end, throwing us into the
midst of the hero's pranks. Monsieur Nikisch conducted this tumult
with a marvelous sang-froid, and the ovation that greeted him and his
orchestra couldn't have been better deserved.[2]

It would be difficult to think of any way of ruining Beethoven's
Fifth! M. Nikisch restored forgotten beauty to some parts of it. During the performance of Schubert's *Unfinished* Symphony, a bevy of
sparrows was rattling against the windows of the Cirque, and they
furiously began a chirping that wasn't entirely devoid of charm. M.
Nikisch had the good taste not to ask anyone to get rid of these
disrespectful music lovers, no doubt intoxicated with azure. Perhaps it
was just a harmless protest against this symphony, which can't decide
for itself, once and for all, to be "unfinished."

Music in the Open Air

> Voici venir le temps où, vibrant sur sa tige,
> Chaque musique militaire s'evapore ainsi qu'un encensoir!
>
> [The time has come when, trembling on its stem,
> All military music will evaporate, as from a censer.][3]

Apologies to Baudelaire! But, seriously, why is the adornment of our
squares and boulevards left solely to the military bands?[4] I like to

imagine more unusual happenings, ones that would blend more completely with the natural surroundings. Isn't military music meant to relieve the tedium of long marches, and to bring joy to the streets? It expresses the patriotism that burns in every heart, and it unites the quiet soul of the little pastry cook with the old gentleman who thinks of nothing but the Alsace-Lorraine question, yet never talks about it. Far be it from me to take away these noble privileges, but I must say that, coming through the trees, it sounds like a childhood phonograph.

For the trees we should have a large orchestra with the support of human voices. (No! Not a choral society, thank you!) I envisage the possibility of a music especially written for the open air, flowing in bold, broad lines from both the orchestra and the voices. It would resound through the open spaces and float joyfully over the tops of the trees, and any harmonic progression that sounded stifled within the confines of a concert hall would take on a new significance. Perhaps this is the answer to the question of how to kill off that silly obsession with overprecise "forms" and "tonality," which so unfortunately encumber music. She could certainly be regenerated, taking a lesson in freedom from the blossoming of the trees. What she lost in the charm of details she would gain from her new-found grandeur. It must be understood that it would mean working not with the "gross" but with the "grand." Neither would it be a question of annoying the echoes by repeating huge clusters of sound ad nauseam, but rather taking advantage of them by using them to prolong the impression of harmony. It would be a mysterious collaboration between the air, the movement of the leaves, and the scent of the flowers—all mingled into music. She would be reunited with all these elements in such a natural marriage that she would seem to live in each one of them. Then, at least, we could prove once and for all that music and poetry are the only two arts that live and move in space itself. . . . I might be mistaken, but it seems to me that here are possibilities for future generations. But for us at this time I've a feeling that music will continue to be rather stuffy.

For those who haven't heard, I have great pleasure in announcing that M. Dukas's sonata, of which I spoke some weeks ago, has been acclaimed by the public with great enthusiasm. Not that it makes

Dukas any the greater, but it does raise in our estimation those we think of as being the "public."

Mme M. Olénine gave a recital of Moussorgsky songs that provided us with an excellent opportunity to increase our affection for this neglected composer, and also to express our infinite thanks to Mme Olénine's fine musical intelligence in choosing and performing these pieces. You couldn't wish for a more faithful interpreter. Everything was pronounced with a correctness little short of miraculous. (A very good audience, too.)

There was a celebration for Wagner's birthday on 22 May at the Cirque d'Hiver under the auspices of Nikisch (already mentioned). My God! How that audience became delirious! You would have thought they were all more or less direct descendants of Ludwig II of Bavaria. (Not such a good audience.)

⌇∾ NOTES

[1] "Boum-Boum" was the name of a celebrated Parisian circus clown, immortalized by Toulouse-Lautrec.

[2] Debussy's ideas on Strauss's music, new to Paris, are among the most vivid of his impressions—immediate personal reactions to this overpowering composer. It was in 1899 that Strauss first conducted in Paris a performance of *Also Sprach Zarathustra*. Debussy was not present on this occasion, but Strauss later gave several performances in the first years of the century, when conducting concerts of his own works in Paris. It is only with the complete edition of Debussy's articles chronologically presented that we are able to assess the French composer's view of Strauss; indeed, this is one of the most important areas of Debussy's taste to be brought into perspective by his magazine and newspaper columns. He was evidently stunned by this, his first encounter with Strauss's kaleidoscopic use of the orchestra. But Debussy conceals his responses behind the mask of the circus clown. His opinion of the composer begins to crystallize later, and we can observe ambivalent attitudes developing, as had been the case with Wagner. As an orchestral colorist with roots not only in Wagner and Berlioz but also in Weber, the orchestrator most admired by Debussy, Strauss found favor. Debussy saw his quickly changing colors as cinemato-

graphic, and as a possible rejuvenating factor for French music. On the other hand, there was an element of teutonic "moonshine" in Strauss that Debussy could not abide. (See pp. 97, 101, 159–161, 168, 270–1, 296, and 302.)

[3] The quotation is from Baudelaire's "Harmonie du soir," the poem whose last lines—"les sons et les parfums tournent dans l'air du soir"—are used by Debussy as the title of one of his piano preludes. Debussy substitutes the words "musique militaire" for "fleur."

[4] Debussy's ideas on "open-air music" are among his most daring and fascinating. They are developed (and, indeed, some repeated word for word) in his later article on pp. 92–4. Evidently the editor of *La Renaissance latine* found them too daring to print, or at least incomprehensible, when he rejected the later article. For the roots of Debussy's ideas on *la musique en plein air,* we might turn to the impressionist painters, often called the "plein-airists," who renounced "studio lighting" in favor of daylight. Debussy's ideas are strangely prophetic, foreshadowing Satie (a complement to his "furniture music"?) and Messiaen, whose *Et exspecto resurrectionem mortuorum,* with its huge clusters of sound, was intended for performance on a mountaintop.

LA REVUE BLANCHE
1 July 1901

Conversation with M. Croche

I T was a pleasant evening and I had decided to do nothing . . . for the sake of politeness let us say that I was dreaming. To tell you the truth, they were not even very noble daydreams that were passing through my mind: not the kind about which one later speaks with great affection and a pretension that they had somehow shaped the future. No, these were quite unpretentious moments; I was just passing a quiet hour.

I was dreaming. Should I not collect my thoughts? Finish off some pieces? All these questions were induced, I fear, by a kind of childish egotism and the need to rid oneself at all costs of an idea that has been in one's head for too long. But all this served only as a thin disguise for that stupid obsession with trying to prove oneself superior to everyone else—a preoccupation that never needed much effort unless it was combined with a desire to better oneself. The alchemy of that is far more complex, for it requires the sacrifice of one's whole precious little personality. High ideals! And quite useless in the end. Moreover, trying to persuade everybody else that one really is superior means a considerable amount of time wasted in manifestation of the fact or endless self-propaganda. All one gains is the right to be one of that packet of famous names which is passed around whenever anyone wants to revive some flagging conversation about art. But let me not press the point, for I wouldn't want to discourage anyone.

A pleasant enough evening, but as you may have noticed I was feeling out of sorts. In fact, I was losing track of myself and drowning in all kinds of twisted ideas.

It was exactly at this moment that there was a ring at the doorbell and I was to make the acquaintance of M. Croche. His entry into my house involved all kinds of little incidents, some quite natural and some rather strange, but I won't bother with the details, as they would only detract from the interest of the matter at hand.

M. Croche was short and wizened. His gestures were visibly cultivated for the purpose of making points in metaphysical discussions, and you would best imagine his manner if you were to think of a jockey, Tom Lane perhaps,[1] or of Monsieur Thiers.[2] His overall manner was sharp as a razor, and he spoke very softly and never laughed. Sometimes he would underline his meaning with a silent smile, which would begin at his nose and gradually spread out in wrinkles all over his face—as if someone had thrown a pebble into some calm pool. It would last for ages and was quite intolerable.

At once he aroused my curiosity with his peculiar ideas about music. He would talk about an orchestral score as if it were a painting, without ever using technical terms. Rather did he use unusual words. His language had a strange ring, faded and with an old-fashioned elegance—it seemed like the sound of old medals. I recall the parallel he drew between Beethoven's orchestra, which he spoke of in terms of black and white (and therefore giving a marvelous scale of grays) and Wagner's, which he said was like a kind of multicolored putty, perfectly evenly spread, where he could no longer differentiate between the sound of a violin and that of a trombone.

How that sinister smile would stretch across his face! Particularly when he was speaking about music. Suddenly I decided to ask him his profession. He replied in a voice that forestalled any comment, "Antidilettante." Then he continued in his monotonous, exasperated voice:

"Haven't you noticed the hostility of concert-hall audiences? Haven't you seen those faces, gray with boredom, with indifference, even with stupidity? They are never the slightest bit involved in the pure drama that is the very essence of symphonic conflict! Never do they even consider the pieces as edifices in sound, and they certainly never breathe so much as an ounce of their beauty! These people, monsieur, give one the impression of being more or less well-brought-up guests. They patiently suppress their boredom, and would leave were it not for the fact that they love to be seen on the way out. You must admit that this is just the way to end up with a lifetime's horror of music."

As I argued that I had not only witnessed but been a part of a genuinely enthusiastic audience, he replied, "No! You are quite mistaken. If you do show true enthusiasm it's only in the secret hope that someday someone will do the same for you! Just remember: something which is truly beautiful commands only silence. Every day we witness the magical beauty of the sunset. Does one think of applauding that? Well, you'll admit that it takes its course in a far less predictable way than any one of your silly little stories in sound. What's more, you feel so overawed that you are unable to be a part of it. But with these so-called works of art you merely make up for their deficiencies with an accepted jargon that enables you to talk about them for hours."

I dared not tell him that I was almost convinced by his arguments (nothing kills a conversation so easily as agreement), so instead I asked him if he was himself a musician.

"Monsieur," he replied, "I do not like specialists. For me, to specialize is to limit the boundaries of one's universe. One becomes like the wooden horses on a merry-go-round: they die to the well-known strains of the 'Marche lorraine.' No, I've heard all the music there is to hear, and all I've gained is a peculiar feeling of being immune to any kind of surprise. Two bars, and I can tell you what a symphony or any other kind of piece is all about.

"Don't you see? For as many composers as could truthfully say they had an obstinate desire to do something new, there are at least as many who have no such desire. They do the same things they've already succeeded at, over and over again. I've no time for that kind of predictability. And we call them 'masters'! We should make sure that it's not just a convenient way of getting them off our chests, excusing them for having done the same old thing too many times. On the whole I try to forget about all that music lest it should hinder me when I want to listen to the music of tomorrow or to pieces I don't know. Why bother with what one already knows too well?"

I spoke to him of the more famous among our contemporaries, but he only became more aggressive than ever.

"You have a tendency," he said, "to give too much importance to things that would have been quite natural, for example, in Bach's time. You talk to me about M. Paul Dukas's sonata. I suppose he is one of your friends, a music critic perhaps? All the more reason to say kind things! But someone has said even kinder things than you. M. Pierre Lalo, in an article in *Le Temps* devoted exclusively to that sonata, would gladly have sacrificed pieces by Schumann and Chopin for its sake. Certainly Chopin's nervous disposition let him down when it came to the endurance required in composing a sonata. But he did make some finely wrought 'sketches,' and it is at least agreed that he invented his own way of handling the form, not to mention the marvelous music he achieved in doing so. He was a man with abundant imagination, and he would flit from one idea to another without demanding a one hundred percent commission on the transaction—which is what some of our more celebrated masters do.

"Naturally, M. P. Lalo does not forget to compare your friend Dukas to the great master Beethoven. But if I were he I'd have been only moderately flattered: Beethoven's sonatas are very badly written for the piano, and are really more like orchestral transcriptions, especially the last ones. Often they seem to require a third hand, which I'm sure Beethoven intended, at least I hope he did. Lalo would have done better to have left Schumann and Chopin alone, though: they knew how to write for the piano. And if that doesn't mean much to him, he could at least have acknowledged that it was they who had prepared the way for the 'perfection' of Dukas, and, if I may say so, several others."

These last words were uttered by M. Croche with an icy coldness. You either accepted all he had to say or you threw it straight out of the window. My appetite was whetted and I let him go on. There was a long silence. You would have scarcely thought he was alive except for the smoke from his cigar, for his eyes were fixed on its blue spiral, watching the curious twists as it rose. . . . Perhaps outrageous plans were forming in his mind. . . . His silence was disconcerting and rather sinister. Then he began again:

"Music contains so many impulses you could write a song about them. My favorite music is those few notes an Egyptian shepherd plays on his flute: he is a part of the landscape around him, and he knows harmonies that aren't in our books. The 'musicians' hear only music written by practiced hands, never the music of nature herself. To see the sun rise does one far more good than hearing the *Pastoral* Symphony. What's the use of such incomprehensible art? Shouldn't all those complications be forbidden? We learn them only because they are as ingenious as a strong-box lock.[3] But you don't agree. Because you know of nothing but music and are subject to her obscure and barbarous laws! A lot of clever words are written about you, but you're merely a cross between a monkey and the *domestique*."

I dared to point out to him that in poetry and painting alike (and I managed to think of a couple of musicians as well) men had tried to shake away the dust of tradition, but that it had only earned them the labels of "symbolists" or "impressionists"—useful terms of abuse.[4]

"It's only journalists doing their job who call them that," continued Monsieur Croche unflinchingly. "That's of no importance. Imbeciles can find something to ridicule in a fundamentally beautiful idea, and you can be certain there is more likely to be beauty in the work of those who have been ridiculed than in those who calmly trail along like sheep to the slaughterhouse for which they have been predestined.

"Remain unique! . . . . unblemished! Being too influenced by one's milieu spoils an artist: in the end he becomes nothing but the expression of his milieu.

"Search for a discipline within freedom! Don't let yourself be governed by formulae drawn from decadent philosophies: they are for the feeble-minded. Listen to no one's advice except that of the wind in the trees. That can recount the whole history of mankind. . . ."

At this point I saw M. Croche in his true light. It seemed that his very words were like some strange music. I do not know how I can express their peculiar eloquence. Perhaps like this:

"Is there a deeper experience than to stumble across a genius whose secrets have lain dormant for centuries? To have been one of these men! There's real glory!"

Dawn broke. M. Croche, visibly worn out, took his leave. I accompanied him to the landing door. He thought no more of shaking my hand than I did of thanking him. It seemed ages while I listened to his steps dying away—staircase after staircase before they were gone. And I dare not hope ever to see him again.

P.S. The Concert Society of the Conservatoire had the chance of having M. A. Messager as their conductor. Needless to say they missed it. The subscribers to this music hall for the soft-headed can continue their sleep.

NOTES

[1] In the mid-nineties Debussy had been a regular visitor to the Bar Reynolds. An Anglophile haunt of Toulouse-Lautrec, this was a Parisian pub complete with horse brasses and a clientèle consisting of stable lads, grooms, and jockeys, many from across the Channel. No doubt it was here that Debussy saw Tom Lane, an English jockey. The wider implications of M. Croche's appearance are discussed elsewhere. (See pp. *x–xii.*)

[2] Ex-premier of France.

[3] In Debussy's puzzling and unpublished play, the *pièce à clef, Frères en Art* (written with René Peter), we find a clue that may point to a source of the primitivistic ideas found in this passage and elsewhere in his articles: his idealization of the "few notes" of an Egyptian shepherd, his recommendation of the "music" of nature—the sunset, the sea—and his later references to primitive music he had actually heard (see pp. 278–9). The principal character of Debussy's obscure play is an English art critic called Redburne, who, as Edward Lockspeiser pointed out in his discussion of the work (*Revue de musicologie*, 1970, no. 2, and "Music and Painting"), contains aspects not only of Swinburne and George Moore but also of Ruskin, who is later mentioned by name in the play. Many of Ruskin's writings, admired by a host of French men of letters at the turn of the century, had been translated into French in various books and articles, including several by Debussy's friend and correspondent Gabriel Mourey. In Ruskin's *Praeterita* there is a curious anticipation of Debussy's *Monsieur Croche*:

> The shepherds on the high Alps live for months in a perfect solitude, not perhaps seeing the face of a human being for weeks to-

gether. Among these men there is a very beautiful custom—the manner in which they celebrate their evening devotions. When the sun is just setting, and the peaks of eternal snow become tinted of a pale but bright rose color by his dying beams, the shepherd who is highest upon the mountain takes his horn and sounds through it a few simple but melodious notes, signifying "Glory be to God." Far and wide on the pure air floats the sound; the nearest shepherd hears and replies; and from man to man, over the illimitable deserts of a hundred hills, passes on the voice of worship. Then there is a silence, a deep, dead silence; every head is uncovered, every knee bowed. . . .

In this custom there is something peculiarly impressive, but it is owing chiefly to concomitant circumstances; and the music of the horn, if it were used for another purpose and in another place, would be heard without any excited feeling. It is the stillness of the solitude, the grandeur of the mountains, the beauty of the twilight, and the simplicity of the worship, which create sensations so sublime in the hearer, which makes so strong an impression on his feelings, and appeal so vividly to his mind.

[4] No doubt Debussy had himself in mind, for he was among the first musicians to be dubbed "impressionist." (The first, according to *Littré*, was a now-forgotten composer by the name of Maupou.) Debussy's "Printemps" had been criticized for its vague "impressionism" at the Académie in 1887:

Monsieur Debussy does not lapse into banality nor is he platitudinous. On the contrary, he has a pronounced tendency—too pronounced—toward an exploration of the strange. One has the feeling of musical color exaggerated to the point where it causes the composer to forget the importance of precise construction and form. It is to be strongly hoped that he will guard against this vague impressionism, which is one of the most dangerous enemies of truth in works of art.

About a Few Superstitions of Ours, and an Opera

LINGERING in the autumnal countryside, all that magic of the ancient forests invincibly came back to me. A gentle, persuasive voice that lulled one into perfect oblivion rose from the falling of the golden leaves—seeming to celebrate the glorious death throes of the trees—and the hollow tones of the angelus, which tolled the fields to sleep. The sun set quite alone, for there was no peasant in the foreground to strike a lithographic pose.[1] Man and beast went to and fro together in peace; the day's tasks were ended. And even those daily chores would have had a special beauty of their own, needing no encouragement and inciting no disapproval. Far, far away were artistic discussions: the names of the Great Men would have seemed like coarse words here; all the artificial hysteria of first nights was forgotten. I was alone and wonderfully carefree. Perhaps I had never loved music more than at this time, when to talk about it was furthest from my mind. Music appeared to me in her total beauty: no longer as tiny fragments of a symphony, nor overblown, complex forms. Sometimes my thoughts would turn to M. Croche, for his neat, ghostly appearance would have fitted into any landscape without spoiling its lines. But I had to leave all this tranquil joy and return, my heart heavy with a mistrust of towns where so many prefer to be slowly broken than to be left out of the "machinery" of which they are unwittingly the wheels.

It was while I was returning along the boulevard Malesherbes, so elegant but monotonous in the dreary twilight, that I caught sight of the wizened figure of Monsieur Croche. Knowing his peculiar ways I walked straight up to him without further ado. He gave me a brief nod of recognition and soon began to talk to me in his forced, asthmatic voice; he pronounced each word so strangely that it reminded one of the rawness of the air itself.

"Among the institutions on which France prides herself, do you know of any more ridiculous than the Prix de Rome? I know this has been said many times and still more frequently written, but it all seems to no avail, for it's kept up with that kind of persistent obstinacy reserved for the stupidest of stupid ideas!"

I dared to suggest to him that perhaps the institution had some value in that it was held in such esteem by certain people. To have won or not to have won the Prix de Rome to some extent allowed one to decide whether one had talent or not. If one wasn't sure, it was a useful pointer. At least it gave the public an easily comprehensible standard by which to judge.

M. Croche whistled through his teeth. I don't think I was meant to hear.

"Yes, monsieur! You have won the Prix de Rome.[2] And don't be mistaken: I'm well aware that it does make it easy for young people to travel to Italy in peace, and even to Germany as well. But why restrict the travels to these two countries? And above all, why this stupid diploma of the kind one awards to prize farm produce?

"One more thing: the cool way in which the academic gentlemen of the Institut decide which of these young people will be an artist strikes me as quite naïve. What do they know about it? Are they so sure they're artists themselves? From where do they think they inherit the right to decide someone's destiny? It really seems that in this case they'd do better if they tried that simple method of drawing lots with lengths of straw! Who knows, chance sometimes yields the wisest results. . . . But seriously, we should look elsewhere for an answer, and not base our judgments on commissioned works of such a form that it's impossible to tell if these young people even know their craft as musicians. If we have to give them something, why not let it be a certificate of higher studies? But not a certificate of imagination—that's worse than useless. With these formalities completed, let them travel across Europe and choose a teacher themselves, if they can find one. Or at least let them find someone who will teach them that art is not necessarily found in state-approved institutions."

At this point M. Croche was interrupted by a nasty fit of coughing, which he excused by blaming it on his cigar. Then, ironically enough, he reprimanded me for having said so much.

"We argue," he said, showing me the butt of his cigar, which had just gone out, and proceeded to warn me that if we were not careful we'd end up buried under a pile of accumulated ash.

"A charmingly pantheistic funeral pyre," he added, "and it serves well as a gentle reminder that we needn't consider ourselves indispensable: the brevity of life is a good enough lesson in itself." Then, turning sharply toward me, he began afresh.

"I was at the Concert Lamoureux last Sunday when your music was whistled .at. You must thank the audience for having been riled enough to bother whistling on their keys: they are not meant to be pressed into service as weapons, you know, they're usually considered to be household implements! And rightly so! The whistling-through-the-fingers of butcher boys is much more to be recommended. But then, we live and learn.

"On this same occasion, M. Chevillard once more showed a marvelous understanding of the music. As for the *Choral* Symphony, he seemed to be playing every part himself, for everything was exactly in its right place. It surpassed all the usual praise that one can give."

I could not help but agree. I added only that if one had undertaken the task of writing music for music's sake, then it was bound to run the risk of being displeasing to those with limited horizons, those who are faithful only to one kind of music, despite all its defects.

"Of course," he agreed, "but you can't blame these people, you know. You must blame the artists. They have to succeed in the fruitless task of both serving the public and at the same time keeping them in a deliberate state of apathy. To this crime, we can add that of knowing how to fight for a place in the market when the time is ripe. But once they're assured of selling their wares they suddenly seem to recoil, asking the public to forgive them for all the trouble they caused when it came to being accepted. Resolutely turning their backs on their younger days, they wallow in their success. Thus they lose all chance of attaining true glory in life—something that is happily reserved for those devoted to the discovery of new worlds of feeling and new forms of expression. They're the ones who end their lives in the happy knowledge that they've fulfilled their true destiny and who, one might say, were successful on their 'last night'—that is, if 'success' does not become vulgar when placed next to 'glory.'

"To cite a recent example: I am sorry to say that it is no longer easy for us to respect a certain artist who claimed to be full of enthusiasm for his work, but who was also a desperate seeker after glory. I detest sentimentality, monsieur, and I prefer not to remind myself that his name is Camille Saint-Saëns."

I simply remarked that I had heard *Les Barbares*. But he replied with such emotion as I wouldn't have thought possible:

"How could anyone go so far in such a wrong direction? Monsieur Saint-Saëns knows the musical universe better than anybody. Has he forgotten that it was he himself who pointed out the tumultuous genius of Liszt and made known his devotion for Bach?

"Why then this sickening need to write operas, following in the tradition of Louis Gallet, or worse, Victorien Sardou, thus propagating the misguided belief that one ought to be 'theatrical'—something that will never go together with being 'musical.' "

I put forward a few timid objections. "But is *Les Barbares* any worse than a lot of other operas you don't mention," I asked, "and should we therefore efface the memory of what Saint-Saëns once was?"

M. Croche cut me short: "That opera is worse than the rest simply because it's by Saint-Saëns! He owed it to himself, and still more to music, not to have set this story in such a hodgepodge fashion. There's even a farandole that has been praised for its archaic perfume: it's a stale echo of "The Cairo Road," which was such a success in the 1889 exhibition, but as a piece of archaism it's doubtful. In all of it there's a painful seeking after effect: each place is suggested by key words in the text, and there are some scenes that make a mockery of music. The singers are a travesty, and the scenery, in the traditional sardine-tin style of the Opéra, completes the spectacle: all hope of achieving anything really artistic is lost forever! Isn't there anyone who cares enough for Saint-Saëns to tell him that he's written enough music and that he'd be better employed in his recently found vocation of explorer?"

Distracted by another cigar, M. Croche then added, in the manner of a farewell, "Pardon me, monsieur, but I don't want this one to go out."

As I was a long way past my house, I retraced my steps, thinking all the time of M. Croche's grumbling impartiality. All in all it seemed to contain a little of that spite which people to whom one has formerly been very close seem to bear. They regard the slightest change in one's affections as an act of betrayal. I also tried to think of Monsieur Saint-Saëns on the first night of *Les Barbares,* and I remember hearing the applause joined by a few of the catcalls that had accompanied the first performance of the *Danse macabre.* I think that he would have cherished this memory.

P.S. The publishers of *La Revue blanche* have just brought out an elegant and precise translation of Wagner's booklet on Beethoven. Those of us who like Wagner will find another opportunity to pay their respects. Those who do not will find much to back up their opinions. Enough said, except that M. Henri Lasvignes' translation is useful to have, whichever view you take.

〜*NOTES*

[1] Probably a reference to the oft-reproduced *The Angelus* by Millet.

[2] Debussy's sojourn in Rome was something of a disaster for the composer. It was in 1885 that he departed for the Villa Medici, the French Academy in Rome that was to become "a prison" for the composer. Depressed by both the teaching and the food, and by his fellow prize winners, he found little to stimulate him save the Renaissance church music of Palestrina. He was desperately homesick, and his letters betrayed a constant desire to return—"to see Manet and hear Offenbach," as he put it. He alludes to the Prix de Rome several times in his articles. (See pp. 167, 198–202, 211–14, 237–8, 303.)

Massenet: From Eve to Grisélidis

I should like to attempt to trace not a portrait of M. Massenet, but rather something of the attitude of mind he was trying to convey through his music. Apart from anything else, the idiosyncrasies of a man's life and the anecdotes surrounding him have to be posthumous before they are of any interest.

It is at once obvious that music was never for Massenet that "universal voice" which it was for Bach and Beethoven; rather did he make it a pleasing speciality.

If one consults a list of his works, already quite long, you will find an overriding preoccupation underlying all of them. Rather ominously, one could say it was destiny, *la marche*. It has caused him to re-work, in his latest opera *Grisélidis,* something of the story of *Eve,* one of his earliest compositions. Can we not conclude that there must be some mysterious guiding hand of fate behind it all? Does it not explain Massenet's insatiable desire to find in music the necessary documents for a complete history of the feminine soul? For they are all there—those females who haunt us in our dreams! Manon, in her billowing petticoats, has a smile that seems reborn on the lips of a modern Sappho—a smile to bring men to tears. And the Navarraise's dagger and the ruthless Charlotte's pistol are brought together. (*Cf. Werther.*)

On the other hand, it is well-known how his music is vibrant with fleeting sensations, little bursts of feeling and embraces that we wish would last forever. The harmonies are like arms, the melodies like the napes of necks. We gaze into the ladies' eyes, dying to know their thoughts. . . . The philosophical, and those in their right minds, inform us that there are none. But we don't have to believe them: M. Massenet proves that there are (at least melodically). With such pre-occupations, he is bound to occupy a position in contemporary art for which, at the very least, he is secretly envied. And that is something which should not be scorned.

Fortune, who is feminine, owed it to M. Massenet both to treat him well and, sometimes, to let him down. So far she has done just that. All this success has meant that for a time it was considered a good thing to copy the idiosyncrasies of Massenet. But then all of a sudden those who had so quietly cribbed from him began to treat him with disdain.

He has been reproached for having too much sympathy for Mascagni and not enough adoration for Wagner. This criticism is as wrongheaded as it is unacceptable. Massenet bravely continues to court the affection of his lady admirers, as he has always done. I must confess that I do not see why it is any better to give pleasure to cosmopolitan old Wagnerian ladies than to those perfumed young ladies, even though they don't play the piano very well. In the end, Massenet is bound to be right. . . . He can be reprimanded only for not having been faithful to the true Manon. . . . There he found the framework that best suited his flirtatious habits, but perhaps he shouldn't have brought them into the opera. One does not "flirt" at the opera: one screams incomprehensible words at the top of one's voice. If one becomes betrothed, then it is with the trombones as witnesses. All the subtle shades of sentiment are bound to be lost in the noise; Massenet realized he could better express his genius in pastel tints and whispered melodies, in works composed of light-ness itself. And that doesn't rule out all artistic depth; it merely demands subtle depth. There will always be those who like their music to be held out at arm's length, while the trumpets bray. Why uselessly augment their number and so encourage this annoying taste for neo-Wagnerian music to develop? This kind of music would do better to return to its country of origin.

Massenet, because of his unique gifts and facility, has been able to do much to counteract this deplorable movement. "It isn't always a good thing to howl along with the wolves" is a piece of advice that could well have been given him by one of his less discreet lady admirers.

To conclude these hasty notes one might add that not everyone can be a Shakespeare, but it does no harm to try to be a Marivaux.

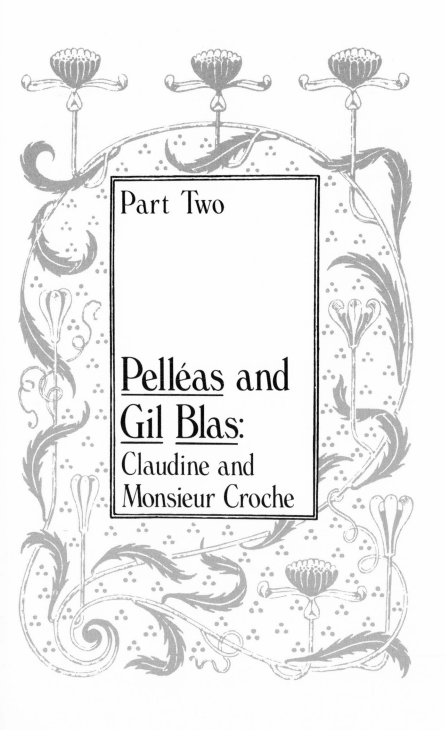

Part Two

Pelléas and Gil Blas:
Claudine and Monsieur Croche

IMMEDIATELY in the wake of *Pelléas,* at the beginning of 1903, Debussy began his second round of music criticism. After only one article and an interview on his opera, he once again was employed as a regular columnist, this time as a weekly contributor to the daily newspaper *Gil Blas.* It was a year for fresh beginnings. After *Pelléas* had received its long overdue first performance in the spring of 1902, Debussy began to search for a suitable sequel in the operatic field. One idea was a dramatization of Edgar Allan Poe's "The Devil in the Belfry." Poe's work, highly regarded in France through the translations of Baudelaire and Mallarmé, and of Debussy's friend Gabriel Mourey, had long been an attraction for the composer. Another, precipitated by a visit to London, where he saw Forbes-Robertson as Hamlet (in July 1902), was a version of *As You Like It,* planned in collaboration with his friend and correspondent Paul-Jean Toulet. But unfortunately both projects remained in an embryonic stage. The following year saw the composition of the two pieces for harp and orchestra—the "Danse sacrée" and "Danse profane"—and the beginnings of two important large-scale works, the *Images* for piano and *La Mer.* In February, at the age of forty-one, Debussy was created Chevalier de la Légion d'Honneur.

With regard to his *Gil Blas* column, as with his earlier contributions to *La Revue blanche,* there were probably mixed motives for Debussy's acceptance of this kind of work. He still felt it important to continue writing reviews, but we have no reason to doubt that the idea of a book was in his mind. At worst, his duties as a critic would mean sitting through works that were odious to him, abandoning work on one of his own compositions for the sake of a second-rate concert. At best, it was a chance to clarify and expound his ideas.

Like several other Paris papers, the editorial policy of *Gil Blas* was to employ several critics of contrasting viewpoints. Frequently two critics would be sent to the same concert and their notices would appear side by side in the same issue, supposedly independent of each other. Debussy's appointment was part of a unique piece of literary matchmaking, for his partner, in a column signed "Claudine," was none other than the thirty-year-old Colette. Their spells as *Gil Blas* columnists were exactly congruent, and it would seem that their pairing was deliberate. In the new year the two critics were introduced to the public for the first time.

Misia Sert's preview of *Pelléas* commented on Debussy's meeting with Colette and her music-critic husband Willy (Henri Gauthier-Villars). The couple were well-known figures on the literary side of Paris musical life, and readers of Colette's biographies will be well-acquainted with the unscrupulous Willy, tyrant to Colette and a celebrated Paris editor who hardly ever wrote a word himself—according to Colette, he had a physical fear of the blank page—and yet who published articles, reviews, and novels with the aid of an entourage of ghostwriters whose talents he exploited for his own ends. By publishing Colette's teenage jottings in his own name—the *Claudine* novels—he had already shown that he was not above including his wife among these ghosts, and no sooner had the first of these books been a financial success than he locked her away in an attic to produce a series of sequels. Still widely read today (and now attributed to their rightful author), the novels are in the "confessions of a schoolgirl" genre, describing a girl's boarding school, Claudine's initiation into the adult life of Paris, subsequent marriage, friendships, and even a full-blown lesbian affair. Willy, seeing the commercial potential of the venture, had instructed Colette to spice up her jottings with a few risqué scandals—a request with which she complied. Despite this (for one feels the novels might have been better had Colette been given an entirely free hand), some passages show the mature writer taking shape. Indeed, she was the first to acknowledge that this early enforced training had in fact done her a great deal of good. Some of the couple's circle of friends at once realized that the true author of these successful books was Colette herself, and for them she had a reputation to live down: the *Claudines* were written in the first person and dangerously auto-biographical. On the other hand, Willy made sure that the image of Claudine was kept alive in the public eye. After all, there was a great deal of money to be made. There can be little doubt that a music critic's column bearing her name was one of Willy's commercially oriented brainstorms.

He succeeded, and Claudine became a type. One memoir of the early years of the century relates how fashionable the Claudine image became, especially after the novels were dramatized with the *café-concert* artiste Mlle Polaire playing Claudine. With the aid of cartoons, fashion photos, posters, and songs, Claudine was successfully publicized. "First in the dance hall, then in the street one would see the bare feet of countless Claudines dressed in their black pinafores and with their hair like a curly-headed shepherd boy."[1] Her appeal? A precarious balance between implicit vice and adolescent innocence.

Willy's style as a music critic was somewhat infectious: his word-play and witty dismissals left their mark on the columns of both Debussy and Colette. Colette's column, like the earlier novels, was a product of the Willy-Colette factory, and was probably written at her husband's request. In her book *My Apprenticeships,* Colette amusingly describes how Willy would arrange for concerts to be reviewed; no doubt Colette was already quite experienced as a ghostwriter by the time she set pen to paper under her own pseudonym:

> For the big Sunday concerts a corps of dispatch riders was mobilized, carefully picked men who galloped from Colonne to Pasdeloup, from Pasdeloup to the Conservatoire, exchanged stalls, snatched a seat from beneath the confederate who had been mounting guard. . . .
>
> Dear Sir, Tomorrow at the Risler concert you are requested to advance swiftly upon stall no. 26 which will be occupied by the backside of a gentleman in black—black, black as my soul! This sombre individual (Aussurasses by name) will deliver up to you some notes (what did you think?) on the concert if you stand him a beer. . . .

Marches and countermarches, passwords, plots, conferences at GHQ, the final fitting together of the jigsaw—what a lot of trouble! Surely it would have been easier for a man who had an excellent ear, who could accompany himself on the piano and sing in a small, pleasantly veiled tenor voice—surely such a man should have found it easier to write? No. Everything was easy to him, everything was lawful, except the task of writing.[2]

For all his lack of literary scruples and his flagrant and cruel infidelity to his young wife, Willy did have his good points. He championed the works of young French composers, including Debussy, from whom he commanded a good deal of respect. According to one writer, Debussy himself remarked that "there is only one music critic and that's Willy. He may not know what a semiquaver is, but it is to him that I owe the best part of my reputation."[3]

In comparing the approaches of Debussy and Colette, we are assisted by the custom prevalent at the time whereby new critics were permitted to state their personal opinions and attitudes. From the outset their differences were clear: Debussy was the expert, Colette the innocent ear. Claudine's lack of insight was to some extent a pose: she had to live up to her image of an ill-bred, tomboyish country girl. Sometimes it is evident that she is not so innocent of sixteenth notes as she makes out, although it is worth noting that when a detailed analysis of Guy Ropartz's symphony was distributed among the audience prior to its first performance, both Colette and Debussy agreed that such priming was a detestable idea. Reading between the lines one feels that the two approaches had a good deal in common; after all, on several occasions Colette lamented the fact that she had missed her vocation as a composer.

Certain writers have suggested Willy's complicity in the column, and no doubt he did add the occasional idea, put a few choice puns in Claudine's mind. But Colette's view of Willy's literary paranoia and her accounts of the pains he took to avoid writing seem to bear out Willy's own answer to the accusation: "If she wrote them or if she signed them," a certain M. Larnac had written, "it was no doubt to please her man-of-letters husband." "Ça m'étonnerait, ça m'étonnerait beaucoup," replied Willy, now divorced, with a wry smile.[4]

While Debussy quotes verbatim critical ideas that opened his first column in *La Revue blanche,* Colette is not afraid to resort to fashionable tittle-tattle: the country girl come to town, impressed by the pearls, diamonds, and chandeliers, commenting on who was with whom, and the latest vogue in gloves. But it is their common ground rather than their differences—Debussy always despised the social element of concert life while Colette constantly reveled in it—that is most illuminating. Colette's excursion into the world of music criticism is often of limited interest, but her literary flair, shining from every column, more than compensates. Besides, from the outset it is clear that each columnist read the other's articles and sometimes—though always with discretion—both allowed themselves a gibe at the other's expense. "I will be discussing established classics very little," Debussy had written. Colette goes one stage further: "Rest assured that I shall be speaking little of music," she writes in her first line of address to her readers, perhaps in imitation of Debussy. "First of all, because it would bore me stiff, and secondly, because Debussy with his ebony curls seems to be more qualified in that respect—better to be Claude than Claudine! My contribution to criticism will be my good faith and coarse upbringing—qualities that have already made me many enemies. Each day I hope to increase their number." Throughout her columns she takes a professional care in preserving her pose: "The experts will tell you *why* that was beautiful. . . . For my own part I am only Claudine, someone frequently overwhelmed by beauty—in music, in painting, and above all in nature. But I have no wish to analyze it." Remembering Debussy's own self-confessed aims, his abhorrence of "parasite aesthetics" and of technical terms, Claudine's ideals of criticism, though less lofty, are basically similar: both writers wish to be themselves, to preserve their immediate reactions and to place them at the center of their writings about the arts.

In Paris at the turn of the century, perhaps the most important hallmark of any music critic was his attitude toward Wagner. In line with a frequently held opinion among French musicians, the orchestral "Forest Murmurs" from *Siegfried* was one of Colette's favorites. Frequently played at this time, it may well have been this piece which Renoir discussed with Wagner when they talked of musical impressionism in 1882. Colette was quick to pounce upon a shoddy performance of the excerpt in her article of 23 February, but apart from a few vitriolic comments woven into her account of Siegfried Wagner's concert in Paris, we have little indication of her feelings. As it happened, she had been expressing them elsewhere. Almost half of *Claudine and Annie* is set in Bayreuth at the height of Wagnermania, and this evocative *roman soufflé* in fact appeared during Colette's spell on *Gil Blas*. Her account of Bayreuth ("The Holy City") is both passionate and irreverent in regard to the Great God. She acknowledges Wagner's immense power—"I was still throbbing, but I concealed my emotion like sensual desire"—but brings Mademoiselle Polaire on the scene for some caustically amusing quips. Relishing her *café-concert* reputation, she appears with a merciless deflation of Wagner's grandiloquence: "Nothing to make you fall flat on your fanny! And as for his music, why, it's just like a band. Makes you want to salute and slap your right thigh." *Der Fliegende Holländer* is held in low esteem—"a piece of sentimental filth, the dregs of Italian-German opera"—but *Tristan* is apparently held in high regard.[5]

In his own articles, Debussy's approach to Wagner is not altogether dissimilar: he hides behind a mask that is frequently frivolous, and only occasionally do real insights shine through. Certainly, we should not take his opinions as expressed in the *Gil Blas* column as a true picture of his attitudes in 1903, by which time French composers had a certain distance from which to look back dispassionately on the French adoption of Wagnerian ideals. In 1893 Debussy had, one recalls, planned a diatribe "on the uselessness of Wagnerism," but by now his ideas had tempered somewhat, giving way to a viewpoint in which *Tristan* and *Parsifal* were rated as the peaks of the German master's achievement. But the Wagnerian "formula" is not recommended for adoption: "Wagner," writes Debussy, "is not a good mentor for the French." Between his bouts of indulgent parody comes a genuine admiration for Richter's performances of the *Ring,* which Debussy saw at Covent Garden. He suggested *Tristan* for performance at the Opéra, and admired *Parsifal* for its harmonic beauty (of which there are many echoes in *Pelléas*) and for its orchestral sound—"as if lit from behind" was how he described these works to André Caplet.[6]

French composers who blindly adopted the Wagnerian formula

were reprimanded by Debussy, who held the view that Wagner's methods were too personal to be followed by anyone else. Quick to recognize the impasse into which Wagnerian imitators would find themselves led, Debussy mercilessly parodied Wagner's more famous pronouncements. "And now I leave you in a vacuum" was what he meant to say. Behind this mask of parody, his mockery of the idiosyncrasies of Wagnerian supermen, an acknowledgment of Wagner's immense power is thinly veiled. And although Debussy's estimation of Wagner as a "sunset" has turned out to be one of the earliest true evaluations of his position in musical history—the culmination of the "symphonic" era—he is nonetheless a figure whose language haunted Debussy until late in his creative life. One clear idea that does emerge is Debussy's early rejection of Wagner's time scale, his superabundance of melody and constant leitmotiv development— the essence of Wagner's operas. Even if, in *Pelléas,* there are certain passages that are harmonically indebted to *Parsifal,* there is a crucial difference in these respects. The endless Wagnerian melody is rejected in favor of a quasirecitative because "symphonic development and character development can never unfold at exactly the same pace." Here is an idea that is several times stressed and that had evidently been in Debussy's mind for some time. In a conversation he had with Ernest Guiraud in 1889, remarkably similar points of view emerge. Speaking of *Tristan,* Debussy said that what he most admired in the work

> is that the themes of the symphony are also reflections of the action. But the symphony never violates the action, nor is it the essence of the plot. There is a constant equilibrium between musical necessity and the thematic evocations, which are only used inasmuch as they are necessary to imbue the orchestra with the appropriate coloring for its decorative role. I fear that in the *Ring* they became tyrants.[7]

Only twice were the two *Gil Blas* columnists diametrically opposed in their attitudes, the major bones of contention being Berlioz and Richard Strauss. Debussy's dismissal of Berlioz has perhaps been overstressed by some of his biographers. Leaving aside his grandiloquence, a quality for which Debussy had little time, Debussy *should* have admired Berlioz as the supreme colorist of French Romanticism, in this respect the direct descendant of Weber (whom Debussy preferred) and ancestor of Chabrier. But as early as 1893 Debussy, in writing to Prince Poniatowski, had described Berlioz as "a tremendous humbug who managed to believe in his own hoaxes."[8] Again, in his article on "Berlioz and Monsieur Gunsbourg" we read that Berlioz is "the favorite of those who know little about music." In view of her strongly pro-Berlioz stand, this may well have been a gibe at the musically naïve Colette. But amidst isolated remarks such as these, often taken out of context to show Debussy's hostility toward Berlioz, we should remember that there are also indications of genuine admiration for certain elements in his work: Debussy holds both the *Symphonie fantastique* and *L'Enfance du Christ* in the highest esteem. Indeed, the overall tone of the article of Monsieur Gunsbourg's adaptation is in defense of Berlioz. And if Debussy was lukewarm about Berlioz the composer, he had at least absorbed something from his *Mémoires,* for several times, as Marcel Dietschy has pointed out, he clearly imitates some of Berlioz's verbal turns of phrase.[9]

Both Debussy and Colette reacted violently to Richard Strauss's appearance in Paris as conductor of his own works. Debussy found himself drawn to the kaleidoscopic orchestrations of Strauss's tone poems, and could forgive the sensationalism of his "extravagant orgies" because of his masterly juxtaposition of apparently disparate musical ideas. For Colette, Strauss was simply "a kind of cuisine [she] detested."[10] Debussy went as far as to say that Strauss "is practically the only original musician of the modern German school," radical because the color itself had become the form. His admiration of Strauss's vivid tonalities shines through; Debussy saw him as "writing in colored images," seeming to "draw the outlines of his ideas with the orchestra"—a phrase that strikingly recalls early criticism of the impressionist painters "drawing their outlines in paint." He went on to compare Strauss's technique to that of the cinema: "It's a book of images, even cinematography." The idea is an important one, for several times Debussy evoked the art of the cinema as one from which music could learn. He himself had been preoccupied with the idea of a book of *images* from the 1890s, when he had considered publishing a series of piano pieces in this form. In fact, the idea came to fruition in the sets of *Images* for piano and the orchestral *Images* composed in the early years of the century. In one sense Debussy saw the art of cinema as being closer to music than was the art of painting. Advising the young composer Raoul Bardac some years later, he clarifies the idea: "Music has this over painting: that it can bring together all variations of colour and light. It is a point not often observed, although it is quite obvious."[11] Debussy's idea seems to be that music's existence in time renders it closer to the art of cinema than to the static, transitory art of painting. With this idea in mind it is not difficult to understand Debussy's attraction to the early cinema—an art he saw reflected in Strauss's use of "rhythmic colors" of the orchestra as a structural element. Eleven years later Debussy goes so far as to suggest cinematographic techniques as a possible force of renewal for symphonic music: "There remains, however, one means of renewing the taste for symphonic music among our contemporaries: to apply to pure music the techniques of cinematography."[12]

Debussy's first article in *Gil Blas,* devoted to d'Indy's *L'Etranger,* highlights another question that has often been misinterpreted by biographers on the strength of a single remark. "D'Indy and I, we are not the same color"—thus René Peter quotes Debussy.[13] But readers of Debussy's articles on d'Indy will find none of the antipathy suggested by this remark, only genuine admiration for d'Indy's piece. In a recent article, Henri Mouton has convincingly argued that the two men—despite claims to the contrary—held for each other a good deal of mutual professional respect, even though the devout, establishment d'Indy felt little in common with Debussy the man. D'Indy, an extremely important figure in Paris musical life, was both leader of the Schola Cantorum, a serious rival institution to the Conservatoire, and influential in securing first performances. D'Indy had severely criticized *Pelléas* both in an outspoken article in *L'Occident* and in his *Cours du composition,* where he accused Debussy of having overemphasized harmony at the expense of the other elements of music. But his criticism was sincere and without a trace of malice. Certainly Debussy did not feel moved to retaliate (as he did with Saint-Saëns), and when he came to review d'Indy's *L'Etranger* he was able to do so with genuine admiration. Indeed, there were many reasons for d'Indy to command Debussy's respect: his resurrection of Rameau and other composers of the French baroque was surely one of them. D'Indy has all too readily been dubbed a conservative, and certainly his music now pales beside Debussy's, but as the power behind the Schola he had shaken the foundations of advanced musical training in France. His ideas of the teaching of composition, based on a far-reaching study of the historical evolution of music, were considered somewhat revolutionary in their day. In addition, there was the fact that d'Indy had himself promoted several first performances of Debussy's pieces at the Société Nationale, and when he later took up conducting, he took several of Debussy's works on tour. D'Indy's "anti-debussyisme" was a myth.[14]

Debussy's *Gil Blas* column emerges as a curious mixture combining some sincere criticism with a good deal of flippant indulgence. Out of the overall picture, one other point is worth bringing to the fore, illuminating the composer's undeniable taste for *la grosse musique:* the music of the open air, circus music, barrel organs, *café-concert,* and music hall. It may seem strange that Debussy devotes space in his column to Sousa's visit to Paris, and that, as a reward for sitting through the *Ring,* he treats himself to a night at the Alhambra music hall in London. Strange, too, that he mentions Paul Delmet, the Montmartre *chansonnier,* as a "truly French" artist. Such asides should not be seen as indulgences in tomfoolery. Those acquainted with the piano preludes, with "Golliwog's Cakewalk," will realize that before the jazz band had made its mark on classical composers (Stravinsky and Ravel in particular), Debussy had himself absorbed a good deal from its precursors, the cakewalks of the Negro minstrels and the brassy circus bands of which (and it was not only Debussy who said this) Sousa was undeniably the king. Think of Seurat's circus pictures, the Montmartre lithographs and circus pictures of Toulouse-Lautrec, Degas's *Miss Lola au Cirque Fernando,* and the clown poems of Baudelaire, Banville, and Laforgue. Steeped particularly in the work of these poets, Debussy created his own musical counterparts to these literary and visual evocations of the entertainment world so colorful in the Paris of that time. A patron of the Bar Reynolds, Debussy met there the celebrated Paris clowns Footit and Chocolat, immortalized by Lautrec. With them, according to his friend René Peter, he discussed the similarities between the arts of music and circus, quoting to Footitt Banville's poem "Le Saut du tremplin" (about a clown whose trampoline projects him into eternity) and discussing his own "harmonic pirouettes."[15] Circuses had a whole host of literary and intellectual devotees at this time, and, as a consequence, some fairly sophisticated parody was incorporated into the acts. One memoir mentions an act that may well have been an inspiration for Debussy's ironic quotation of Wagner's *Tristan* in the middle of "Golliwog's Cakewalk" from *Children's Corner.* Wagner was parodied on a tightrope, accompanied by a warped medley of his own leitmotiv played by the circus band.[16] In Debussy's piano piece, the love motif from Wagner's greatest opera is similarly debunked through a series of cakewalk *gruppetti.* Through his absorption of the music of popular entertainment, a side of Debussy's imagination to which the present articles afford us a glimpse, he foreshadows the Cocteau era, of Satie's *Parade* and Stravinsky's *Petrouchka,* in a way no other music had done.

The attention Debussy paid to open-air music was more than cursory. It demonstrates his fondness for circuses, and it shows us his involvement in certain aspects of the socialist movement. Little is known of Debussy's politics. His attitude to the Dreyfus case has already been mentioned in connection with the anarchists on *La Revue blanche* (again hinted at in the *Gil Blas* article on the Opéra). Less well-known is his youthful participation in a revolutionary political movement known as the "Black Snake." This side of Debussy's character is expanded further in his articles on the Théâtre du Peuple and his mention of Bernheim's widely discussed book, *Trente Ans de théâtre.* Ideas of a people's theater were brought to a head in 1903 with the publication in book form of Romain Rolland's *Le Théâtre du peuple,* in which he advocated the establishment of a true "people's theater"—not merely an offshoot company from one of the established theaters, but a totally new concept. In Debussy's ideas on the Théâtre Populaire the imprint of Rolland's socialist ideas on the arts is unmistakable. Rolland criticized Bernheim's effort, accusing it of breaking no new ground. His own idea was more visionary and idealistic. Parallel to these run Debussy's thoughts on open-air music —bold sketches, not practical plans. In a later edition of his book Rolland included Debussy's *Gil Blas* articles in his bibliography of works on the people's theater. Debussy had not only echoed Rolland's radical vision of a totally new kind of popular spectacle but had also echoed his ideas of a theater that would break down the barriers of class. It is in this light that we should view his comments on "bringing together the most insignificant little pastry cook with the old gentleman who thinks of nothing but the Alsace-Lorraine question."[17]

๛NOTES

[1] Willy, *Les Célébrités d'aujourd'hui* (Paris, 1904).

[2] Colette, *Mes Apprentissages* (Paris, 1936); in English, *My Apprenticeships* (London, 1957).

[3.] Sylvain Bonmariage, *Willy, Colette et moi* (Paris, 1954).

[4] Willy, "Claudine Musicographe," *Mercure de France,* 15 December 1927.

[5] Colette, *Claudine s'en va* (Paris, 1903); in English, *Claudine and Annie* (London, 1962).

[6] Debussy, *Lettres inédites à André Caplet* (Monaco, 1957).

[7] Maurice Emmanuel, *Pelléas et Mélisande* (Paris, 1926).

[8] Prince Poniatowski, *D'un siècle à l'autre* (Paris, 1948).

[9] Marcel Dietschy, *La Passion de Claude Debussy* (Monaco, 1962).

[10] *Gil Blas,* 23 March 1903.

[11] Debussy to Raoul Bardac, 25 February 1906. Quoted in Edward Lockspeiser's *Debussy.*

[12] *SIM,* 1 November 1913. See p. 295.

[13] René Peter, *Debussy* (Paris, 1944).

[14] Henri Mouton, "Les Rapports Debussy-d'Indy," *Schweizerische Musikzeitung,* July-August 1973.

[15] Peter, *Debussy.*

[16] A. de Saint-Albin, *Les Sports à Paris* (Paris, 1889).

[17] The most extensive discussion of these ideas comes in Debussy's play *Frères en Art*. There, the character Maltravers bears out Debussy's later statement that "too wide a diffusion of art can lead only to the greatest mediocrity":

> MALTRAVERS: I come from the working classes and I'm not ashamed of it. I also believe that from this melting pot of suffering and hatred, from this power of the people alone, great works may emerge. The only trouble is that the working classes are not drawn to art. They feel they are intruders or a poor relation. In almost all the documents of anarchy isn't it true that there is never any question of the popularization of art? Is this unfortunate? I don't think so.

April 1902

Why I Wrote Pelléas

*(Note written by Debussy at the beginning of April 1902,
at the request of Georges Ricou, the manager of the Opéra-Comique)*

MY acquaintance with *Pelléas* dates from 1893. Despite the enthusiasm of a first reading, and perhaps a few secret ideas about possible music, I did not begin to think seriously about it until the end of that year (1893).[1]

For a long time I had been striving to write music for the theater, but the form in which I wanted it to be was so unusual that after several attempts I had almost given up the idea.[2] Explorations previously made in the realm of pure music had led me toward a hatred of classical development, whose beauty is solely technical and can interest only the mandarins in our profession. I wanted music to have a freedom that was perhaps more inherent than in any other art, for it is not limited to a more or less exact representation of nature, but rather to the mysterious affinity between Nature and the Imagination.

After some years of passionate pilgrimages to Bayreuth, I began to have doubts about the Wagnerian formula, or, rather, it seemed to me that it was of use only in the particular case of Wagner's own genius. He was a great collector of formulae, and these he assembled within a framework that appears uniquely his own only because one is not well enough acquainted with music. And without denying his genius, one could say that he had put the final period after the music of his time, rather as Victor Hugo summed up all the poetry that had gone before. One should therefore try to be "post-Wagner" rather than "after Wagner."

The drama of *Pelléas*—which despite its atmosphere of dreams contains much more humanity than those so-called documents of real life—seemed to suit my purpose admirably. It has an evocative language whose sensibility is able to find an extension in the music and in the orchestral setting. I also tried to obey a law of beauty that seems notably ignored when it comes to dramatic music: the characters of this opera try to sing like real people, and not in an arbitrary language made up of worn-out clichés. That is why the reproach has been made concerning my so-called taste for monotonous declamation, where nothing seems melodic. . . . First of all, that's not true. In addition, a character cannot always express himself melodically: the *dramatic* melody has to be quite different from what is generally called melody. . . . The people who go to listen to music in the theater are really like those crowds whom one sees gathered around street musicians! There you can have your emotions-in-melody for a couple of sous! You can also be sure of a greater degree of attention than is usually found among the patrons of our state theaters, and you will even find a greater wish to understand—something totally lacking in the above-mentioned public.

By a unique stroke of irony, this public which demands "something new" is the same one that is bewildered by, and which jeers at, anything new or unusual, whenever someone is trying to break away from making the customary hullabaloo. This may seem hard to understand, but one must not forget that with a work of art an attempt at beauty is always taken as a personal insult by some people.

I do not pretend to have discovered everything in *Pelléas,* but I have tried to forge a way ahead that others will be able to follow. These are the fruits of my experience, which will perhaps release dramatic music from the heavy yoke under which it has lived for so long.

Pelléas was completed for the first time in 1895. Since then I've reset parts of it, modified it, and so on. It represents some twelve years of my life.

NOTES

1 Although the errors of certain of Debussy's biographers concerning the origin of Debussy's acquaintance with Maeterlinck's *Pelléas* can be confidently refuted (Laloy, for example, in his biography of 1909, "approved" by the composer, claimed that Debussy first read the play in 1892), a certain amount of doubt still surrounds the exact chronology. Marcel Dietschy (in *La Passion de Claude Debussy*) has carefully presented the evidence. On 13 April 1893 a performance of Maeterlinck's play was announced for the twenty-first at the Vaudeville. Several times postponed, it was finally given, with Debussy in the audience, at the Bouffes-Parisiens on 17 May. Several important literary critics prepared for the impending performance with articles on the little-known poet-playright. The "first reading" of which Debussy speaks in the present article was probably prompted by the attention given to the poet at this time and by the recommendation of friends included in the "score of people in Paris acquainted with the work of the Flemish poet," as *Le Figaro* summed up the extent of Maeterlinck's reputation in Paris.

The composer Ernest Chausson, at this time something of an artistic father figure to Debussy, and his brother-in-law the painter Henri Lerolle, were both interested in Maeterlinck's work, and Chausson was about to embark on a setting of the poet's *Serres chaudes*. In July Debussy asked the poet Henri de Régnier to contact Maeterlinck with a view to obtaining his permission to set *Pelléas*. "My friend Claude Debussy," wrote Régnier, "who is a most sensitive and ingenious musician, has begun to compose some charming music for *Pelléas et Mélisande,* delicately adorning the text while scrupulously respecting it. He would like your authorization to proceed before continuing further with this considerable task" (Georgette Leblanc, *Souvenirs* [Paris, 1931]). Maeterlinck wholeheartedly gave his blessing to the idea.

It seems likely that Debussy had begun a few sketches for the project at once, and as early as 6 September he announced to Chausson the completion of the last scene of the fourth act. Henri Lerolle evocatively recounted to Chausson the circumstances of the first hearing of early drafts of the opera:

> Yesterday we had a little reunion. . . . D'Indy was there, the hero of the feast, Poujaud, Benoît, Debussy, the Denises [Maurice Denis, the painter] and the Arthurs. I had asked Debussy to bring *Pelléas,*

but when he arrived he said he had not brought it because he would have had to carry too much. Then, after dinner and cigarettes and cigars, d'Indy began with his piece. In his peculiar way he recounted the subject of the third act of *Fervaal,* then he played it to us and sang extracts like a little schoolgirl reciting her lessons. Then, at a quarter to twelve, when Benoît was about to take Poujaud home— he'd rather have gone to bed—Debussy began tinkering at the piano, seemingly thinking of other things. "Go on then," we urged. "But I've nothing to play." I saw that he desperately wanted to play something, so I told him I didn't believe him, saying I'd found some of *Pelléas* in his briefcase. At this he began to play it, and we all gathered around the piano—except Benoît, who was lying down on the divan fuming.

Thus Debussy first shared his new creation with his friends.

2 The theatrical projects of Debussy's earlier years bear careful scrutiny in that they provide a key not only to the development of his musical ideas but also to the literary themes that attracted him. All through Debussy's life the boundaries between the theatrical work, the cantata, and even the pure orchestral piece were unclear, breaking down completely in the *Prélude à l'après-midi d'un faune,* which was originally conceived as a theatrical project. Perhaps the largely unsatisfactory outcome of these early theatrical projects led him to seek other means of incorporating literary ideas into his music, for in 1890 he was thinking in terms of a "symphony whose theme would be taken from the tales of Poe, in particular 'The Fall of the House of Usher.' " The following is a brief list of Debussy's early theatrical projects:

Diane au bois. The most complete and successful of the early projects, this setting of Théodore de Banville's poem is extant in short score. Its subject, the conquest of Diana by Eros, was originally taken from Ovid, and Banville imbues the landscape setting with Watteauesque half-lights and ambrosian perfumes. Eros charms Diana with a seductive flute solo foreshadowing both Mallarmé's and Debussy's *Après-midi.* Musically, the orchestration of *Pelléas* is already there, and so is a certain amount of the later opera's declamation.

Zuleima (1885–88). A dramatization of the central character in Heine's play *Almansor.* Two scenes were completed during Debussy's unhappy stay in Rome and eventually submitted to the Académie. Shortly after his arrival there he wrote to the bookseller Vasnier, who supported him during these difficult years, *"Zuleima* is decidedly not for me. It's too old and fusty. The long stupid lines—great only in length—bore me and my music would be stifled by them." The following year, on 19 October, he writes that *"Zuleima* is dead and I shall certainly not be the one to bring her back to life again. It's not the kind of music I wish to write—too much like Verdi and Meyerbeer." The *Journal officiel,* which passed judgment on works submitted by holders of the Prix de Rome, declared the work "bizarre and unperformable."

Axel (1890). One scene from this influential play of Villiers de L'Isle-Adam was completed by Debussy but has since been lost. Debussy wrote the music before the play was first staged, and he must have been well acquainted with Adam's work, which was published extensively in various reviews, such as the celebrated *Revue Wagnerienne.* The play, which has much in common with Wagner's *Parsifal,* tells of Axel's relinquishment of reality in favor of the pursuit of dreams. He, like Golaud, is the inhabitant of a remote medieval castle, and, were the music to be found, it seems likely that one would recognize some ideas that later came to fruition in *Pelléas.*

Rodrigue et Chimène. This setting of an adaptation of *El Cid* by Catulle Mendès seems to have been undertaken largely on the strength of a chance meeting between Debussy's father and Mendès. Debussy was unwillingly pushed into the project, and in 1892 he wrote to Robert Godet of his inability to work on the opera: "My life is sad and frantic because of this opera where everything is against me." Debussy finally abandoned the project. *El Cid* was not for him.

Debussy also wished to set Maeterlinck's *La Princesse Maleine* to music, but the poet refused to grant him permission to do so.

LE FIGARO
16 May 1902

Pelléas et Mélisande: *A Reply to the Critics*
(*Interview by Robert de Flers*)

CRITICS? They're fine people, very fine! Or so I would like to believe. Certainly they are a contented lot—perhaps I envy them. In their battle, the odds are all on one side: they have the right to pass judgment on the several years' struggles and labors of a work's gestation—all in one hour.

For twelve years, sir, I have had Pelléas and Mélisande as my everyday companions. Of the length of my labors, I have no complaints. For me, above all, it has been a joy. I have experienced an inner contentment that nobody's comments or accusations could erode. Moreover, certain critics have perfectly understood my intentions. I have only thanks for M. Gaston Carraud (*La Liberté*), M. Camille de Sainte-Croix (*La Petite République*), M. Gustave Bret (*La Presse*), M. André Corneau (*Le Matin*), and M. Henry Bauër for his fine article in *Le Figaro*.[1]

M. Catulle Mendès, after a host of eulogies that I must admit confused me, judged that I had not conveyed the "poetic essence" of the play and that my music remained independent of this. I did in fact concentrate all my efforts on trying to identify the one with the other. Above all I respected the characters themselves—their ways. I wanted them to have their own expression, independent of me. I let them sing within me. And, hearing them, I tried to present them faithfully. That is all.[2]

M. Gauthier-Villars—I admire the technical expertise and honesty that allows him to afford the ninth of the chord some unexpected publicity—reproaches my score because the melodic lines are never found in the vocal parts but always in the orchestra. My wish was that the action should never be halted, continuing uninterrupted. I wanted to dispense with parasitical musical phrases. On hearing opera, the spectator is accustomed to experiencing two distinct sorts of emotion: on the one hand the *musical emotion,* and on the other the emotion of the characters—usually he experiences them in succession. I tried to ensure that the two were perfectly merged and simultaneous. Melody, if I dare say so, is antilyrical. It cannot express the varying states of the soul, and of life. Essentially it is suited only to the song that expresses a simple feeling.

I have never allowed my music to precipitate or retard the changing feeling or passions of my characters for technical convenience. It stands aside as soon as it can, leaving them the freedom of their gestures, their utterances—their joy or their sorrow. It is this that one of my critics understood so well—M. Fourcaud of *Le Gaulois*—perhaps without realizing it, when he spoke of *Pelléas et Mélisande* in terms of a "declamation in notes, scarcely accompanied."[3]

I know I caused M. d'Harcourt grave doubts. I am so sorry. He spoke of my characters as loud and noisy. Well, he can put his mind at ease. He evokes the "Holy Trinity" of music—"Melody, Harmony, and Rhythm"—whose laws may not be infringed upon. Nicely put. But is there really any law that prevents the musician from combining these three elements in one given proportion rather than another? I think not. Moreover, despite two careful readings, I wasn't able to penetrate the meaning of all M. d'Harcourt's comments. They must be infinitely profound. The same critic speaks of Mélisande's "awakening." Perhaps he is confusing it with Brünnhilde's.

The Interviewer
Imprudently Mentions the Name of Richard Wagner

CERTAINLY my method of composing—which consists above all of dispensing with "methods of composing"—owes nothing to Wagner. In his work each character has, one might say, his own "calling card," his image—his leitmotiv—which must always precede him. I must confess that I find this procedure somewhat gross. Also, the symphonic development that he introduced into opera appears to me to conflict continually with the moral argument in which the characters are involved and with the play of passions, which alone is important.

What shall I say of the other critics? No doubt M. Gaston Serpette has excellent grounds for declaring my score to be the "negation of everything musical." This indulgent writer forgets that a negation is very often worth several affirmations. *La Vie Parisienne* and *La Libre Parole* luckily did not concern themselves with artistic matters, so I need not concern myself with them. What is more, by some regrettable oversight, the editor of this latter journal forgot to sign his article.[4] It makes one laugh . . . or at least smile. What a joy for me to have colleagues such as MM. Albert Carré and André Messager, interpreters such as those in *Pelléas et Mélisande,* and to remain, after the fray, their devoted and grateful friend.

⤳*NOTES*

[1] Carraud's article (*La Liberté,* 2 May 1902) began with a lengthy criticism of Maeterlinck's play, questioning the success of the numerous short scenes and the overabundance of seemingly trivial detail "contaminated with symbolism." He noticed several "unfortunate features" that lent themselves too readily to parody. No doubt Debussy was pleased with Carraud's recognition of his almost complete originality. Denying any influence of Wagner (a view we can no longer hold today), Carraud suggests that "the only discernible artistic influences were from certain Russian composers, and even then they are only superficial. There is nothing, neither in the expression, the color, nor the musical substance that is not entirely personal."

To Camille de Sainte-Croix it was Debussy's rhythmic fluidity that was most impressive. "The richness of the rhythms," he wrote, "is found afresh at every new detail, and it follows, syllable by syllable, the melodic shape of the dialogue, adapting itself to it in the most supple way."

In *La Presse,* Bret wrote of the "sober declamation where not a word was lost and [where an] orchestra [was] used with the utmost discretion, from whence rise up the most exquisite and ingenious sonorities."

Like Carraud, André Corneau (one of the two critics who had preceded Debussy on *La Revue blanche*) found discernible influences "no
more of Wagner than of Gounod or Massenet." He stressed the importance of the orchestra:

> You will search in vain through the two hundred and eighty-three
> pages of the score for any fragment of melody. Your beloved ro-
> mances are nowhere to be found. The characters do not declaim, and
> they avoid singing. They speak what they have to say in a summarily
> notated melopoeia. It is to the orchestra alone that the task of
> expressing everything is reserved, or to put it better, of making
> everything felt.

Along with several others, he thought Carré's scenery the best he had ever
seen, but strangely enough he found Mary Garden's interpretation of
Mélisande dull.

Bauër's article, published under the anonymous name of "A Gentleman
of the Orchestra," was especially devoted to Carré's fine scenery. Alongside appeared a more hostile review by Eugène d'Harcourt.

[2] Mendès hoped for great things from the collaboration between Debussy
and Maeterlinck: "the best possible match because of a certain resemblance, almost a brotherhood." He was disappointed, especially with the
recitative, which (like many others) he found monotonous.

Willy, almost seeming to parody Debussy's own style of criticism, wrote
that "to analyze such works? I don't know how. The very special sugges-
tiveness of this work is perhaps best explained by a comparison. Old
Byzantine frescoes clumsily encased between Roman pillars. . . ." His
image, developed at some length, seems purposefully obscure, thinly
veiling an overall disappointment with the work. "Impressionistic? Yes,"
he adds, "a word that suits Debussy as long as it is not used pejoratively."

[3] Fourcaud found in Maeterlinck "the philosophy of passivity carried to its
furthest extreme: a mixture of *Geneviève de Brabant,* Shakespeare and
Tristan und Isolde." He found it utterly unsuitable for music and admired
Debussy for his tentative approach, his "notated declamation, with scarcely
any accompaniment."

[4] *La Libre Parole* was particularly hostile, talking of the work's "perpetual
cacophony" and of its "denial of all that constitutes musical good taste."

MERCURE DE FRANCE
January 1903

German Influence on French Music

G E R M A N influence never had any ill effect on anyone except those people easily impressed, or, to put it another way, on those who take the word "influence" to mean "imitation."

Besides, it is always difficult to be precise about influences, whether it is of Goethe's second *Faust* or of Bach's B Minor Mass. These works will remain monuments of beauty, unique and incapable of repetition. Their "influence" is like that of the sea or the sky, universal rather than especially German.

Closer to our own time, is not Wagner perhaps an example of the subjugator? However, musicians should be grateful to him for having left us an admirable treatise on the uselessness of set forms—that is, *Parsifal* . . . a masterly contradiction of all that is in the *Ring*.

Wagner, if one may be permitted a little of the grandiloquence that suits the man, was a beautiful sunset that has been mistaken for a sunrise. There will always be periods of imitation and influence, but one can never foresee how long they will last, still less their nationality; truth moves at the same speed as the laws of evolution.

These periods are necessary for those who like to follow easy, well-trodden paths. But they allow others to go further into realms where they will suffer for having found Beauty. So everything is for the best. It is not a question of money—something unfortunately inseparable from art.

MUSICA
October 1902

The Orientation of Music

*(Reply to a question posed by Charles Joly in the first issue
of* Musica: *"Is it possible to predict what the music of tomorrow
will be? The paths which have already been well-trodden now
seem to be deserted. Where do we go from here?")*

Q U E S T I O N S of this sort are usually answered by very reputable
people who know scarcely anything about music, who thus can approach the subject with great detachment. But their opinions are of no
importance, and, happily, nothing is explained.

The best thing one could wish for French music would be to see
the study of harmony abolished as it is practiced in the conservatories.
It is the most ridiculous way of arranging notes. Furthermore, it has
the severe disadvantage of standardizing composition to such a degree
that every composer, except for a few, harmonizes in the same way.
We can be sure that old Bach, the essence of all music, scorned harmonic formulae. He preferred the free play of sonorities whose curves,
whether flowing in parallel or contrary motion, would result in an
undreamed of flowering, so that even the least of his countless manuscripts bears an indelible stamp of beauty.[1]

That was the age of the "wonderful arabesque," when music was
subject to laws of beauty inscribed in the movements of Nature herself. Rather will our time be remembered as the era of the "age of
veneer"—although here I am speaking generally and not forgetting the
isolated genius of certain of my colleagues.

Contemporary dramatic music, however, embraces everything from

Wagnerian metaphysics to the trivialities of the Italians—not a particularly French orientation. Perhaps in the end we will see the light and achieve conciseness of expression and form (the fundamental qualities of French genius). Will we rediscover that abundant fantasy of which music alone is capable? It seems to have been forgotten under the pretext of research, which at first sight makes it seem as if the days of music are numbered.

Art is the most beautiful deception of all! And although people try to incorporate the everyday events of life in it, we must hope that it will remain a deception lest it become a utilitarian thing, sad as a factory.[2] Ordinary people, as well as the élite, come to music to seek oblivion: is that not also a form of deception? The Mona Lisa's smile probably never existed in real life, yet her charm is eternal. Let us not disillusion anyone by bringing too much reality into the dream. . . . Let us content ourselves with more consoling ways: such music can contain an everlasting expression of beauty.

I hope this letter does not arrive too late to be of use. At least it gives me an opportunity to wish you every success in your enterprise.

❧ *NOTES*

[1] In 1880 Debussy had enrolled in Ernest Guiraud's composition class at the Conservatoire. A close friend of Bizet, Guiraud was a traditional teacher but reasonably open-minded and likable; Debussy kept in contact with him until well on into the nineties, finding in him a sympathetic if not uncritical listener to his own revolutionary ideas of harmony and the approach to composition. In a remarkable account, in the form of a dialogue between Debussy and Guiraud, Maurice Emmanuel records how the young Debussy, seated at the piano, would expound his ideas in front of Guiraud's class, shaking the foundations of Conservatoire harmony with his deliberate series of parallel fifths and unresolved dissonances. To Guiraud's accusations of "theoretical absurdity," Debussy's reply was that "there is no theory. . . . Pleasure is the law." But when Guiraud reminded Debussy that he had himself been at the Conservatoire for ten years, Debussy agreed "that he can feel free because he has been through the mill, and that he doesn't write in the fugal style because he knows it."

2 "Sad as a factory"—Debussy's image was one to which he returned several times. As Robert Godet has pointed out, the "factory" image is strongly reminiscent of Laforgue. Elsewhere Debussy writes, "Je croupis dans les usines du néant dont se plaignait notre Jules [Laforgue]." (See Godet's article "Debussy 1918" in *Revue de musicologie,* Special Issue, 1962.) The endless assembly line of a factory becomes an image of boredom and sterility.

Vincent d'Indy's L'Etranger

Théâtre royal de la Monnaie—
L'Etranger: *music drama in two acts;*
poem and music by Vincent d'Indy
(*first performance 7 January 1903*)

N o t so long ago, I wrote a piece of music criticism for *La Revue blanche* preceded by a few explanations that went something like this:

"What you will find here are sincere and heartfelt impressions rather than 'criticism,' which is all too often no more than a brilliant set of variations on the theme of 'you didn't do it as I would, that's your mistake,' or even, 'you have talent, I have none, and that certainly cannot go on.' I shall try to see the works I discuss in perspective, to discover the various seeds from which they sprang, and what they contain of inner life. Isn't that just as interesting as that game which consists of taking them apart as though they were curious old watches?" Certainly there is at present a strange mania that demands that the music critic explain, take things to pieces, and, to put it bluntly, kill in cold blood all the mystery or even the emotion of a piece. Some we can excuse because of their complete ignorance, and others—the more spiteful of them—because of their malice. It's a bit like the "murder considered as one of the fine arts" of which Thomas De Quincey, the celebrated opium eater, spoke.

I shall be discussing established classics very little, no matter if they are popular or traditionally famous. Once and for all, Meyerbeer, Thalberg, Reyer—they are men of genius. But that's as far as their importance goes.

I hope that music and the gods will forgive me, but my opinions have hardly changed. In this column, which *Gil Blas* has so kindly given me, I will try to continue a "criticism of impressions," as free as possible from arbitrary aesthetics.

L'Etranger is what the dogmatists would call "a pure and lofty manifestation of art." In my humble opinion it is much more than that.

It certainly unfolds itself in pure and lofty forms, but they have all the intricacy, the coldness, the hardness, even the blueness of a machine of steel. The music appeared to be very beautiful, but it was as if veiled; its workmanship struck one so powerfully that one scarcely dared let oneself be moved—an uncomfortable feeling.

Whatever has been said about it, the influence of Wagner on d'Indy never went very deep: the heroic clowning of the one was never really compatible with the artistic integrity of the other. If *Fervaal* still comes within the Wagnerian tradition, it is excused by its morality and its scorn for the grandiloquent hysteria that consumes so many Wagnerian heroes.

I am well aware that Vincent d'Indy will be reproached for freeing himself and for not being fond enough of the "rendezvous of themes" —that delight of the old Wagnerians, who are warned of its impending occurrence by way of special signals.

What he is not quite free from is the need to explain and underline everything—something that occasionally makes the most beautiful scenes of *L'Etranger* somewhat heavy.[1] What is the good of so much music for a customs officer, a secondary character whose interest, I can see, lies in the contrast with the boundless humanity of the Stranger? One would wish him more comic, more like one of those people who are only concerned for their own skins.

The dramatic action of *L'Etranger* is by no means trivial, despite its simplicity. It takes place in a little fishing village beside the sea. A man has just come to set up house in the village, and they call him l'Etranger ("the Stranger") for want of a better name. He is highly antisocial, and neither associates with nor speaks to anyone. He wears an emerald in his cap, and this naturally earns him the reputation of a wizard. But he does try to help people: he gives some of his fish to those who haven't been able to catch any, and he tries to save some poor fellow who is about to be carted off to prison—but authority does not like symbolists, nor do fishermen.

With two simple linear phrases Vincent d'Indy very clearly expresses the character of the Stranger. He is a Christian hero, one of a line of martyrs who have fulfilled on earth some charitable mission imposed upon them by God. The Stranger is thus the faithful servant whom the Lord tempts with the love of woman. His heart succumbs; and death alone can redeem him. Never before has modern music been more deeply pious, more full of Christian charity. In fact, it is d'Indy's own deep conviction that makes these two phrases so absolutely right: they illuminate the profound meaning of the drama better than any kind of symphonic commentary.

However, a young girl, Vita, is attracted by the mystery and the sad thoughtfulness of this man, and what's more, she deeply loves the sea—the usual confidante for all her sorrows and secret desires. But Vita is already betrothed to André, a handsome customs officer who in a domestic scene shows himself to be self-centered and arrogant. He is the kind of official who could never understand that a young girl might dream of something other than a handsome customs officer.

In a scene where Vita and the Stranger meet, Vita confesses her love. Since the Stranger's arrival, the sea has no longer been her confidante. He in turn, deeply troubled, declares his own painful secret: "Adieu, Vita, may all happiness be thine! Tomorrow I must leave thee, for I love thee, knowest thou this, I love thee with all my heart!"

Vita is young and betrothed, and, in uttering these words of love, the Stranger has lost the purity of heart in which lies his strength, for an ascetic solitude is necessary for the mission of redemption he has undertaken. Being devoted to all things prevents him from being devoted to one alone. But it isn't much fun having to do miracles everyday, and after all the Stranger is old now. I must say that this most human quality was more than welcome in such a holy character!

Having forgotten his mission in a single moment, he will henceforth be prevented from continuing his acts of charity. He gives Vita the emerald, which is useless now, and bids her good-bye forever.

Weeping, Vita throws the sacred emerald, the cause of all her anguish, into the swirling sea—from whence rise mysterious voices. The sea swallows up the stone, its waves taking a savage delight in reclaiming the sacred charm, which once had been able to calm it against its will. A storm breaks, and a ship is in distress: even the good fishermen of the first act dare not attempt to save her. André, the handsome customs officer, takes advantage of the general chaos to show Vita his stripes of promotion and offer her a fine silver bracelet. He oversteps the bounds of egotism, and Vita, by her silence, shows him just how intolerable he is, but he goes off shamelessly. Then the Stranger, sensing the danger, appears on the scene, and demands that a lifeboat be brought. He is about to set off alone, for no one dares go with him. Vita, uttering one of the most beautiful love cries that has ever been heard, rushes forward to join the stranger. They launch themselves and disappear into the raging billows, which they no longer have the power to calm. An old sailor watches their plight. Suddenly, the line holding them to the shore snaps. The old sailor takes off his cap, intoning the words of the *De Profundis*. These two souls have found repose in death, which alone took pity on their impossible love.

Let he who will, look freely for unfathomable symbols in this play. I like to see it as a human tale that d'Indy has clothed with symbols only in order to render more deeply the eternal gulf between beauty and the vulgarity of the masses.

Without dwelling on technical questions, I want to pay homage to the serenity that runs right through this work, to the deliberate avoidance of all complication, and above all to d'Indy's quiet determination to excel himself.

And if earlier I was complaining that there was too much music, it's just that, here and there, it seemed to inhibit the marvelous blossoming of unforgettable beauty that flows from so many pages of *L'Etranger*. Thus the work is an admirable lesson to those who believe in that crude, imported style which reduces music to dust under a pile of realism.

The Théâtre de la Monnaie and its directors are to be warmly congratulated for staging *L'Etranger* with an artistic care worthy of the highest praise—although perhaps we could have had more forceful scenery. We should be grateful for what amounts these days to an act of courage.

I cannot but praise M. Sylvain Dupuis and his orchestra for their remarkable feeling for the music. M. Albert and Mlle Friché played their part too in this triumph for Vincent d'Indy. Everyone showed a touching enthusiasm, and I see no reason why the city of Brussels should not be congratulated.

৵*NOTE*

1 Debussy was not alone in his opinion of *L'Etranger:* Camille Bellaigue agreed that d'Indy's excellent craftsmanship was sometimes *de trop.* "He practices his art both as a science and a virtue," wrote this critic in the *Revue des deux mondes.* As for the influence of Wagner on d'Indy, Debussy considerably oversimplified the case, almost seeming to come to d'Indy's defense on this point. Like so many others, d'Indy came strongly under the spell of Wagner in his early years, and in 1873, with the aid of an introduction to Cosima Wagner from Liszt, he was allowed to enter Wagner's house at Bayreuth, where he silently watched his idol at work through the doors of his study, too busy to be disturbed. But d'Indy had written of *L'Etranger* that it was as different from *Fervaal* (his highly Wagnerian earlier opera) as was *Nina* or *La Folle d'amour* from *Götter-dämmerung.* He had aimed at a texture that would allow the recitatives to be heard—another reason to bring him professionally close to Debussy.

GIL BLAS

19 January 1903

Thoughts on Music in the Open Air

N o one in France cares any more for the barrel organ! It is virtually only at the annual flag parades on Bastille Day, or in remote areas more used to the cries of hooligans than the fleeting reveries of music lovers, that they still dare grind their melancholy pipes on wheels.

Something to be regretted? Should we conclude that it signifies a lowering of our musical taste here in France? Far be it from me to say, nor to point the accusing finger, whatever the answer may be. But M. Gavioli, the celebrated maker of these instruments, doesn't seem to have achieved all that he should. Is it really enough just to have made organ rolls of the Entr'acte from *Cavalleria Rusticana,* the "Valse bleu" and a few other masterpieces these past years? Why so many reservations? Could he not have turned his attention to the need for popularity felt by some of the more famous of our contemporaries? Is there not a great deal of out-of-date music played at our Sunday concerts that would find itself pleasantly renewed on the barrel organ? If only M. Gavioli wasn't so desperately impervious to the needs of our time. One must keep up to date, sir! Do not leave the charm of perfect instruments to the kings of Africa. And let me tell you, the Shah of Persia has an electric organ that can give a fine rendering of the Pre-lude to *Parsifal,* and if you think these harem performances would have flattered Wagner, you're wrong! Admit, in spite of his taste for the mysterious, that that is going a little far. Moreover, has it not been proved time and time again that he will never be understood except in France? Come, M. Gavioli, can you not see where your duty lies? M.

Gailhard did not hesitate to put on *Pagliacci* at the Opéra; well, hurry up and make instruments that can play the complete *Ring*!

But to be serious, the futility of these thoughts is only too apparent. It shows that one thinks about things being banal only in order to criticize them—never to help put them right. To those who will find this defense of the barrel organ ridiculous, one could reply that it is certainly no mere dilettante pleasure: it's something one could offer as a remedy for the mediocrity of most people's minds.

Without defending the people who attend open-air concerts any more than those who go to the Concerts Lamoureux, one must confess that both have a right to their own emotions. . . . But there are others, too: those who can be stirred only by "music in the open air," something which, as it's practiced today, is just about the most mediocre thing one can think of.

But seriously, why is the adornment of our squares and boulevards left solely to the military bands? I know there is the music of the Republican Guard as well, but that is something different: it is practically an instrument of diplomacy.[1]

I like to imagine more impromptu happenings that blend more completely with the natural surroundings. Isn't military music meant to relieve the tedium of long marches and to bring joy to the streets? It expresses the patriotism that burns in every heart, and it unites the quiet soul of the little pastry cook with the old gentleman who thinks of nothing but the Alsace-Lorraine question, yet never talks about it. Far be it from me to take away these noble privileges, but I must say that, coming through the trees, it sounds like a childhood phonograph.

Imagine a large orchestra augmented with the sound of the human voice. (No, not a choral society, thank you!) Here would lie the embryo of music especially designed for the open air: new ideas flowing in broad lines both from the orchestra and voices. It would float from the tops of the trees, through the light of the open air, and any harmonic progression that sounded stifled within the confines of a concert hall would certainly take on a new significance. Perhaps this is the answer to the question of how to rid music of all those petty mannerisms of form and tonality—arbitrary questions with which music is unfortunately encumbered.

It must be understood that it would mean working not with the "gross" but with the "grand." I don't mean that it should produce echoes by repeating huge clusters of sound ad nauseam, but that it should take advantage of them by using them to prolong the crowd's feeling of harmony. The mysterious collaboration between air currents, the movement of leaves, and the perfume of flowers would combine together in such a natural marriage with the music that it would seem to live in each one of them. . . . And the tall, still tree trunks would not be left out: they would be the pipes of a universal organ. Hordes of children would play on their branches, singing the rounds of yesteryear, for which the feeble rhymes that disgrace our gardens and towns today make such a poor substitute. We might also redis-cover counterpoint: something we have currently invested with the stiffness of a mandarin, but from which the old masters of the French Renaissance could raise a smile.

If all that did happen, I admit that I would shed no tears over the disappearance of the barrel organ, but I have a feeling that music will continue to remain somewhat stifled.[2]

Concerts

THIS brings me, somewhat irreverently, to express my regret at not having been able to be present at last Sunday's concerts. What makes it worse is that they were going to play some charming pieces —among them, I am happy to say, the Orchestral Suite from *Namouna,* such marvelous ballet music—but the antimusical manage-ment under the direction of M. Gailhard insisted on replacing this with a selection of imported music, of the kind that seemed to be a cross between a bazaar and a bawdy house. Heaven knows why, but they're trying to infect music with the microbes of bad taste.

Mentioning *Namouna* reminds me that when I was very young I went to one of the all-too-rare performances of this work—and I showed a noisy but forgivable enthusiasm. M. Vaucorbeil, at that time director of the Opéra and a very kind man, showed me to the door forthwith. I can't help it, but the recollection of this little event is very dear to me, and nothing has ever reduced my sincere and joyful ad-miration of this work. So, in passing, I salute the name of Lalo.[3]

Yesterday, at the Concert Colonne, was the last performance of *La Damnation de Faust*. It will soon be easier to count the stars in the sky than the last performances of *La Damnation de Faust*! And I don't find that so funny! At the Concert Chevillard was the first performance of the Symphonic Prelude that precedes the second act of *L'Etranger*, that wonderful music drama by Vincent d'Indy. I have already confessed, perhaps a little too hastily, my respect for this work, which seems to mark the beginning of a new era in M. d'Indy's sincere and honest career. There one can breathe with ease, far away from d'Indy's cares about whether his friends will admire the masterly craftsmanship of his writing—something that sometimes mars the beauty of his ideas. On the other hand, he was bound to come to the following profound truth: that the actual writing, however well it is done, is never a substitute for the emotional effect, and that the work will never achieve beauty except by doing away with any kind of abstract cleverness in the craftsmanship.

The Prelude was given the warm reception it deserved. For my own humble part, I was not as impressed as I had been in Brussels. D'Indy really does stick too rigidly to the conciseness and single-minded plot of this play; all the theatrical timing falls to pieces in a concert-hall performance. The piece is like pages torn from a very beautiful old book to which one no longer has the key: even if they are still beautiful, they no longer have any meaning.[4] That is not too harsh a criticism. . . . There was also the first performance of a piano concerto by M. Léon Moreau. The mixed reception this concerto received indicates, better than any critic could, in which direction M. Moreau should now turn. It had charming orchestral qualities, but ironically it was the piano part that prevented them from showing themselves to their full effect. And without sharing the opinion of one section of the public, who showed their disdain in true Parisian fashion, I would say that the piano concerto, treated in this way, calls for the piano to be banned once and for all! M. Léon Moreau certainly has the power to take his revenge; his friends would like that.[5]

Meanwhile, M. David-G. Henderson sang, with a distinguished quaver, a song by Beethoven bearing the somewhat old-fashioned title of "Adelaide." I think the old man must have forgotten to burn this piece, and we must put the blame for its exhumation on his greedy heirs. After a triumphant performance of Berlioz's *Roméo et Juliette*, I left. So I am prevented forever from telling you about the rest of the concert.

Prince L.-F. of Bavaria

IN *Le Temps* of 15 January 1903 you can read the following news:

> Prince Ludwig-Ferdinand of Bavaria has just sent the following reply to the Committee for a Monument to Wagner in Berlin: "I accept, with the greatest of pleasure, the honorary presidency of the committee for the inauguration of a Wagner monument, as well as for the foundation of the international musical Congress. I sincerely thank you for having chosen me for this honor, for it is to the glory of the first and the greatest composer of Germany."

So what! There's no need to brag about it! Certainly Ludwig-Ferdinand of Bavaria is better at being a prince than he is at writing about music. And I will not dwell on the historical impossibility of Wagner being the first real German composer. What about Bach? Just a man who had a lot of children? Or Beethoven? A man who was so ill-bred that he decided to become deaf so that he could better annoy his contemporaries with his last quartets? As for Mozart, it would be better if we did not mention him—a mere sensualist who wrote *Don Giovanni* to aggravate the Germans.

But for heaven's sake! These people are the very glory of Germany, and of such tremendous genius that few names can rank with them.

Wagner, on the other hand, never did anything of real service to music, and he never did much for Germany either. At present, it is busy arguing: one side is blinded by the last rays of the Wagnerian sunset, and the other frantically holds onto the neo-Beethovenian formula bequeathed by Brahms. It is like the *Ring* come to life! And when Wagner in a stupid outburst said, "And now you have an art," he might just as well have said: "And now I leave you in a vacuum; it's up to you to get out!"

It is not my concern to discuss Wagner's genius here. His force was undeniably dynamic. But its effect was all 'the greater because the way had been prepared by cunning magicians whose guile knew no bounds. For a long time, music suffered from what you might call a fever—incurable in anyone who ventured near the marshy stench. A stable of worn-out cart horses, Wagner-crazy, followed willingly after his egotistical need for glory. But it is perhaps the extraordinarily anguished groaning in his music that is responsible for the deep impression made by Wagner on the contemporary spirit: he has awakened the secret thirst for the criminal in some of the most famous minds of our age.*

To conclude, Wagner's works suggest a most striking image: Bach is the Holy Grail; Wagner is Klingsor, who wants to destroy the Grail and take his place. Bach reigns as king over music, and in his infinite bounty he desires that we should wait to hear his words, as yet undecipherable—a great lesson he has bequeathed to the pure and noble glory of music. . . . Wagner vanishes. A fearsome darkness, black as soot.

* Among the Germans, M. Richard Strauss is unique. We gather from his orchestral music that his method is merely an extension of Liszt. And does not his need to underline the plot of his symphonic poems ally him with Berlioz? Certainly, there is no trace of a Wagnerian influence.

⌇*NOTES*

[1] In the introduction to this chapter we mentioned Debussy's taste for *la grosse musique,* the music of the circus and fairground. The predilection for popular music by the sophisticated artist reveals, as Cosima Wagner put it, "a whole world that makes you shudder" (she was speaking of the music of Chabrier), and she could admit this ironic use of street and café music into the temples of great art. Debussy's defense of the barrel organ (as well as his asides on Sousa) must be seen in the context of literary evocations of popular music, particularly those of Laforgue. The composer's close friend and correspondent G. Jean-Aubry wrote of Laforgue's taste for the street organ, shown both in his poetry and his letters, and of his ideas on music, considering them to be central to an understanding of

Debussy's art. "Les orgues de Barbarie," were, wrote Laforgue, "mes bons amis de Paris," and one of his *Complaintes* is that of the barrel organ:

> Orgue, orgue de Barbarie
> Don Quichotte, Souffre-Douleur
> Vidasse, vidasse ton coeur
> Ma pauvre rosse endolorie.

For Laforgue, the sad, autumnal sounds of the grinding street organ were full of irony. Perhaps Debussy's most "Laforguean" piece is the moon-struck Sonata for Cello and Piano.

[2] Evidently Debussy was pleased with this somewhat prophetic description, for it is a repeat of a passage that originally appeared in *La Revue blanche* (see pp. 40–1).

[3] The exuberant enthusiasm of the seventeen-year-old Debussy for Lalo's ballet *Namouna* probably depended largely on the vivid orchestration of the work. Martin Cooper has aptly described the music as "decorative"; it has a superficial exoticism that never penetrates below the surface.

[4] Colette's second notice contained her views on d'Indy's *L'Etranger*, which she had also heard at its first performance in Brussels. She assumed none of the admiring detachment in which Debussy phrased his comments on this important occasion. Instead we have a list of the more famous members of the audience and a little bitching: "All the Schola were there, listening as if it were the Mass." So, too, mentioned Colette, was Octave Maus, the important Belgian impresario who promoted French music and founded the *XX*, a salon that fostered all that was new in the arts. Colette absorbed *L'Etranger* conscientiously, but found herself intimidated by all the "superhuman characters, the larger-than-life sentiments—larger than my poor little life in any case. Apart from moments where I, along with everyone, was carried away by such beauty as was appreciable to lowly mortals, I said to myself, 'Well, if it's for me, I'd rather have one size smaller!' "

[5] Colette agreed with Debussy about both *Namouna* and Léon Moreau's concerto. The former she affectionately dubbed "an oriental fairground without the clowning or the belly dance: ingenious music this!" and the latter she noted "was played on a dry old Gaveau that won no enthusiasm. Nor did M. Moreau."

At the Opéra-Comique

First performance of Titania,
music drama in three acts;
libretto by Louis Gallet and André Corneau;
music by Georges Hüe

As its title indicates, this play takes place in the domain of the fairies. It is the story of one of Titania's many flirtations. This one ends very badly, since Oberon, deceived to the full (if I may put it thus), becomes angry, commands thunder and lightning, and plays his piccolo. This causes Yann, a poor sneering little fellow, one-time lover of Titania, to come tumbling down from his seventh heaven. He learns, a little too late, while he is dying in the snow, that one should never fall in love with fairies. Except when one is very young, and in books generally bound in red.

The success of this piece has been immediate. One could sense how well the first night audience understood Monsieur Georges Hüe's intentions: to please them, without disturbing them too much.

Mme Raunay was commanding yet deliciously feminine; MM. Maréchal, Allard, and Delvoye didn't fail us in their capacity as perfect artists; and Mme Marguerite Carré delicately portrayed the slightly shy character of Yann's lost little girl friend. All had the purity and freshness of an early fresco. Mlle de Craponne was as sharp as an imp who sings like an angel.

So—"Rule Titania"!

Titania

THESE past foggy days have made me think of London and of that wonderful play *A Summer Night's Dream,* whose real and more poetic title used to be *A Midsummer Night's Dream:* that being the shortest night of the year. A sultry night, alight with stars! But fleeting, transitory: its charms encased between a twilight reluctant to fade and a dawn impatient to break . . .

A night of dreams that one dream alone could fill! And to Oberon, king of the fairies, fell the task of organizing the activities of the night. It did not prevent him from becoming royally jealous, and he even took the opportunity of testing Titania's none too secure virtue aided by Puck (or Robin Goodfellow), merry vagabond of the night, artful and mischievous, that fine joker whose aid could be procured simply by calling, "Hobgoblin! Gentle Puck . . ."

But I am reminded above all of a man now almost forgotten, at least in the theater. I saw him trudging the streets of London, his body aflame with a luminous glow and his brow having that special radiance of those who have left behind them a trail of beautiful things. There he went, upheld by a determined resolution not to die until he had heard performed the work that was to be a testimony to his whole life, painfully wrought from every drop of lifeblood in his veins. How was he able to recapture the mettle of his youth, those romantic galloping rhythms which had so suddenly filled his youthful heart with the spirit of genius? Nobody will ever know. . . . The music had a kind of dreamy melancholy quite unique at this time, never for a moment weighed down with that indigestible Germanic "moonshine" indulged in by nearly all his contemporaries.

He was perhaps the first to have concerned himself with the relationship that must surely exist between the all-embracing spirit of nature and the soul of the imaginary character. Certainly it was he who had the idea of using the legend as a background against which the music could express real actions. For it is music alone that has the power to evoke imaginary scenes at will, to conjure up the intangible world of fantasies secretly shrouded within the mysterious poetry of the night, the thousand indistinguishable noises made by moonbeams caressing the leaves.

All the known ways in which music can describe the fantastic were under the command of this man's mind: even in our time, so rich in orchestral chemistry, he has hardly been surpassed. If one could perhaps reproach him for too strong a taste for panache and showy arias, one must not forget that he married a singer. And he probably adored her. It's nothing to be sentimental about, the less so because the usual matrimonial concern for tangling the wedding ribbons in a flurry of elegant semiquavers doesn't prevent him from finding, at the least opportunity, effects that are really beautiful, above all natural and free from useless embroideries. This man (have you all recognized him?) was Karl Maria von Weber. The opera, his last, brilliant work, is called *Oberon,* and its first performance was given in London. So you can see my excellent reason for mentioning this town.

A few years earlier, *Der Freischütz* and then *Euryanthe* were performed in Berlin. That's how he became the father of the so-called romantic school, to which we owe our own Berlioz, so in love with romantic color that he sometimes forgot about the music; Wagner, the great entrepreneur of symbols; and, closer to our time, Richard Strauss, who, for a romantic, has such a remarkably organized imagination. To Weber goes the honor of fathering such a lineage, and he will have to console himself with the glory of these sons of his genius, for it is virtually only the overtures of his operas that are nowadays performed.[1] It is the duty of M. A. Carré, as artistic director of the Opéra-Comique, to revive, at least, *Der Freischütz*—such a beautiful work. He alone would be capable of understanding how its scenery could be realized in its fully legendary light.

Unfortunately, Weber is dead—and the dead are a closed book. But Georges Hüe is very much alive, fortunately for us. (I will not mention Louis Gallet, for he is dead, and has left no titles of enough importance to be the "father" of anything in the realms of art.) Thanks to M. Georges Hüe and M. André Corneau, we were able to breathe once again that atmosphere of magic, essential to all who know how to remain grown-up children and whose imaginations are whetted more by the unreal than by current affairs. Besides, done well, the adventures of Titania will always be more interesting than those of the *Casque d'Or.* If the loves of the queen of the fairies end in ways that are more or less similar to those of a courtesan, let us admit that their setting is far more pleasing. But I do not think that Weber (to whom M. Georges Hüe is bound to be a little indebted) would have been fully satisfied with the way in which he re-creates certain figures in the Titania legend—in particular the all too solemn Oberon, who, in a grand explanatory duet with Titania, becomes angry about her behavior and bellows away in a manner suited rather to the rages of Wotan than to the scorn of the king of the fairies! And all for the sake of a poor word-spinning poet, who cannot after all be blamed for following the flights of his imagination. Neither you nor I would have had the courage to punish such a respectable desire. Could Oberon not have punished the poor dreamer for his foolishness by some other means than death? And his earthly girl friend is struck down at the same blow—a character full of human weakness whose gentle complaints are a useless encumbrance to the action of the play. What's more, it's probable that Weber would have insisted more on the fairytale side of things: he wouldn't have missed the opportunity to envelop the character of Titania in a halo of lightness and fantasy. In M. Georges Hüe's hands she is almost too human; her mood sometimes contradicts her words. The character who comes off best turns out to be a minor figure—an old shepherd who in the first act clearly describes the plot. He also brings it to its conclusion with a most touching recitative, to the gently monotonous sound of a heavy snowfall.

One has the impression of the death of a landscape, so desolate, so cold that even the simple act of asking for his overcoat becomes something of a moment of truth. But this old shepherd should have been the only really human character of the play! The rest should have remained in the land of make-believe, without ever trying to justify the work's title of a music drama.

M. Georges Hüe knows exactly how to produce the effect he wants: he is a very good musician. He controls the orchestral chemistry with a sure hand. But why, especially when he is concerned with light, charming things, does he have the slightly bored air of someone who has invited people to a feast where all is joy and gaiety, but who is himself put out by any overt expression of happiness? He thus detaches himself from the party spirit and makes it clear that his own heart is heavy. Perhaps fate has not yet given M. Georges Hüe the chance to show his real nature. But he has a real feeling for the sadness, even the tragedy of people and their daily affairs, and for proof of this I have only to cite the striking way in which he has set the desperate cry of his hero, "Death is the final hope—for him who cannot live out his dreams." This cry contains such a deep and true expression of torment that it seems to crystallize in a few bars M. Georges Hüe's attitude of mind. It makes one think that he would only be at home in pure tragedy. Life and its affairs are not necessarily all play. Not everyone can live with just the strains of the "Marche lorraine," and in the life of an artist there are mornings when the prospect of writing or painting is not exactly a rosy thought.

I'm not claiming the right to draw any moral conclusion from all these thoughts. I would rather just express my hope that in the future M. Georges Hüe's music will achieve the tragic depth of which he seems capable.

I must humbly excuse myself for not having known how to write about this piece—a grave shortcoming in any critic worthy of his name. I'll try to make up for it by getting back into rigorous training.

In the preceding, all too hasty account, I have already spoken of the perfection of the artists who contributed to the success of *Titania*, so I will here only say that all the usual praise is due to M. Albert Carré. The sure and informed mastery of his contribution has long been unquestionable.

M. Jusseaume's scenery has been called Shakespearean; I will not deny it. But don't you think Shakespeare would have gone berserk if he could have seen the pole that, in the theater of his youth, bore the simple indication, "A Forest," transformed into one of the luxurious forests for which M. Jusseaume is famous?

We should not forget M. Luigini, impeccable as a conductor, who obtains a wonderful sense of rhythm from a delicately supple baton. He is a very necessary bridge between the action on the stage and that of the orchestra.

Concerts

THERE are in Paris six series of Sunday concerts. Where is the logic of allowing them all to take place on the same day? It is most impractical for those who possess only one pair of ears to hear with, and one pair of legs to get them there. The choice was so difficult to make that I decided not to go to any of them!

Rest assured that my absence did not prevent M. Chevillard from conducting the *Choral* Symphony by heart. [La symphonie avec choeur, par coeur . . . pardon!][2] And even if that seems easy, I wouldn't try it if I were you. At the Concert Colonne there was the first performance of a Concertstück for harp and orchestra by Gabriel Pierné. That is an occasion which should certainly have enhanced M. Pierné's reputation for charm and delicacy. Perhaps they'll repeat it next Sunday. It is the least one could hope for.[3]

At the Jardin d'Acclimatation, someone sang "Les Vallons" (Gounod), the aria from *Guido en Ginevra* (Halévy), and the trio from *William Tell* (Rossini). I do hope that these young composers, so honorably received before now, commanded success with these new and so little known pieces! Of all the locations for Sunday concerts, this spot is one of the nicest, because it gives you the alternative, if the music bores you, of watching the animals. And they are certainly not musicians!

❧ *NOTES*

[1] Hüe's opera *Titania,* though forgotten today, prompts from Debussy some interesting insights into an area of his imaginative mind where the imagery of Shakespeare and the music of Weber play an important part. These two articles should be seen alongside a detailed memoir, published by Debussy's close friend Robert Godet, entitled "Weber and Debussy" (originally published in *The Chesterian* [London, June 1926]). The interview with Godet, which took place while Debussy unwound after the dress rehearsal of *Pelléas* (i.e., about six months before the present article), includes a remarkable portrait of Weber and the magic world of *A Midsummer Night's Dream.* It is worth quoting at length:

> Night was already falling when the author of *Pelléas* was accompanied back to his door. He insisted that I should go up for a cup of tea. It was then, in a quiet tête-à-tête, in which he did not make the slightest allusion to his work or the somewhat tumultuous reception it had received, that he began to praise the "horn" of Oberon as only he knew how, with all his heart and all his soul. . . .
>
> "Do you know who kept faithful company with me just now? No, you will not guess. This so-called visitor, Heaven be praised, has no part in the 'event of the day.' I am even embarrassed to introduce him to you, he so detests ceremonies. Let us call him, if you will, Oberon's horn. Fascinated at all times by its melancholy call, perhaps I would have ignored its real power of evocation if the echo of its three distant notes, coming at a moment I least anticipated it, had not most unexpectedly revived in me the feeling of that magic world with which Weber was pleased to enrich our art, and which he opened so wide with so sober a gesture. What a refuge for an artist of this world, especially when he is bent on relinquishing his dream and exposing it to reality's revenge! Let us not insist. We know the reserve of Oberon's horn, and how much it forbids any emphasis. And yet, as one thing follows upon another, Weber, while preserving me from my personal vicissitudes, made me think of the multifarious revelations of music: serious, lively, passionate, mystical, of those which refresh the style, of those which unsettle the expression, and I asked myself if his music, above all, were not pre-eminently the 'revealer' in a certain sense and a certain domain, it being well understood that neither its effect nor (I imagine) its

motive is to found an undiscovered aesthetic order or to determine an unknown type of passion. That which it inaugurates, without any pretension to innovation, is the musical reign of a kind of poetry that hitherto had only spoken, or, if you prefer it, had merely hummed between its lips. Weber lends it his magnificent voice, and then, as if by the phenomenon of spontaneous combustion (I had this chemical metaphor from Dickens's *Bleak House*), a truth which nothing had announced bursts forth, a truth whose discovery appears to me more important than that of the most ingenious rhetoric. Weber sings and thereupon the voice of this Orpheus renews the harmony of nature with the human soul in a visionary kingdom which has no difficulty in persuading us of its reality, since the law which governs it secures for art a life of its own, far better balanced than ours. In this accord which he constructs so harmoniously, note that Weber begins instinctively by transposing its two terms: it is in the measure, when matter unloads its weight, that it impresses him so that he succeeds in animating it with his breath when he sets it down. And if, for example, he turns his landscapes into living beings, one might even say individualized in their characters, and if he transforms his characters, even those that are supernatural, into elementary types of innocence and malice akin to the tree and the flower, it is the genius in him, in spite of himself, that transfigures them until they are knit one within the other. Do you not admire in that a delightful miracle? Certainly in *Oberon,* the ground was prepared for the music by the fable. Still, for the miracle to take place a special magic was necessary, the bewitching enchantment of Ariel 'more rapid than thought,' of Puck, equally adept at suddenly descending to the ground as in vanishing into space with a flap of his wings. But look at *Der Freischütz.* Between his forest, vibrating with the terrors and rather heavy and childish joys of the Germanic legend and, for example, this forest in the Ardennes, so resolutely fictitious, where the confetti of *As You Like It* bursts forth like rockets, there is certainly an insuperable distance. Now, is it not all the more strange that, barely touched by the wand of the magician Weber, the realistic and natural scene for the most German of melodramas assumes a grace and freshness, a mystery worthy of Shakespearean fantasy? Any manufacturer of the picturesque would have deemed it shrewder and more expeditious simply to imitate the given surroundings. But Weber is a poet: he re-creates his surroundings, and he re-creates them (as for instance his Max, his Agatha, who are very human, with flesh nourished by his blood but rendered volatile by his dream) by exercising a sovereign independence which is the privilege of masters in transposition.

"In order to understand well the kind of quality I mean, remember the passages of Wagner (of the first period and even the second) when that other sorcerer, but Klingsorian (Klingsor whose digestion would be equal to his appetite), borrows inspiration from our sober magician. It immediately loses its airy grace, its innocent freshness, and its mystery is injured by excessive emphasis. Adorned beyond measure in order better to attract, it adapts its gestures, which had expressed an ethereal nostalgia, to the expression of the most violent desires. Perverted in that fashion, one is pained to recognize it under its luxurious trappings, even without considering that they defend it badly against the caprice of fashion. One must go as far as *Parsifal*—to the perfect 'enchantment' which, in its essential being, owes nothing but to itself—to find again among much that is unequalled, that simplicity of harmony and especially that pureness of tone with which we associate in our dreams the eternal youth *Oberon* or *Der Freischütz,* in contrast to the wear and tear of the too-usual Wagnerian idiom.

"Now, supposing a visitor from Mars were to come this evening to pay us a musical call—all the stars having fallen, as you know. I willingly leave to you the controversial subjects: theory of sound, scales, chords, form, the whole group. But let us take note of the word 'timbre' which just escaped me. It would take care of the question of orchestration and it would hardly give me any trouble: Weber alone would undertake the whole. Barring one or two postscripts, his work is the best of instrumental treatises. What is a clarinet? I would not know how to instruct the Martian better than by referring him to Agatha to learn the virginity, not of that young girl, but of the instrument, which would reveal to him in the Concertstück one of the most beautiful secrets of its deep register. The flute? There I should be embarrassed in my choice, but there is a duo which would reveal to the Martian one of its latest possibilities—notwithstanding the period—the thirds accompanying the 'casting of the bullets' or those not less nocturnal but so different in shade, which are introduced in Agatha's adorable air in the second act of *Der Freischütz*; and in this same act he would hear in the 'hunting scene' the piccolos which have lost nothing of their fierceness. He would hear in addition a quartet of horns which remains a model of wildness, whilst that of the overture has not been surpassed for sylvan charm and birdlike sweetness. As foreshadowing our modern brass, I could find nothing better, offhand, than the song of the trumpet to the sunrise in *Oberon* and those breathless exclamations of the trombones in the overture of *Der Freischütz.* Now if the Martian had not had enough of the wind instruments, well! we would have to abandon all hope of going to bed early. . . . Who has made better use of the strings than Weber, associating them, contrasting them, choosing amongst them the most expressive, entrusting an E string with a 'cantilena' that makes the most of the bowing, varying the attack and the style of the tremolo? He has resplendency, he has delicacy, and I think he is without a rival in the art of subduing—that is to say, notably in the use of the mutes: think of those with which he tempers the violins in the prelude of *Oberon* in order better to illuminate the answer of the violas and violoncellos; think of the ethereal quality of the different violins in Agatha's aria already mentioned, and in the octet of *Euryanthe* so mysteriously darkened for the appearance of the ghost. . . . It is not sufficient to say that the instrumental resources are familiar to him to a rare degree. It would be necessary to say that he scrutinizes the soul of each instrument and exposes it with a gentle hand. Deferential to his resources they yield him more than he appears to demand. Also, the most daring combinations of his orchestra, when he makes himself most deliberately symphonic, have in particular the tone color preserved in its original quality: colors that are superimposed without mingling, the mutual reactions which enhance rather than abolish their individuality. A predilection for the voluminous, if not corrected by aversion to neutral tone, is fatal. Weber, when he gathers together his forces, knows well how to be formidable, but as a colorist he has too great a sense of values and as a musician too much taste for quantity ever to matter more with him than quality. Only one example more, not of the first but of the second, a quite minute example but a very delectable one, and then good night (already the Martian has vanished): re-read the four or five introductory bars to Max's air in G, after the waltz in *Der Freischütz,* and listen intently for the hammering of the clarinet, which insinuates itself into the frail sonorous edifice between the tone colors of the flutes that crown it and the tones of the oboe that support it. Then you will tell me what you think of it . . . but not on the evening of a dress rehearsal!"

This evocative passage underlines similarities with *Pelléas*, whose setting has much in common with the dark forests of Germanic legend. Debussy's phrase "very human, with flesh nourished by his blood but rendered volatile by his dream" could equally well have been a statement about his own opera, written, as it was, after the first full rehearsal of *Pelléas*; indeed, several times he stressed the ambiguity between his desire for realism and the dreamlike atmosphere of the opera. In addition, the composer's attraction to the magical side of Shakespeare is emphasized—a preoccupation that bore fruit in the piano prelude "La Danse de Puck," and which Debussy had intended to explore in a projected opera of *As You Like It*.

In its literary style the passage (though rather clumsily translated—the original is lost) would seem to be reminiscent of the evocative writing of *Monsieur Croche*. The two visitors—Oberon's horn and M. Croche—have much in common. Again, Debussy's ambivalent attitude toward Wagner is better clarified than in the confused picture we glean from the articles. Klingsor, satirized in the article of 19 January, is seen as an unsuccessful reworking of Weberian characterization overburdened by Wagner with "excessive emphasis and luxurious trappings." But once again Debussy is careful to counterbalance his distaste for what he calls "first and second period" Wagner with his sincere admiration for *Parsifal*, especially with regard to the "pureness of tone"—presumably the subtle orchestration for which Debussy expressed admiration elsewhere.

[2] Neither Colette nor Debussy could resist a pun on the "Symphonie avec choeur." Collette recalled one of her husband's weaker gibes and elaborated: "Willy, whose puns often annoy me, succeeded in more than wordplay the day he called the Ninth the 'cardiac symphony,' for I now imagine this 'Symphonie avec "coeur" ' as a huge funeral urn where the heart of Beethoven is still palpitating."

[3] Colette liked Pierné's harp piece: "It was acclaimed and deserved it," she wrote. "But between ourselves, I never know whether it is just a nice tickle I get from harp concertos or whether they make me to go *pipi*." (The *Gil Blas* editor softened "faire pipi" to "faire autre chose," but Willy restored the original in his article "Claudine Musicographe" in *Mercure de France*, 15 December 1927.)

At the Schola Cantorum

A performance of the first two acts of Castor et Pollux;
music by J.-P. Rameau (1683–1764) ;
under the direction of Vincent d'Indy[1]

M. Charles Bordes is universally known, and for the best reasons in
the world. He is an accomplished musician in the fullest sense of the
word, and his personality could be compared with that of one of those
old missionaries whose courage grew the more they were faced with
danger. Certainly, it is less perilous teaching the masses the catechism
of Palestrina than teaching the savages that of the Gospel. But in
both cases there is often a similar hostility, only reaction is different:
in one case they yawn, in the other they have your scalp!

Charles Bordes, choirmaster of Saint-Gervais in Paris, organized
the Holy Week series at that church. It was such a success that the
highest-ranking clergy were riled: they considered the concerts to have
distracted the faithful! (Though the good Lord above never complained that *He* was shocked!)

This made Bordes decide to found the Association des Chanteurs
de Saint-Gervais, a society for the promotion of old choral music.
His enthusiastic campaign dates from this time: there are few towns
left where he has not preached his gospel. You can be sure that one day
he will be preaching it on the North Star! It would not surprise me.

Bordes was also the founder of the Schola Cantorum, which was
initially formed for the preservation of church music, but which has
become, since the expansion of its aims, an advanced school of music—

the nightmare of our state Conservatoire! At the Schola Vincent d'Indy teaches composition in a way which some find tainted with dogmatism. But nobody can fail to notice his high ideals and individual approach.

For some years this school, with just its own pupils and the addition of a few chosen performers, has not only restored to us all the beauty of early music, but has also presented to us the works of young, unknown musicians.

When so many others inexcusably lag behind with constant repetition, or make no progress at all, one cannot but respect this little corner of Paris where a love of music is everything. How comforting it is to see these young boys and girls devote their good little hearts to the cause of music, and set themselves the task of living up to the ideals of perfection that Vincent d'Indy, smiling encouragingly, has set them! Even in the simple act of beating time one can feel his paternal influence on these young people.

It's a strange thing, but at the Schola, side by side, you will find the aristocracy, the most left wing of the bourgeoisie, refined artists, and coarse artisans. But there is little of that empty space too often found at the more famous establishments. One feels they understand. . . . I don't know if it is because of the smallness of the room, or because of some mysterious influence of the divine, but there is a real communion between those who play and those who listen.[2]

I said at the beginning how justly celebrated is the name of Charles Bordes. I wish I could say the same for the name of Rameau. For many people, he is merely the composer of the famous Rigaudon from *Dardanus,* and nothing more.

It's an example of a peculiarly French streak of sentimentality: we cling frantically to certain set ideas about art just as we do to certain styles in clothes—even if they do not suit us at all.

We all know about the influence of Gluck on French music. It was an influence that would never have taken place were it not for Marie Antoinette, the Austrian Dauphine. Incidentally, it was much the same in Wagner's case, for we owe the first Paris performance of *Tannhäuser* to another Austrian—Mme von Metternich. However, Gluck's genius was deeply rooted in the work of Rameau. *Castor et Pollux* contains in embryo the initial sketches for much that Gluck was to develop later on. On close comparison it appears that Gluck could not have taken Rameau's place in French music without immersing himself in Rameau's beautiful works and making them his own. But why on earth is the Gluck tradition still alive? His pompous and artificial way of treating recitative is enough to show us that it is, and there is also that habit of suddenly interrupting the action: Orpheus, having just lost Eurydice, sings an aria that is hardly in keeping with his sad state of mind. . . . But then that's Gluck all over, and everybody bows down to it. Rameau should have changed his nationality—it's his own fault that he did not!

We have, however, a purely French tradition in the works of Rameau. They combine a charming and delicate tenderness with precise tones and strict declamation in the recitatives—none of that affected German pomp, nor the need to emphasize everything with extravagant gestures or out-of-breath explanations, the sort which seem to say, "You are a singular collection of idiots who understand nothing and would easily believe that the moon was made of green cheese!" At the same time one is forced to admit that French music has, for too long, followed paths that definitely lead away from this clearness of expression, this conciseness and precision of form, both of which are the very qualities peculiar to French genius. I've heard too much about free exchange in art, and all the marvelous effects it's had! It is no excuse for having forgotten the traditions founded in Rameau's work, unique in being so full of wonderful discoveries.

But back to *Castor et Pollux*. The scene is the burial place of the kings of Sparta. After the overture, which makes sounds appropriate for the display of the flowing costumes in all their silken glory, we hear the lamenting voices of a choir intoning the funeral odes for Castor. At once we are enveloped in an atmosphere of tragedy. But it's still a human one—that is to say, it's not just an atmosphere of ancient Roman tunics and helmets. People weep, just like you or I. Then Telaira comes in, Castor's lover. There unfolds the sweetest, deepest lament that was ever wrought from a broken heart. Pollux appears leading some warriors who have just avenged Castor. Then the choir perform a wonderfully warlike interlude, with superbly powerful music and trumpet fanfares. And that finishes the first act.

In the second act we are at the entrance to Jupiter's temple, where everything is prepared for a sacrifice. It is simply a marvel, but one would have to quote it all . . . Pollux's solo aria: "Nature, amour, qui partagez mon sort" ("O Nature, O love, you who share my fate"), so unique in feeling and so novel in its construction that all sense of time and space is suspended. Rameau seems like one of our contemporaries whom we could congratulate as we left the theater.

It really was most disturbing! . . . The scene that follows, in which Pollux and Telaira are to sacrifice the greatest of loves to the desires of the Gods, sees the entry of the high priest of Jupiter and then Jupiter himself, who appears enthroned in glory. In his sovereign goodness he has compassion on the human torments of Pollux, the poor mortal whom he, as chief of the Gods, could crush at will. But, I repeat, one would have to quote it all. . . .

Then we come to the last scene of this act. Hebe leads the heavenly Graces in a dance, their hands filled with garlands of flowers with which to capture Pollux—Jupiter has commanded this magic to wean Pollux from his desire to die. Never has such a delicate feeling of the voluptuous found such perfect expression! It fills the heavenly air with such light that Pollux needs all his Spartan energy to withstand the spell and remember Castor. And, I must admit, *I* nearly forgot him for a moment.

To the end, this music preserves its fine sense of elegance. It is never affected, and it never uses dubious effects. Have we continued in such good taste? Or have we replaced it with our Byzantine locksmiths? I dare not say. Let us thank the Schola, MM. V. d'Indy and Bordes, and the artists they assembled for such a restoration of beauty.

I hope I will be forgiven for having written so much on a subject that is not really of our time. My excuse is first and foremost Rameau himself, who is well worth it. And moments of real joy in life are rare: I wouldn't want to keep them to myself.

A suitably passionate performance of the wonderful *Der Freischütz* Overture by Weber. The play of sonorities in this work is stupefying, and the return to the initial key of C major is one of those moments which one finds stronger and more vivid each time one hears it. Good colors, these. They will never fade.

Of Lalo's orchestral suite from *Namouna* one can say straight away that it is a masterpiece of rhythm and color. . . . Then on the first level a piano and a lady and on the second M. Chevillard and his orchestra. And the battle began! Sometimes the orchestra won, sometimes the piano. After twenty-five minutes' struggle the battle ceased. Nobody won, because Mlle Fanny Davies plays the piano well. . . . It was a Fantasy for piano and orchestra by M. R. Lenormand.[3] The concert ended with Beethoven's Ninth Symphony: I wouldn't do you the injustice of doubting your admiration for this symphony. M. Chevillard conducted with the surest hand.

Obituaries: Mme Augusta Holmès, Robert Planquette

MME Augusta Holmès died suddenly last week. The world of music should be truly saddened. She was extremely beautiful and probably had all that one needs for happiness, but she preferred to devote herself to music, despite all the trials and tribulations that entails.

She was so much of a Wagnerian that she all but married the man; the reasons why she didn't are unclear to this day. Nonetheless, she maintained her worship of Wagner, although she was not unsusceptible to the charms of Massenet. She bequeaths to us countless songs, which testify to her sensuous nature and intense musicality. One opera, *La Montagne Noirse,* was not at all successful. But that's of no importance, for it does not make us forget what we owe her for her charming and robust music.

Apropos of Augusta Holmès, M. V. Joncières, in an interview published in *Le Petit Bleu,* holds that I regarded both Wagner and himself as bores.

First, that is untrue. It's contrary to my customary respect for old people. Perhaps M. Joncières will do me the honor of believing that it was impossible for me to apply to Wagner himself an epithet that is justly used for those who imitate him a little too closely. Monsieur Joncières has every right to deplore this, and with more authority than I.[4]

I never saw or knew M. R. Planquette, and only heard *Les Cloches de Corneville* in Russian.

〜*NOTES*

1 As early as 1882, d'Indy had been working on new editions of old French music, reviving works by Rossi and Destouches. The early years of the new century saw d'Indy editing more substantial works by Rameau and Monteverdi and staging these operas at the Schola Cantorum. *Castor et Pollux* was the first of these ventures, to be followed in 1905 by editions of *Zaïs, Les Indes galantes, Hippolyte et Aricie,* and *Dardanus.*

2 Debussy's mention of the Schola Cantorum not only clarifies his opinions on the educational ideals of this important institution, but also confirms suggestions that, despite d'Indy's inability to accept certain aspects of *Pelléas,* Debussy still regarded him with considerable respect. This probably stemmed less from his music than from his other activities—his revivals of early music and his composition class at the Schola, which for the first time offered a serious alternative to the Conservatoire as a training ground for certain aspects of musicianship. For his important work in these fields, it seems that Debussy was able to forgive d'Indy the less appealing sides of his personality: his anti-Semitism and dogmatic belief in his own ideals.

The Schola, founded by Bordes, had opened its doors for the first time in October 1896. Initially aiming to be nothing more than a school of church music centered upon a study of plainsong and Renaissance church music, the Schola soon expanded its aims, offering a full course in composition. For this d'Indy alone took full credit, and it seems to have been largely his commitment to the institution that caused it to become such an important force in the early years of the century.

By the time Debussy reviewed *Castor et Pollux,* d'Indy's *Cours de composition* had already been published in book form, and when Debussy mentioned d'Indy's composition, "which some find tainted with dogmatism," he was probably recalling opinions of the book. Based on a rigorous study of the historical development of musical (and visual) forms reaching right back to medieval music, d'Indy's course opened up little-known areas of early French music and offered detailed analyses of Beethoven and Wagner; if Debussy found such an approach dogmatic, it was probably because the rigorous historical method opened few doors onto the future. But there can be little doubt that Debussy had great respect for d'Indy's restorations of French baroque music. As something of a French Arnold Dolmetsch, d'Indy had given performances of Lalande, Destouches, and

Rameau on the harpsichord, as yet unrevived, in 1896 at the Libre Esthétique in Brussels.

[3] Colette's viperish tongue was again in evidence with regard to Lenormand's concerto, which she linked with that of Léon Moreau. "I was forced to swallow . . . a concerto by M. René Lenormand for which no matter what epithet would be sufficiently nasty. But where were you, rowdies in the gods? You were there last week, kicking up a terrible racket in reply to M. Léon Moreau's concerto—unquestionably better—and for this one we merely had a stony silence. Hardly a single catcall! I'm ashamed of you! Fanny Davies did well out of your indulgence, for she played with a weighty left and a pretentious right hand."

[4] Augusta Holmès seems to have been as famous for her charms as for her compositions. The cynical old Saint-Saëns once admitted that "we were all of us in love with her," and after hearing the Irish Augusta sing the first version of this composer's *Danse macabre,* d'Indy admitted that he was "completely infatuated with the beautiful Augusta." (She was an accomplished singer as well as something of a pianist, poetess, and stunner.) But as Léon Vallas has pertinently suggested, it was on César Franck that Augusta had the most radical effect. Best known as an organist and composer of what Colette appropriately called "musical rosaries" (his oratorios), Franck suddenly produced an intensely lyrical piano quintet at the age of fifty-eight, so passionate and freely expansive in its form that it disgusted Saint-Saëns for musical reasons and Franck's wife because she knew what had produced this sudden change of heart, this upsurge of invigorated romanticism in the aging man. Once overhearing one of his pupils describe him as a mystic, old man Franck replied, "A mystic, huh? Ask Augusta!"

GIL BLAS
16 February 1903

Monsieur F. Weingartner

L A S T Sunday was an irresistibly pleasant day. The first sunlight of the year seemed to forestall any attempt to listen to music, no matter what it was. A day for the swallows to return . . . if I may express myself thus.

M. Weingartner chose this day to conduct the orchestra at the Concert Lamoureux. Well, we can't all be perfect!

All the famous ears of Paris were there on the alert: eccentric rich old ladies, corseted young dilettantes, and wizened old men—the very best of audiences, ripe for anyone who knew how to use it. Weingartner has for a long time known how to be certain of an enthusiastic reception. First of all, he conducted the *Pastoral* Symphony with the care of a meticulous gardener. Every weed, every caterpillar was painstakingly removed! It was all done with such refinement that it seemed like one of those glossy, finely detailed paintings where the gentle undulation of the hills is made of twopenny velvet and the trees are formed with curling irons.

All in all, the popularity of the *Pastoral* Symphony rests upon the common and mutual misunderstanding that exists between man and nature. Look at that scene by the brook! . . . A brook where, apparently, the oxen come to drink. At least, that's what the sound of the bassoons suggests to me. Not to mention the wooden nightingale and the Swiss cuckoo-clock cuckoo—more like the art of M. de Vaucauson than drawn from nature's book. All such imitations are in the end useless—purely arbitrary interpretations.

But certain of the old master's pages do contain expression more profound than the beauty of a landscape. Why? Simply because there is no attempt at direct imitation, but rather at capturing the *invisible* sentiments of nature. Does one render the mystery of the forest by recording the height of the trees? It is more a process where the limitless depths of the forest give free rein to the imagination.[1]

Elsewhere in this symphony, Beethoven shows himself to be of a time when one never saw the world of nature except in books. This is proved by the "storm," which forms part of this same piece. The real terror of man and beast in the face of a storm is hidden beneath the folds of a romantic cloak, and the thunder is hardly severe.[2]

But it would be stupid to think that I have no respect for Beethoven. It's just that a musician of genius, such as he, can make unconscious mistakes greater than anyone else. There is no man who is bound to write only masterpieces, and if we class the *Pastoral* Symphony as one of these, then we have no yardstick with which to measure the others. That's all I want to say.

Next, Weingartner conducted a Fantasy for orchestra by M. C. Chevillard. A highly individual way of developing ideas is served well by a singularly solid handling of the orchestra. One gentleman, who is himself fond of music, whistled the fantasy on an old key. . . . Extremely unfortunate! How do we know whether this gentleman was criticizing the piece, or just Weingartner's interpretation of it? And, you know, a key is not meant to be a weapon of war, it's a household utensil. M. Croche preferred the far more elegant way of whistling used by butcher boys—between the fingers. It makes more noise. Perhaps the gentleman in question is still young enough to learn the art.

Of three songs by Weingartner himself, delicately sung by Mme Raunay, it was really only the third that got off the ground. The over-rich orchestration drowned them, and it threw into relief a lack of inspiration surprising in a man of Weingartner's stature. They were pitilessly long too, and seemed to inhabit keys where it was raining.

M. Weingartner made up for this with his marvelous conducting of Liszt's *Mazeppa*. This symphonic poem is full of the worst faults; it is sometimes even vulgar, but all that tumultuous passion which never lets up for a moment exerts such force that you end up liking it, without knowing why. (You can always *pretend* to be disgusted as you go out—that is the done thing, and believe me, it's nothing but hypocrisy!) The undeniable beauty of this work of Liszt's shows, I think, that he valued music above everything else. And if he sometimes seems almost too familiar, "sitting his music squarely on your knees," it's considerably better than those whose music announces itself with the pomposity of some opening address. I suppose that way is more polite, but it lacks fire. Fire and chaos, so much a part of Liszt's genius, are infinitely preferable to that manicured perfection.

Physically, Weingartner looks at first sight like a brand-new knife. His gestures have an elegance that is almost geometrical. Then, suddenly—wild, incomprehensible gestures, which make the trombones roar and the cymbals go wild! It is most impressive and little short of miraculous; the public no longer knows how to show its enthusiasm.[3]

Revival of La Traviata *at the Opéra-Comique*

T H E triumphant revival of *La Traviata* at the Opéra-Comique is more significant than the fact of the revival itself. Certain things are restored to their rightful place—in particular that peculiarly Italian "realism" which, it is held, might influence French music. Well, I suggest that it stay in Italy.

At least, these are the kinds of things said in the cafés, to liven up bigoted discussions about the so-called Latin temperament.

In *La Traviata* one meets with certain preoccupations dear to the young Italian school: the inevitable interlude, the tear-jerking romance, and so on.

Has anybody noticed their curious need to borrow French subjects of already established fame? First, there is Verdi, who used *La Dame aux Camélias*. And, closer to our time, MM. Puccini and Leoncavallo are both setting *La Vie de Bohème* to music. It is not my place to pass judgment on the literary merit of these two works, but they do represent a period that was particularly sentimental in France, and they could certainly do without being tarted up in music. Verdi is at least straightforward, going from romances to cavatinas, but there are a few pleasures to be encountered on the way, and here and there, real passion. It never pretends to be deep; it's all just a façade, and however unhappy the situation becomes, the sun always shines in the end. The aesthetics of this type of art are certainly ill-founded, for real life is not best expressed in songs. Verdi, however, speaks of a life that is perhaps more beautiful than the attempted "realism" of the younger Italians. But Puccini and Leoncavallo pretend to character study, even to a kind of crude psychology that in reality goes no deeper than mere anecdote.

The two *Bohèmes* are striking examples. In one there is nothing more solid than triviality, with sentimentality rendered in that nasal manner peculiar to Neapolitan songs. In the other, even if M. Puccini is attempting to recapture the atmosphere of the streets and people of Paris, it is still an Italian noise he makes. Now I wouldn't hold the fact of his being Italian against him. But why the devil choose *Bohème?*

In M. Mascagni's universally celebrated *Cavalleria Rusticana* we are again faced with triviality, only it is made worse by the declamation, which attempts to be lifelike but is nothing but double Dutch! How tiresome it all is!

The French tend to look for subject matter in much the same way as the Italians. But how often must it be repeated: good books often become bad plays. It does not take much deduction to conclude that they do not improve as operas.

That's just about all the so-called Italian influence consists of; and it's still only partial. As for the French public acquiring a taste for these Italo-French tales, that's another matter, and it's almost cause enough for war! There are men, and pieces, whose peculiarly French brainpower can provide an answer to these niggardly questions. And we should say so! The Italian "realism" is a factory that produces nothing! It's not the way to get our music out of the rut and restore it to its natural beauty.

Let us congratulate M. A. Carré for having revived the somewhat faded charm of *La Traviata* with such ingenious and elegant scenery. Congratulations also to M. A. Messager for having had the necessary vigor when the time came, and the ardent passion so necessary for this music. It made us forget how false it all was, and that's quite an achievement.

Mlle Garden was the star of the evening: she deliberately avoided all the traditional interpretations of the role of Violetta. Her delicate and fragile crystal voice sometimes seemed at the breaking point, before being reborn almost supernaturally.

All the human suffering of a heart full of sacrifice was contained in this voice, and an understanding of art that went far beyond the written music.

It remains only to congratulate MM. Beyle and Fugère and all the rest of the cast.

NOTES

[1] Here Debussy's comments on program music would seem to provide a key to those of his own works that deal with the natural world. See also similar ideas expressed in the article on *Pelléas* (pp.74–5).

[2] Debussy may well have had Berlioz's enthusiastic response to the *Pastoral* Symphony in mind when he spoke of Beethoven's piece as symptomatic "of a time where one never saw the world of nature except in books." In his *À travers Chants* Berlioz had put forward precisely the opposite view: "Let us understand that Beethoven was not concerned with the rose- and green-garlanded shepherds of M. Florian, still less of Lebrun, author of *Le Rossignol,* nor those of Rousseau, author of *Le Devin du village.* It is with Nature herself that he is concerned here."

[3] Colette agreed that Weingartner was

as much to be watched as listened to. Such a tall man, too! And with that pallid, clean-shaven face that suddenly blushes like an enlightened Jesuit. A stunning conductor whose gestures were either magnificent or ridiculous. His tails were too short and would bob up and down in response to the ataxic jerkings of his arms, flutter in time with his hammering fists. This German becomes completely intoxicated with the music he is interpreting in an almost epileptic way. I envy him! . . .

. . . A little later we heard the Overture to *Die Meistersinger.* Again a blind fury of gestures! Invisible missiles hurled at the violins! Repeated bending of the knees and a rolling of the loins! And barbed banderillas hurled at the bellowing brass! Could it really have been this same gesticulator, this Don Quixote wheeling his arms, who concocted those sickly romances so excellently translated by Mme Chevillard and sung by Mme Raunay? What a contest!

An Open Letter to Monsieur le Chevalier C. W. Gluck

SIR,

Should I write to you or should I summon your spirit? No matter, for my letter will never in fact reach you. Why should you agree to leave the glades of the Blessed, merely to come down and discuss with me the fate of music, an art in which you yourself were so excellent that you deserve to be exempt from such interminable discussions. I will therefore alternately address you in person and invoke you, but you must forgive me if I bestow upon you an imaginary life that allows a certain license. I must beg you also to excuse me for having little admiration for your work. It does not mean I will forget to pay you the respect deserved by a man as illustrious as yourself.

To begin with, you were a court musician: royal hands turned the pages of your manuscripts, and powdered smiles lauded you with praise. You were a trifle aggravated by a man called Piccini, who had written more than sixty operas. But you were reassured by that well-known maxim about quality being better than quantity, and with the fact that Italians had always cluttered up the musical market. This above-mentioned Piccini is now so forgotten that he had to take the name of Puccini in order to be played at the Opéra-Comique. Furthermore, these discussions between elegantly erudite ecclesiastics and dogmatic encyclopedists really shouldn't have bothered you at all, for the former are as bad as the latter when it comes to incompetence in talking about music—an incompetence surpassed only by present-day critics. And if you asserted your independence by conducting the first performance of *Iphigénie en Aulide* without your wig but in your nightcap, it was only for the sake of pleasing your king and queen. Do you not see that almost all your music has been tainted with a certain pomposity from moving in such high circles? If someone falls in love, it's only with an air of courtly propriety, and even suffering is preceded by humble apologies. If I were asked whether it was not more elegant to please King Louis XVI than to please the world of the Third Republic, only your being dead would prevent me from answering in the affirmative.

Thus, your art was essentially full of pomp and ceremony. The common people only participate at a great distance, watching the lucky ones, the satisfied, going about their business. For them you represent that wall behind which they know something to be going on.

Well, Monsieur le Chevalier, we have changed all that! With our social-mindedness, we want to strike home at the hearts of the masses —not that there's any particular virtue in that! You cannot imagine what troubles we're having in trying to found a popular opera.

But despite the "deluxe" side of your art, it has had a great influence on French music. One finds it first in Spontini, Lesueur, Méhul, and so on, but, worst of all (you will see why later on), you contain the seed of many of Wagner's ideas. And between you and me, your prosody is awful: you turn French into an accented language when it is really a language of nuances. (Yes, I know you're German.) Rameau, who helped to form your genius, had some examples of fine and vigorous declamation that could have been of use to you—but I will not bother you with what a marvelous musician Rameau was, lest you suffer by comparison. We must acknowledge that it was you who made the action of the play predominate over the music. But was that such a good thing? On the whole, I prefer Mozart to you; he was a fine man who ignored your influence completely, thinking only of music. In order to dominate the music in this way, you chose Greek subjects, giving everybody the opportunity to say the most solemn and ridiculous things about the pretended rapport between your music and Greek art.

Rameau was far more Greek than you! (Don't get angry, I'll be leaving you soon!) What's more, Rameau was lyrical, and that suits the French spirit from all points of view. We should have continued this tradition of lyricism before, not waited for a century to pass before we rediscovered it.

From having known you, French music gained the unexpected benefit of falling straight into the arms of Wagner; I like to think that, had it not been for you, it might not have happened. But then French music shouldn't have had to ask the way so often of people only too ready to lead her astray.

Finally, you have been the subject of all the many varied and false interpretations that people give to the word "classical." But the invention of this dramatic hullabaloo, at the expense of all real music, is not enough to warrant this label. There are far more grounds for bestowing it upon Rameau.

Mme Caron's performance was another reason to lament your death. She made your Iphigenia into a figure of purity—someone much more Greek than you ever imagined. Not a gesture, not a pose that was not of the most perfect beauty. All the inner feeling you left out was rediscovered by her. Music was in her every step. If only you could have seen her in the third act! The way she sat down beside the sacred tree before the sacrifice would have had you weeping, so great was the anguish in her simple gesture.

And when, at the end, you unite the tender Iphigenia with the faithful Pylades in the bonds of marriage, Mme Caron's face became so radiant that one forgot the banality of her outpourings. All one could think of was the violet color of her eyes, a color very precious to those who dream eternally of Greek ideals of beauty.

Sung by this lady, your music took wing. One couldn't pin it down to any one century; she has a gift that makes one believe in the survival of the ancient gods—a tragic soul that lifts the dark veil of the past and reveals those forgotten cities where art went hand in hand with beauty.

M. Cossira would have pleased you with his charming voice, and M. Dufrane with the convincing way he made Orestes roar with fury. I didn't care for the Scythian divertissement in the first act. Were they Cossacks? or taxi drivers fooling about? And, if I may say so, the warlike episodes are most difficult to realize, for there is not enough to grasp in either the music or the rhythm. You can rest assured, however, that everywhere else M. Carré found exactly the right setting.

And with that, Monsieur le Chevalier, I have the honor of remaining your obedient servant.

At the Société Nationale

LAST Saturday, the Société Nationale gave its 308th concert. If you recall that the society was founded in 1871, you can imagine how many pieces they have played. The majority of respected musicians (and also probably those who will be recognized by our grandchildren), were heard there for the first time. There is always something interesting to be found at the Société Nationale, and so it was on Saturday, when we heard excerpts from an organ symphony by M. Vierne, in which outstanding musicianship was combined with ingenious discoveries about the special sonorities of this instrument. Old J. S. Bach, father to us all, would have been pleased with M. Vierne. Next came an interesting trio by M. P. Coindreau, and some charming songs by R. de Castéra, substituted for those by H. Duparc listed in the program, about which there is nothing more to be said, since they are perfect. Under the title of *Quelques danses* we heard again the individual music of E. Chausson. One ought to like all these dances, but my preference is for the Sarabande. Why is it that my feelings for this music grow all the more acute in the knowledge that he is no longer with us, and that we will never again feel the warm reassurance of his smile?[1]

After an amusing scherzo by Borodin, the concert ended with the beautiful Finale in B Flat of César Franck.

At the Concert Lamoureux

THE main attraction of the day was the first performance at this concert of the *Symphony on a Breton Chant* by M. Guy Ropartz.

On this subject, I would like to protest against a custom that is prevalent each time a modern symphony is performed: that is, that a four-page thematic analysis containing the text as well as numerous illustrative examples is distributed among the audience. It tells everyone how a composer should should treat his theme, and puts the secrets of composing a symphony at the disposal of the public. There is nothing to prevent the dilettante listener from being attracted to the idea of composing his own little symphony! Being unable to contain himself, he might even take it, still warm, to M. Chevillard. It's an encouragement to all the horrors of the symphony. Moreover, I believe that it is dangerous to initiate laymen into the secrets of musical chemistry. Some people do treat these little analyses with suspicion, as if they were explosive, others treat them with a puzzled stupefaction, but the most sensible people send them gently away on the north wind, or quite simply put them in their pockets—and there is the real moral of the story.

Music owes a great deal to Guy Ropartz. We know that he has a following in Nancy, where he directs the Conservatoire. There, with an untiring enthusiasm, he works for the cause of beautiful music. The *Symphony on a Breton Chant* contains many qualities that prove Guy Ropartz to be an energetic and productive man. But why does he seem ill at ease, even a little dumbfounded? Is it not because this preoccupation with the form of "the symphony," common to all our contemporary musicians, inhibits the free flow of ideas?

By alternating fast and slow sections, Guy Ropartz has certainly tried to loosen the solid marble block that the symphony represents. In doing so, however, he has immediately destroyed the unity of the composition; the first piece could take the place of the last and vice versa, for there is nothing to choose between them.

I must confess that the words "on a Breton Chant" had made me imagine the opposite of what it meant to Guy Ropartz. I envisaged Brittany with its hard, stark countryside and its deep green sea, which is more beautiful than anywhere else. And I saw the Breton chant as her fiercely religious soul, of the kind that makes one awestruck, as if by an old cathedral. Then I was handed a little brochure to enable me to follow the whimsical pranks of the chant. In all seriousness I am not making fun of symphonic form. I know that Guy Ropartz could have written a brilliant piece. If only he hadn't thought it necessary to wrench a symphony out of this Breton chant! After all, it had done him no harm. He should have respected it like the true Breton he is. I hope he will pardon me if I seem to be giving him a lesson, but his example is a lesson for all of us concerned with music.[2]

Mozart's E-flat Symphony, coming after the Ropartz, seemed full of a luminous lightness, like a group of lovely children laughing joyfully in the sunshine! The rest of the concert consisted of pieces played by M. Chevillard in such a way as to be beyond praise.

～NOTES

[1] Debussy's cursory tribute to Chausson's music and to his "warm smile" recall the early 1890s when Chausson and Debussy were on close terms. The older Chausson was, as the correspondence between the two composers shows, something of a father figure to Debussy in his late twenties, and their letters betray Debussy's sensitivity to the older composer's criticisms of his work and also suggest that the widely read, wealthy Chausson, whose assets included a substantial collection of paintings, including impressionist and post-impressionist canvases, was a source of artistic stimulation for the younger composer, his tastes and ideas in the arts commanding Debussy's respect. Unfortunately, the manner in which Debussy used money borrowed from Chausson caused a rift to develop between the two men, added to which was the older composer's disapproval of Debussy's short-lived engagement to the singer Thérèse Roger. The two men had not been on speaking terms since 1894.

[2] On Guy Ropartz's symphony, and what must surely be one of the earliest examples of a detailed thematic analysis included on a program, Claudine has this to say:

> Guy Ropartz, of your symphony I will leave Debussy to comment. Myself, I cannot. I could sense its beauty; it gripped me but I am unable to say why. But then the program did its best to explain. . . . How obliging of it! It said, for example, "The rhythmic transformations of figures 4 and 5 lead theme 1 through progressively increasing note values." (Do minor, re minor—it must be the abduction of minors!) Then a restatement of the introduction, reexposition, etc. There are, perhaps, people for whom such artifice aids comprehension; it merely makes me feel a fool.

For the People!

FOR some time now there has been a widespread concern to develop in the hearts of the people a taste for the arts in general and for music in particular. Just for the record, I shall mention the Conservatoire de Mimi Pinson, where that young genius M. Gustave Charpentier preaches the ideas dear to his heart. In this way he instills the taste for freedom, in life as well as in art, in young girls whose likings would otherwise be limited by the following boundaries: on the north by Paul Delmet and on the south by Pierre Decourcelle. Now, however, they know such names as Gluck and A. Bruneau, and their pretty tapering little fingers, so adept at tying ribbons, can caress the strings of Monsieur G. Lyon's chromatic harp. Instead of becoming impertinent *bourgeoises,* they are thus fashioned into nice young ladies.

At the same time the fame of the *Noces de Jeannette* is waning, and as for *La Dame blanche,* she has not much longer to go.

> *Chevaliers félons et méchants*
> *Qui tramez complots malfaisants . . .*

You knights won't have to bother guarding yourselves against this old lady any more. (I will not mention those romances where "Mignon misses her homeland," and other young people sorrow over their "wilting posies": they are now at the bottom of the coolest of thy lakes, O Norway!)

We also have the Théâtre-Roulotte of M. Catulle Mendès. That, by the way, is a good idea. Then there's the book *Thirty Years in the Theater,* in which M. A. Bernheim imagines himself taking all the solemnity of the Comédie-Française into the most incongruous places.

In my own humble way, I have been connected with attempts to take the arts to the people, but I must confess that I recall them only with the deepest depression. In general, the people who make such efforts act with a kind of condescending good will that ordinary people feel to be both forced and artificial. Certainly these people seem to be able to produce tears or laughter as the occasion demands. It's dishonest! There is an instinctive feeling of envy hovering over this vision of luxury, brought for a single moment into their dull lives: the women pass judgment on the costumes with a hollow laugh, and the men, a little embarrassed, make comparisons and dream up the most inconceivable fantasies. And believe me, others lament the loss of their ten sous and go home to eat their soup—sure to be spoiled a little that night, and tasting somewhat salty with tears!

Certainly, I recognize the goodheartedness of these social ambitions and pragmatists' enthusiasms; nothing is more exciting than pretending one is some little Buddha, living on an egg and two glasses of water a day and giving the rest to the poor, mulling over ideas of "nature naturing" and pantheistic thoughts about the cosmos, and indulging in those attractively confusing arguments about the self and the not-self. All bound together, of course, by the theory of the Universal Consciousness. . . . All very nice as conversational topics, but unfortunately not worth a penny in practice, and possibly even dangerous.

If it really is right to provide performances for the masses, then we must agree upon the best way of putting them on. It would perhaps be most fitting to revive the old circus games of the Roman emperors. We have the zoological gardens, which would be bound to lend some of its best inmates. The yawning old lions, bored stiff with watching endless drummer boys and old maids, would soon recover their natural ferocity. But could we so easily find dilettanti keen enough to let themselves be devoured? Well, you never know! If the price were high enough . . .

But let us not concern ourselves with that any longer and get back to the Théâtre Populaire. They used to fulfill everyone's needs simply by putting on old plays from the regular repertoire or highly romantic dramas. Not such a noble attempt.

What they should find, it seems to me, is an art form that could adapt itself, in tone as well as in décor, to suit the greatest possible number of people. Now I'm not pretending to have all the answers, but why not remember what the Greeks used to do?

In Euripides, Sophocles, and Aeschylus, do we not find all the great human emotions drawn in such simple lines, and with such naturally tragic effects, that they could be understood by the most virgin and uncultured minds? (To be convinced of this, I would recommend you to envisage the performance of Aeschylus's *Agamemnon,* so admirably translated by Paul Claudel.)

Would not such things strike home more directly than all the mundane psychological subtleties of the present-day repertoire? When it comes to making people forget their daily chores, the means of achieving this cannot be too refined. If the aim is to tear them away from their daily lives, then it defeats the object if we show them events that are too lifelike, however well they're done.

This brings me to the question of the Opéra Populaire—a recent obsession, but one that presents serious problems. At a pinch, we can muster up a comic actor, like one of those from the old Théâtre Libre. But we haven't as yet got powerful enough means to compel the first passer-by to step in and have a go at the double bass. Although it may not seem like it, this little fact is of the greatest importance. For an opera you need an orchestra, but where do you get it from? You need singers and a chorus, what about them? And which operas should be done? Ones from the old repertoire as usual? *La Juive* or a dusty old *Muette de Portici?*

Well, if for a moment we put aside any ideas of a voyage to Utopia, there is still a way of making everybody happy: by uniting the Théâtre Populaire with the Opéra Populaire. And, as I said earlier, that could be achieved by going back to the theatrical ideas of the ancient Greeks. Let us rediscover tragedy, and enhance its primitive musical accompaniment with all the resources of the modern orchestra and a chorus of innumerable voices! Let us not forget the possibilities of a combined use of pantomime and dance, heightened by an extreme use of lighting effects to render it more suitable for a large body of people. One could learn much about this from the entertainments given by the Javanese princes, where the command and seduction of a language without words is taken to its furthest extremes, unfolding in acts rather than set patterns. It is the pity of our theater that we have limited it to verbal means of expression.

This way would be so beautiful that we would find it impossible to tolerate any other. . . . Paris would be a place where pilgrims of Beauty would flock from all over the world. So we must be generous—no small-minded enterprises based upon hypocritical speculations! A theater would have to be built, for none of the existing ones would do. If only the municipal council and the state authorities would get together for once—they need not make a habit of it!

Let us not have a theater with unpleasant gilded décor, but a bright and cheerful room where everyone would feel at home. And I needn't mention that the seats should be entirely free. If need be, a loan must be raised: never would such a loan have been made for nobler reasons, nor so much in the national interest.

Finally, we should not forget that Beauty has its own laws. Despite the efforts of some people, we seem to be almost oblivious to them, for in the music societies of today there are far too many followers of mediocrity—that monster with a thousand heads. That's why all men of good will must be united, forming an invisible but powerful force. Then, those booths where the sinister Mr. Nobody is advertised will be closed down, once and for all.

M. Siegfried Wagner at the Concert Lamoureux

M. SIEGFRIED WAGNER is well aware of the heavy burden of glory left him by his illustrious father. Even so, he does not seem marked by it, for his neat, scrupulous manner has a quiet assurance of its own. His resemblance to his father is apparent, but he lacks the stamp of genius. Evidently, he was destined to be an architect when he was young; we shall never know how great was the loss to architecture when he subsequently turned to music. Moreover, we cannot easily estimate how much music has gained. One thing is clear: he is certainly a respectful son, having decided to continue where his father left off. Only it's not so easy to do this in music as it is, say, in the millinery business. It's not that Siegfried ignores what he finds unacceptable in his father's work, but the fact that he has turned elsewhere shows a childishness complicated by the desire to dedicate his work to the memory of his father.

On the other hand, it was difficult to escape from the bewitching atmosphere of Bayreuth and not to thirst for what remained in the old magician's chalice! Unfortunately, only the dregs of the magic potion remained; and they smelt only of vinegar. These were the thoughts that came to me while listening to fragments of *Herzog Wildfang*, a musical comedy in three acts by Siegfried Wagner. It's respectable music, but that's all; it's like a student exercise by a pupil of Richard Wagner, but not one in whom the master was very interested.

M. Siegfried Wagner, in conducting the "Siegfried Idyll"—which, by the way, he does very well—should perhaps have listened to the message of motherly love that flows so sweetly from this work. It advises him to be free and happy in life, to be carefree and immune to the deceptive desire for fame. His name is already uttered in hushed tones, and he is surrounded by an aureole of light that may never cease to shine. What more does he want? Why strive for further glory? He will always be a special case, and, in my opinion, just to be the son of Richard Wagner is enviable enough in itself.

But the mind of another man is a dark forest where we should tread with care. Siegfried Wagner probably has his own reasons for what he does, stronger than those which I have put forward. As an orchestral conductor, he would seem to me to be inferior to Germany's usual exports in this field. Among the others, Weingartner is more comprehensive, and Nikisch prettier to look at. Why such a finicky performance of Beethoven's Seventh Symphony? It weakens it, and even makes it a trifle ridiculous.[1]

Next Monday I will talk of *Les Béatitudes* of César Franck, given yesterday by the Concert Colonne at a curiously situated establishment in the Place de l'Opéra.

⮥*NOTE*

1 Colette was not especially indulgent toward Siegfried Wagner:

Siegfried Wagner snobbery at the Nouveau-Théâtre: a young man
with Papa pulling the strings. The *Herzog Wildfang* Symphony—by
an architect.

Disgusting! My opening phrase is rather good, don't you think?
A little bitchy and contrived, somewhat pretentious—all the makings
of an excellent "lead," as the typesetters would say. . . . The wind,
that inescapable March wind that has had us shaking for a week,
blew in through the window. And from my beautiful "lead" you
can see what it left behind. . . .

This impish hurricane—an ill wind—annoys me. . . . But then
I'm off the point, far from that bloated young man who conducted
Chevillard's orchestra so "exceptionally." Allow me to make myself
clear: for him, conducting seems to be the "exception" rather than
the rule.

Siegfried Wagner and I are old acquaintances, although we seldom
speak to each other. How many times must I have bumped into him
at Bayreuth, near the Gasometer Theater, in the restaurant, or on the
long pavements of the Operastrasse. A shoulderless silhouette (he's
built like a bottle): how many times must I have avoided his
glance. . . .

Believe me, this precocious young genius can outstare women as if
he were a tenor! As if to say, "Now if I wanted . . . but then I
don't." Nor I, thank you, monsieur!

No, if Cosima conducts the finances as her son conducts the
Seventh Symphony, then he wouldn't be such a good catch as he
makes out. It is all right for him to be smart and take the Scherzo at
120 kilometers per hour, but when the thirds reappear in the woodwinds, he has to slow down and wait for them.

But to be fair, Wagner junior conducted *Mazeppa* like . . . well,
like a real conductor. It had a tumultuous ending, which could even
be recommended to Chevillard himself. Because he did this Liszt so
well we can pardon him, and I'll say no more than that his *Herzog
Wildfang* bored me stiff.

GIL BLAS
9 March 1903

The Opéra and Its Connections with Music

MONSIEUR P. Gailhard has for some years managed the establishment I mentioned at the end of my column last Monday. With regard to this, I have been accused of the most evil designs! If some mischievous anarchist had the imagination to blow up the Opéra, it's certain that I would at least be accused of having been the inspiration of this eloquent but brutal action. But such foul crime is far removed from my nature, and so would be any notion of a premeditated attack on one of our national institutions. It's just that as music is played at the Opéra, a musician is the man to worry about it; it's even his duty to do so. I have no need, I hope, to assure you of my complete innocence of, and sincere disdain for, any such idea!

The Opéra has for a long time been called "the greatest lyric theater in the world." No mean title, but it's hardly worthy of it anymore. Without being too emotional, and keeping an open mind, what I write today will try to discover the reasons for this. First of all, let us look at the way M. P. Gailhard manages things at present. We find serious shortcomings and a naïve lack of any precise policy. Everything is determined more by chance than by what the audience would probably like. One such example, among others, is the way *Pagliacci* was imported. In fact, the universal success of this work was due to causes that were really rather vulgar and of little artistic merit; it didn't deserve all the attention it was given. Such directorial whims only give validity to the irreverent opinions our foreign visitors gleefully take home with them and whatever M. Gailhard may think, that's not such a good idea. I shall not mention the "revival" of other outmoded operas; one never knows how much these resurrections are controlled by underhanded motives and administrative obligations. But once and for all, the Opéra ought to be a model theater, not a place where all that impressive plush serves only to conceal the poverty of what is performed. The purely mundane spectacle of beautiful ladies descending the celebrated Grand Staircase in a rustle of silk is hardly worthy of the title "music"!

And, what right has M. Gailhard to get rid of artists such as MM. Alvarez and Renaud? I don't want to take sides, but simply from the business point of view it would seem wasteful—all the more so because he could have avoided several recent evenings when the public forcefully showed its displeasure. The presence of a great artist merely throws into relief the mediocrity of all that surrounds him.

All in all, they do very little work at the Opéra, and I know from a reliable source that they revive pieces and add new elements without sufficient rehearsal because they don't consider it necessary to bother the orchestra. And as for this orchestra, it is a curious fact that its performance is hazy: although nearly all its members are respected teachers, a wavering uncertainty is combined with a most disturbing lack of care.

But, for all this, I'm not attacking M. Gailhard personally, for I'm deeply convinced that the greatest willingness in the world would be shattered there, when it came up against that solemn brick wall of red tape. It is a place that has resolved to grow old peacefully, sheltered from any attempts to shake up its deliberate apathy.

The rot within the Opéra has deeper causes: they lie in the principles of management that govern the place. It is all too easy to attack M. Gailhard alone, but I don't believe the previous managements were by any means beyond criticism. It is absolutely ridiculous that one man should have to bear so much responsibility; he would need the energy of Hercules, the craft of Ulysses, and the artistic genius of Apollo all rolled into one! He would have to be God himself to be able to achieve this. And that would make things very difficult for the chorus. Without setting him such an impossible task, one can accuse him of a baser motivation.

You can be sure that he intends to put on *L'Etranger,* that fine piece by Vincent d'Indy; the considerable success with which it was received in Brussels guarantees that it will cause a sensation here. He would also be doing a service to French music. And he will no doubt be putting on Gluck's *Armide* again; it's an acknowledged masterpiece. Also in that vein, he would want to do something for Rameau, our own genius; perhaps he'll revive *Castor et Pollux,* such a fresh and convincing piece. Or *Les Indes galantes,* so gracefully French! He is certainly considering Moussorgsky's *Boris Godunov,* or a few other operas of the young Russian school of whom the French know only the symphonic works. . . . Only, of course, they do not work very hard at the Opéra, and M. Gailhard has already had a lot of difficulty in reviving *La Statue.*

Why not let the Opéra be governed by a board of people too rich to be worried about making money, but who would, on the other hand, be proud to spend it on beautiful things? It would only be a question of tactful choice. . . .

There should also be a director of music who is completely free and independent; his function would be, first, to be up-to-date in artistic affairs, and then to plan in advance a comprehensive program of carefully chosen works. And when the operas of Wagner are put on, why not invite Richter to conduct the orchestra? (I merely mention this as one example.) It would certainly be an attraction for the public and it would ensure a good performance. Without laboring the point, what I have proposed would not be an innovation: it's almost a rule of thumb at Covent Garden, where the performances are perfect in every respect.[1] It's a pity they can't do so well at the Opéra, let alone any better. I don't believe it's merely a question of money.

To summarize, they should put on a great deal more music, and not keep the public in a deliberate state of complacency.

It's a pity, but certain artists are to blame for this; they know how to fight for a minute or so when it comes to haggling for a place in the musical market, but once they're assured of selling their wares, they suddenly seem to recoil, asking the public to forgive them for all the trouble they caused when it came to being "accepted." Resolutely turning their backs on their younger days, they shelter themselves in their own success. Thus they lose all chance of attaining true glory in life, something that is happily reserved for those devoted to the discovery of new worlds of feeling and new forms of expression. They

are the ones who end their lives in the happy knowledge that they
have accomplished all they meant to, and who, one might say, were
successful on their "last night"—if success doesn't become a vulgar
word beside "glory." I don't pretend to hold that the Opéra ever did
anything for these latter, but it ought not merely to cater to the
former. I have tried to show that the faults aren't all on one side. If
M. Gailhard is guilty of a share of them, then we shouldn't forget
that he receives guidance from others, some of whom reside in high
places. . . . An unhappy conclusion, and one that leaves me reflect-
ing on the uselessness of all such debates.

At the Société Nationale

L a s t Saturday the Société Nationale gave one of its annual orchestral concerts. Given the huge mass of people who flocked to this
concert, one is tempted to ask oneself a rather terrifying question: Do
they all really like music? So great was their enthusiasm that the
question was no sooner posed than it was answered in the affirmative.
They brought the house down, and called for the composer to reappear. One would have thought oneself in Italy! There's nothing
ridiculous about such enthusiastic applause; it's wonderful, and it
gives warm encouragement to all those young people who are preparing "to enter the profession, when their elders are no longer there."
    This little musical party began with a symphony by P. de Wailly.
In his hands, this generally rectangular form became triangular. I
found none of his usual delicacy, but an almost stifling concern with
being robust. Not that it didn't have some worthwhile qualities, but
I firmly believe that the title "symphony" has such connotations of
seriousness and gravity that it inhibits anyone bold enough to attempt
the form.
    Afterwards, we heard a Ballade for piano and orchestra by the
Master of Charms, Gabriel Fauré. It was almost as lovely as Mme M.
Hasselmans herself, who played the piano. She kept having to
straighten her shoulder straps, as they fell down at every scale that
was a little too fast. And she made the most charming movements
whenever she performed this little task! I don't know why, but I

somehow associated the charm of these gestures with the music of Fauré himself. The play of fleeting curves that is the essence of Fauré's music can be compared to the movements of a beautiful woman without either suffering from the comparison.[2]

Everyone has seen the famous flying Scheffers, the kings of the gymnastic mats. Their acts included a myriad different ways of jumping onto one's partner's back, of vaulting over him, and of using him as a magic springboard. The Variations for Piano and Orchestra on an Aeolian Theme by M. Rhené Baton could easily be taken for such gymnastic exercises. . . . The Aeolian theme jumped and leaped so much that it seemed neither here nor there. Its tricks became more complex with each successive variation, suddenly disappearing and then, to everybody's surprise, reappearing again. In the end it turned up in the cloakroom, in someone's overcoat pocket. But all this did not prevent these exercises from being very skillful: M. R. Baton already knows the best ways of impressing his public. He will go far. I have kept till last M. Jean Huré's Symphonic Prelude with its unusual strength of form and superior orchestration, and the "Chant des âmes de la forêt" by M. P. Ladmirault: the fine dreamy music of this, if a little loose-knit, testifies to his being of a genuinely artistic nature. But be careful, M. Ladmirault! Dreamers are not very popular these days, when we are all in such a hurry that we have invented automobiles! He will be laughed at, but I'm sure he won't be deterred; I wish him the best of luck. After all this enthusiasm, added to the heat of the hall, I was overcome with an insatiable desire to take refuge in a cool glass of beer, without waiting for the rest.

M. Albert Cahen died last week. He was a pupil of César Franck, which in itself is an indication of his profound love of music. He adored it enough to make it his constant preoccupation, and he has left us no mean number of works. *La Femme de Claude* is the most famous, but its fate has been out of proportion to the effort that went into it. A pity, but it makes one realize how cruel Music is. Perhaps cruelest to those who love her most of all.

❧ NOTES

[1] Debussy had presumably been to Covent Garden in 1902 when he had visited London at the invitation of Messager, then musical director at the Royal Opera House. *Tristan* was in the repertoire, and it seems likely that Debussy attended a performance. On 15 July he saw *Hamlet* at the Lyric Theatre, and, according to Mary Garden, was profoundly moved. "He seemed like a child in a trance," she recalled. "So profoundly was he affected that it was some time before he could speak."

[2] This is one of the few recorded opinions of Debussy on Fauré's music.

AN INQUIRY IN LA PLUME
15 March 1903

The Artistic Education of the Public Today

T H E artistic education of the public seems to me to be the most useless
thing in the world!

From a musical point of view, it is impossible, not to say harmful. Far too many people quite mistakenly concern themselves with
art without having a thought in their heads. How, in effect, can
anyone claiming to have some degree of artistic education be prevented from thinking himself at once able to take up art? It is that
which makes me think that a too wide diffusion of art will lead only
to a greater mediocrity. Were all the great flowerings of Renaissance
genius ever appreciated in their time, in the ignorant atmosphere into
which they were born?

And did the dependence of music on the Church or on some
princely patron make it any less beautiful?

In reality, the love of art is as difficult to procure as it is to explain.

GIL BLAS
16 March 1903

At the Concert Colonne:

MM. C. Saint-Saëns and Alfred Bachelet

M. CROCHE, an old friend of mine, had the habit of solemnly removing his hat whenever he spoke of Saint-Saëns. In his distant, asthmatic voice he would say, "Saint-Saëns is a man who knows music better than anybody in the whole wide world." Then, lighting one of his frightful cigars (which were blacker than a young crow), he would continue:

"This scientific approach to music has meant that Saint-Saëns will never allow himself to overload his music with too many of his own personal feelings. We are indebted to him for having recognized the tumultuous genius of Liszt, and we should remember that he professed his admiration for old Bach at a time when such an act of faith was also an act of courage. But let's make no mistake: Saint-Saëns is, by definition, the essential traditional musician. He has accepted tradition's harsh discipline, and he never allows himself to overstep the limits set by those he considers to be the great masters. This is proved marvelously by his Variations for Two Pianos, which he based on a theme of Beethoven. He recaptured Beethoven's style so accurately that it is only Beethoven we think of. . . . It's such a disinterested mark of respect. I know of no better example. This respect for form has also governed the composition of his symphonies, which are such perfect models of logical development that one asks oneself how he could ever have made the mistake of wanting to write operas. He fell into the tradition of Louis Gallet and, worse, Victorien

Sardou, thus spreading the misguided belief that one ought to be 'theatrical'—something that will never go together with being 'musical.'

"God in his infinite wisdom has put countless opera writers on this earth! In making the number still greater, Saint-Saëns becomes one too many. And what he has done can only encourage the commercial success of the rest of them: it's wicked! How can he be blind to the fact that it is bound to lose him the respect of all those young people who are counting on him to open new roads to freedom, toward a purer air. . . ."

M. Croche broke off for a miserable coughing fit, blaming it on his cigar, which all this eloquence had put out. Then he began again, with an emotion unusual in this spectral and dogmatic old man:

"I detest sentimentality, monsieur! And I prefer not to remind myself that the man who wrote *Les Barbares* is called Camille Saint-Saëns."

I timidly put forward a few objections: "But is *Les Barbares* any worse than a lot of other operas you don't mention?" and "Should we therefore efface the memory of what Saint-Saëns was like?"

But he cut me short. Unperturbed, he continued in icy tones: "This opera is a bad example because it comes, as it were, from 'above.' Saint-Saëns owed it to himself, and he owed it still more to music, not to write such a pastiche; there are forms in it which are quite contrary to his nature. There's even a farandole that has been praised for its archaic feeling—that's nothing but cold-blooded ignorance of the kind peculiar to music critics. In reality, it's just a rather stale echo of the old Exposition of 1889. Wasn't there anyone who cared enough for Saint-Saëns to tell him that he'd written enough operas, and that he'd be better employed in his more recently found vocation as an explorer? The contemplation of new areas of sky might suggest to him a more useful kind of music. . . .

"Without knowing him, one can tell that he cares nothing for the public! This obsessive need to build a brick wall between himself and the above-mentioned public at each of his first nights is undeniable proof. Lamentably, he redeems himself by making any concessions he feels he ought with his tongue gently in his cheek."

M. Croche's dogmatic grumblings let up a bit when he thought of the *Danse macabre,* and he gleefully recalled the catcalls that greeted it at its première. One felt that he had formerly liked Saint-Saëns very much, and he was riled now only because the composer had changed and for him this amounted to an act of treason. At this point in the proceedings, M. Croche would usually be distracted by another cigar and say, in the manner of a farewell, "Pardon me, monsieur, but I don't want this one to go out." I forgot to say, too, that M. Croche didn't like to talk music for too long; he considered that it was not in his interests as a professional antidilettante.

The music for *Parysatis* was written for the play by Mme Jane Dieulafoy, and first performed at the Théâtre des Arènes at Béziers in August 1892. I was not fortunate enough to be present at this performance and I'm deeply sorry, for the idea of music in the open air interests me.[1] It seems to me to be one of the best opportunities for a musician to bring together all the resources of music. To have the natural scenery and the beautiful sky at one's fingertips! To be able to make an orchestral commentary on the daily miracle of the sunset! What a marvelous chance for anyone with a feeling for the harmony that so powerfully links Art with Nature herself! I have myself spoken, in these very columns, of my hopes as regards open-air music. But to return to *Parysatis:* I will never know if it was better in its original open-air setting than in the confines of the concert hall.

It seems to me to be a work that is more concerned with charm than with grandeur. Although at one time one could count upon Saint-Saëns for a confident mastery in the handling of the voices, I must say that I did not find the simple lines I was waiting for here. To put it another way, I found the choral parts extremely well written, but there seemed to be a certain lack of enthusiasm in the choir. In short, it was pleasant concert-hall music. But it should not have been! It was written for the open air! I would have liked to have seen a way to escape from this cruel dilemma, but for the sake of a pitiless logic (which if not pitiless does not merit the title "logical") I could see none.

One episode of the ballet from *Parysatis,* "The Nightingale and the Rose," is a sort of dramatic recitative for soprano, with the other voices interjecting chords. It's a game whose pleasure is in the difficulties it causes a singer. Afterwards there's another dance, in which the harps imitate a rippling stream and evoke the freshness of the young priestesses emerging from the water. Just the thing to ravish the amateurs! I almost forgot to mention a song with choir, based on a rhythm that almost seemed to be Spanish. A strange archaeological find, this! I really don't understand the use of the tambourine: the Persians are well-known for their warlike temperament, but I didn't know they used this alluring percussion instrument! Apart from this, the music of *Parysatis* more willingly takes its roots in Handel than in a really ancient tradition: I know that M. Saint-Saëns will not take offense at that observation. As for the question of open-air music, this piece doesn't seem to provide an answer; there is plenty of room for competition, and there should be no lack of it. Mlle Korsoff could have battled with any nightingale, and MM. Rousellière and Guillamat have voices that are pleasingly resonant; these were the performers responsible for the success of *Parysatis*.[2]

M. Alfred Bachelet won the Prix de Rome in 1890, since when we have heard extremely little of his work. I don't expect it is entirely his own fault, but rather of those who decide what music is played. One could voice the usual complaints once again; they wouldn't be out of place, but by any stretch of the imagination they can never hope to prevent this dreadful state of affairs. It continues inexorably, as do all stupid and false ideas. It's deplorable!

The symphonic poem *L'Amour des ondines*, heard for the first time yesterday, must have remained in a dark drawer for some time. M. Bachelet probably went back to it time and time again, and even if it hasn't lost its charm, it positively vibrates with recognizable influences, both old and new. Its orchestration uses all the tricks of modern orchestral chemistry, and the music itself is still weighed down and dominated by Wagnerianism. The voices sometimes sing what are really distraught clarinet parts, and I would have preferred them not to have sung any words (which are by Jean Rameau). The water sprites (*ondines*) don't speak at all, and it is this which distinguishes them from their mortal sisters. M. Bachelet, as with so many distinguished spirits, seems to be in love with the idea of the dream. Why, then, did he not extend it further into the realms of the supernatural? The setting of this piece is the most successful thing about it. There is a sensation, drawn from the music itself, of moonlight caressing the rustling leaves, that shows a very special feeling for the sounds of the night. This is not to say that the rest is despicable: the general feeling of the poem is one of poise, but it is tainted with the precious. It reminds one of someone who pins orchids onto his nightshirt! All the same, M. Bachelet may take his place in the future, among those who will render a service to music. He is sensitive and has an instinctive scorn for the facile effect; this will secure him the admiration of real artists. *Parysatis* and *L'Amour des ondines* have suffered different fates in the hands of the public. And they are both the wrong ones.

When M. Bachelet is as old as M. Saint-Saëns, he will know how to command success. I hope that he will be content with a sympathetic reception at present, and that it will be given him. I hope, too, that he will not learn the demands of glory until later.

Meanwhile, we heard M. Léopold Auer, violin soloist to His Majesty the Emperor of Russia. He showed enormous talent playing a concerto by Brahms and a melancholy serenade by Tchaikovsky. These two works competed with each other in boredom. If I were His Majesty the Emperor of Russia for one minute, I would threaten M. L. Auer with immediate Siberia if he persisted in putting his virtuosity at the service of such finicky trivialities.

Apropos of this concert, it gives me the opportunity to pay my respects to M. Colonne, who celebrated his thirtieth birthday last Sunday. Whatever one's point of view, he represents a man committed to his task, and he has an unflinching devotion to music. The overwhelming enthusiasm of the audience was by no means unjustified, and I am proud to associate myself with it.

At the Concert Lamoureux

FOR no apparent reason, this concert began with the Overture to *Sigurd*. I hope that Monsieur Chevillard considered the occasion to be an attempt to prove the superiority of his orchestra over that of the Opéra. If so, he proved his point . . . but it doesn't make the overture to *Sigurd* any the better! He made up for it with a dynamic performance of *Antar,* the symphonic poem by Rimsky-Korsakov. Never has the beauty of this music been so admirably conveyed! It is a pure masterpiece of renewal, in which Rimsky-Korsakov sends the traditional form of the symphony packing. Nothing can describe the charm of its themes, nor the blossoming of the rhythms and the sounds of the orchestra. I defy anyone to remain indifferent to the power of this music. It makes you forget everything else—your life, the person sitting next to you, and even the correct thing to do, because you have an intense desire to shout for joy. You don't even want to make that ridiculous noise with your hands; certainly that is poor thanks to a man who has given one such genuine moments of happiness.[3]

After that, Mme Teresa Carreno played a concerto by Grieg. Has anyone noticed how awful people from the north become when they try to be Mediterranean? The end of this concerto, which reminds one of Leoncavallo, is a striking example. The piano "tootles," if I may take the liberty of putting it like that. And the orchestra accompanies it with such a brilliant blaze of color that one thinks one will come away with nothing less than a suntan! But Mme Teresa Carreno has much talent. Much more, for example, than Grieg, who seems to me to abuse his Norwegian birthright.

ᏁᏆ*NOTES*

[1] The Arena Theater at Béziers, mentioned by Rolland as an example of the *théâtre populaire,* was an open-air spectacle that mounted two operas by Saint-Saëns as well as one by Fauré. In addition it staged Greek tragedy. Rolland considered it rather second-rate.

[2] Debussy's relations with Saint-Saëns were openly antagonistic, the older composer venomously waging war on Debussy—both the man and his music. A section of this article repeats the invective of Debussy's earlier attack in *La Revue blanche,* after which Saint-Saëns had begun his campaign in earnest. Staying in Paris for the première of *Pelléas,* he maliciously confessed that he had foregone a visit to the country especially to speak ill of Debussy's opera. His legendary comments on Debussy's *Prélude à l'après-midi d'un faune* summed up his hostile attitude: "Debussy did not create a style. On the contrary, he cultivated the absence of style and of logic and common sense. But he had a name with a euphonious sound.

Had it been Martin nobody would ever have spoken of him, though it is true that in this case he would have taken a pseudonym." Even when Debussy was on his deathbed, Saint-Saëns, carefully maneuvering behind the scenes, successfully prevented his election to the Institut. James Harding, in his biography of Saint-Saëns, rightly restores the balance by quoting Rolland's summary (to Richard Strauss) of the commonly held opinion of Saint-Saëns at this time: "He has become the great musician of the universities, and it's to them he goes to gather laurels now the musicians think of him as more or less dead—deader than Mendelssohn and perhaps even deader than Brahms. It's odd how one can talk with musicians for hours about French music without thinking of once mentioning the name of Saint-Saëns."

³ The Russian influence on Debussy's music has not as yet been sufficiently studied from a musical point of view, although André Schaeffner has probed extensively into the biographical affinities between Debussy and Russian music. In the summer of 1882 Debussy visited Moscow, where, according to Laloy's biography, of which Debussy "approved," he came into contact with the music of Rimsky-Korsakov and other Russian composers, bringing back the score of an opera by Rimsky-Korsakov among other things. Rimsky-Korsakov directed two concerts of Russian music at the Pan-Russian festival in Moscow including *Antar* and fragments of *Prince Igor*. On Debussy's return to Paris he may have attended one of the first performance of *Sadko* in France, between 1878 and 1883. Apart from these, virtually none of the Russian composer's music was heard in Paris before 1884. *Sadko* had been coolly received, and it was not until the nineties that the tables turned and his music began to achieve popularity. In fact, the criticisms leveled against Rimsky-Korsakov's music (before the 1893–94 fever for Russian music) were strikingly similar to those leveled against Debussy's own music: "looseness of form," "harmonically contrived," etc.

Colette herself testified to Debussy's love of Rimsky-Korsakov. In her book *My Apprenticeships* she described how Debussy was bowled over by the first performance of *Schéhérazade:*

> Debussy, at the end of the concert, had not had his fill of Rimsky-Korsakov. His lips hummed, he made reedy noises through his nose trying to recover a theme on the oboes, he drummed with his fingers on the lid of the grand piano, echoing the deeper notes of the kettledrums. Still pursuing, he jumped to his feet, snatched up a cork and rubbed the window with it to imitate a pizzicato on the

double bass. So does the satyr, erect on his goatlegs, his eyes fierce between the twisted horns, pluck his favorite briar from the thicket. Debussy had something of the followers of Pan. With the help of the piano I sang him the passages he wanted, and his eyes lost their haunted look, glanced at me humanely, as though he saw me for the first time. "Good memory! Good memory!" he said, and my heart warmed.

In her own review of *Antar*, Colette was as enthusiastic as Debussy:

I ran straight for *Antar* without looking back, just as I do for all my strongest passions. *Antar:* my intoxication! My too intense of pleasures! In spite of all my prayers, Chevillard rarely does this piece more than once a year. How I pity those who can coldly analyze this music, like that meddlesome old busybody L'Ouvreuse [another of Willy's pseudonyms].

After giving a description of the "plot" of *Antar,* Colette despairs, "Oh how colorless and weak are words! You would be dazzled if my phrases could recapture all that this sketch does through its orchestration, whose beauty changes more than a hundred times, reawakening my abandoned imagination."

GIL BLAS
19 March 1903

At the Opéra-Comique
First performance of Muguette,
comic opera in four acts after a story by Ouida;
libretto by Michel Carré and Georges Hartmann;
music by Edmond Missa

I F subtitles were still in fashion, the comic opera performed last night might well be called: *Muguette, or Beware of Painting*! The action takes place in Flanders in about 1820, and also in Paris. It concerns a French painter called Lyonel who is looking for an ideal model. He finds it in Muguette, a young Flemish girl with beautiful eyes. Naturally, they fall in love with each other—something that happens too often to cause us any astonishment! And, of course, we don't see them united until the last act. Muguette finds Lyonel, and, thanks to an old pedlar, marries him. All is according to the formula that has made the Opéra-Comique its fortune.

The music and story of this work evoke a time when everything seemed to be shrouded in old lace. It's as touching as when one finds an old, faded photograph of one's great-grandmother. Young girls who have their bread sliced and buttered for them will derive great pleasure from this (if there are any of them left). Apart from a bohemian who impertinently smokes his cigarette, it's all "solid family stuff." There are some touching episodes, including an "Ave Maria" sung by Muguette and four little girls, an Antwerp carillon, and some nicely melancholy waltzes. It all leaves one rather defenseless. MM.

Michel Carré and Edmond Missa are good-hearted men who would never even lightly abuse the traditions of the past.

And do not think they were wrong! *Muguette* has been very successful. Mme Mary Thiéry endowed the part of Muguette with all the fluid charm of her voice, and Mme J. Passama gave fine conviction to the part of Line Krebs, a milkmaid, whose faithful customer I'd willingly become. Mmes de Craponne, Pierron, Costès, and Perret made pleasing subsidiary characters.

M. Muratore is handsome, but that doesn't prevent him from having a fine voice. M. Fugère gave much character to the rôle of the old pedlar, representing the lovers' good fortune. MM. Cazeneuve, Mesmaecker, Imbert, and Viguié do "three turns each and then go out," like little puppets. The scenery, the costumes, and the production were all according to the best traditions of the Opéra-Comique, and M. A. Luigini conducted the orchestra in his usual experienced way. . . . I hope I haven't forgotten anyone. And if *Muguette* is no better than *Mignon,* its grandmother in the realm of comic opera, it's simply that we no longer have any respect for the saner traditions of our own dear old France.

GIL BLAS
23 March 1903

LAST Saturday, 21 March, spring began. . . . That wouldn't seem to have much to do with music: one generally considers that this season is merely the one when the poplars are ornamented with those little shoots that resemble electric light bulbs, or the season when young ladies are allowed to show a little décolleté! But that's a big mistake. . . . Spring, stage-managing the summer, urges official Music to pack her bags. The Sunday concerts have only a few weeks more to go, and they are already preparing for their emigration to the casino-studded coasts.[1] All the same, I hope you didn't miss hearing, at Colonnes, the singer who is a little narrowly described as the "Wagnerian tenor," although he sings all kinds of music very well indeed. I mean, of course, M. E. van Dyck, who combines an impeccable vocal technique with a rare understanding of what he is singing, two qualities that are rarely found together in any one singer. At this same concert Saint-Saëns's *Parysatis* and *L'Adonis* of M. Th. Dubois were played again, the latter being directed by the composer. *L'Adonis* is a work in which the gray, severe style of this master should have given way to something rather more pagan, if I understand the title correctly. I would very much like to talk to you for longer about all these gems but nobody has asked me to as yet, I don't know why. Somehow I do not think it is an oversight I'm going to regret for the rest of my life.

To celebrate the coming of spring, and so as not to get out of practice, the Opéra has put on *Les Huguenots* once again. . . . There's a touch of irony in linking *Les Huguenots* with the spring, for the opera can hardly pretend to offer any kind of "renewal." Rather is it to be classed as one of the most miserable of the crosses we have to bear, together with such things as epidemics, the three percent devaluation, and the excavations for the Métro. But the need to put on *Les Huguenots* does seem to me to be a special case. This opera is one of the most tiring to listen to, and to perform. It is music that gets you by the throat, and it cannot be excused just because of the massacre of the poor Protestants! How nice it is for those in the audience (the Protestants . . .), for there are still some left! And despite Meyerbeer's genius, I would hold that gunfire is not a very praiseworthy effect to use. But let us not dwell on the subject; there are more important things to shoot into oblivion (*La Juive,* if I may dare to say so). Or, should such a thing exist, an opera about the dwindling of the Catholic congregations! I suppose these things have their place, though—as in that wonderfully indigestible dictum of Carlyle: "Without Evil, there would be no Good, for victory is only possible through battle."[2]

Apropos de Muguette

S O M E of my readers, as diligent as they are faithful (I humbly beg the pardon of the others), have written to reproach me for not having clearly stated my point of view on the music of M. Ed. Missa. They have even insinuated that I seemed to be afraid of discussing it. That's not quite the case. It's just that M. Ed. Missa is a good and devoted friend of mine, and even if he doesn't write exactly the kind of music I like, that's not to say that I ought to discourage him. Moreover, the fault I find in him—persisting with worn-out ideas that are never his own—is not peculiar to M. Missa. Others in fact pilfer even more. They spice up worn-out ideas as eagerly as everyone else does with their "modern-style" sauce! With a little luck, and a good deal of promotion, that's what happens, and before you know it, you are crowned Sacred Master. It's one of the faults of our age that, when one has the opportunity of going so far in Art, one must get out (that's to say, before one has gone *too* far). The elevated respect that one ought to have for Art has become nothing but a ridiculous sham for many people; think of those who regard Art as just one of many roads to success! M. Ed. Missa sings his songs, frail and wan; his sensitive soul shrinks from howling with the wolves, from dressing frivolities up so that they resemble a crazed kind of drama, raging with lyricism. I believe he is best described as sincere and loyal, for which, even if these qualities have nothing to do with music, we must admire him. At the same time we can be sorry that his undeniable craftsmanship and sensitive touch are not put to better use. That is not to say that operetta hasn't enough devotees already, but I think M. Missa will soon occupy an enviable position.

At the Concert Lamoureux

T H E R E were two nauseating moments during this concert: one was the *Reformation* Symphony, by that elegant but complacent man Mendelssohn. This symphony was written for the festival of 25 June 1830, celebrating the three-hundredth anniversary of the Augsburg Confession. Perhaps the mention of this date sets many a noble heart aflame! I must confess that mine is quite impervious to the Vaseline that oozes from all three movements of this symphony.

However, the festival in question never took place because of the political troubles of 1830, and Mendelssohn's symphony remained in his bottom drawer. Oh, that it had stayed there! Together with your famous canticle, O Luther! The second, even more nauseating moment was the Concerto for Piano and Orchestra by M. Emile Sauer. Although he is not an evil man, he has written a pitiless concerto. By a diabolical artifice, it sometimes seems to have finished, but then it begins again with a whole lot of crazy, charmless ideas. Occasionally an infernal waltz intervenes, and during this M. Emile Sauer infuses his hands with the spirit of a juggler; this gives the music-loving spiders on the ceiling quite a shock! But take note: he does play the piano very well, and he has an incredible understanding of the different ways of playing scales. But why does he feel obliged to write concertos? Has he made some kind of vow? Or was he just born that way?

The crowning work of the evening was M. Alf. Bruneau's *Penthésilée,* a choral and symphonic poem with voices to words by M. Catulle Mendès. In this work we again find all M. Alf. Bruneau's gifts: naturalness in declamation as well as great skill with orchestration. He seems to me, however, less preoccupied here with "naturalism" than he is in his lyric dramas. On the other hand, I know that he has reached great heights by pursuing this preoccupation with "naturalism." We have a high opinion of him for this, and also for having had the artistic courage to keep his musical imagination in check for its sake. I'm a little reluctant, therefore, to confess my admiration for this poem, and also the fact that he seems more at home here than in the dramas written for him by Emile Zola. Not that these dramas do not contain very beautiful and highly original sections: for example, the third act of *L'Ouragan,* in which the music captures the spirit of ancient tragedy by expressing all the terrible feelings the characters express and portrays that other character, reeling and surging—the sea! Also, certain pages of *Rêve* have a fine tenderness, and much else that I find myself unable to pinpoint today.

However, it seems to me that although music was never meant to confine itself solely to the world of dreams, it doesn't gain anything by concerning itself too much with everyday life. It is weakened by trying to be too human, for its primary essence is mystery. Nothing is more mysterious than a perfect chord! Despite all theories, both old and new, we are still not sure, first, why it is perfect, and second, why the other chords have to bear the stigma of being imperfect or dissonant. Music ought therefore to free itself as quickly as possible from these little rituals with which the conservatories insist on encumbering it. I don't believe that this liberation can be achieved by absorbing more and more elements from everyday life; music has a life of its own that will always prevent it from being too precise. It says everything that one cannot put into words; thus it is logical that to emphasize it is to diminish it.

It's always the same old question: should music dominate or be subservient? I'm pleased to note that in *Penthésilée* Bruneau has chosen the former. How right he was! As a result we have some richly musical orchestral interludes that embellish with passion the "white spots" of Catulle Mendès's text. I particularly remember the one that precedes the verse: "Les festins te plaisaient après les chocs d'épées, . . ." in which the music takes on a ferociously caressing tone. Then afterward, the brutal warlike fanfare that leads Penthésilée to her destiny strikes up again, gradually fading away with her destiny. She dies with that heroic beauty to which only music can do justice: "en jetant au vainqueur beau comme une guerrière, un regard moins chargé de haine que d'amour!" This poem does a great service to French music: we should thank M. Chevillard for having understood it so well and for having conducted it with such ardor. Thanks also to Mme Félia Litvine for having given it such a perfect interpretation. Earlier she had sung the aria from *Der Freischütz* in a voice whose full richness seemed to be stifled, but in *Penthésilée* and Yseult's death she was perfect.

At this concert Saint-Saën's *Danse macabre* was given another airing. Regarding this symphonic poem, I share the opinion of my old friend M. Croche, who could never hear it without experiencing a very special feeling. Looking back, I think he was right. The amusing rhythms and timbres are still as fresh as ever, and I hope M. Saint-Saëns will forgive me if I dare say that there he gives every sign of being a very fine musician. This same M. Croche believed that. But never mind! He's just an old fool who loves music inexcusably as well as intolerantly.

⮀ NOTES

[1] Colette also began her column with a lyrical evocation of spring, beside which—to her as well as to Debussy—music seemed pale: "To the concert hall, alas! When spring is bursting forth as from a ripe seed pod, her casual splendors taking place before our eyes and her cruel light illuminating the ugliness of our lives in comparison with those ethereal clouds that sail by far above. And when I stop to look up, I say to myself: 'How nice it must be up there!' " Her sentiments echo Debussy's twice-uttered plea for a music of the open air to refresh the stuffy, stale atmosphere of a music imprisoned within the confines of a concert hall.

[2] Debussy seems to have been fairly well acquainted with the writings of Carlyle; possibly he was introduced to Carlyle by Maeterlinck, whose plays (especially the ideas of silence in *Pelléas*) were strongly influenced by Carlyle's *Sartor Resartus*. (See E. Lockspeiser, *Debussy et Edgar Poe* [Paris, 1962])

GIL BLAS
30 March 1903

The Mozart of Saint-Maur

LE PETIT BLEU has recently informed us of the existence of a
child prodigy whom it calls, a little prematurely, "the new Mozart."
Pierre Chagnon, this prodigy, was born in 1893, so now he is nearly
eleven. At that age Mozart had written an opera; certainly it was a
trifle primitive, but even so it is not something that comes easily to
every child. Thank God! Until now our prodigy has been happily
coupled with portraits of Mozart and George Sand (why this photo-
graphic flirtation, which can only annoy poor old Chopin?). And he
has written an "O Salutaris," "very successfully performed at the
church of Saint-Maur," says his father.

In any case, the existence of a child prodigy can leave no Frenchman indifferent. Generally, they are the prerogative of rival countries,
so it is comforting therefore to see that we gain some lost ground here,
and even if it doesn't make up for our having lost two provinces, at
least it's something. We're a little at loose ends these days. We waver
between the two extremes of difficult complexities and deliberate
inertia. We are going rotten, but we will not accept the leadership of a
chef d'école at any price.* (That would probably be absolutely no
good at all, but at least it would be convenient.) Since we look for
direction from our neighbors across the borders, we can't have much
faith in ourselves. It will thus be necessary, even essential, for some

---

* Meaning that talented men are numerous, and untalented men innumerable; something that makes the choice of a "great man" very difficult. He
would be a luxury and a special favorite.

young genius to come along and put things in order and restore our dwindling confidence. I hope that this young Pierre Chagnon will be the one to point the way, but I do wish he wasn't so popular already. Without wishing to know how the editor of *Le Petit Bleu* discovered him, one is disturbed to see so much fuss made of such a young child. It can only cause him unnecessary worries, and might make him forget that his true glory lies in the future; he is being given too much success on a plate.

Of the genius that falls upon a person, a large part is bound to remain untapped because there is a sort of fearful delicacy about revealing so much of oneself. One should not forget this, for fear of offending the terrible divinity who stamps our heads with the sign of the "chosen," or to put it more simply, "those who aren't quite like everybody else."

Monsieur Chagnon, the father, complains that his son hasn't got a good enough piano, and that he can go to the Conservatoire only once a week. . . . These two problems are easily remedied: let his son not go to the Conservatoire at all, and let him spend the money thus saved on a better piano. That would be ideal for both his son and his pocket. (I hope I make myself clear.)

At the Société Nationale

LAST Monday, the Société Nationale gave a concert at the Salle Pleyel. E. Risler, one of the most marvelous pianists of our time, and Mme J. Raunay were the performers. M. Risler played a Beethoven sonata for horn and piano, with M. Pénable the younger. It must have been written in the early days of the horn, and the sonata.

If you only knew "comme le son du cor est triste au fond de la Salle Pleyel."[1]

Next came a suite for piano by M. G. Samazeuilh . . . a work full of good intentions, but which did not seem to me to have "aged" enough. That is to say, it was a little green: M. Samazeuilh has been a bit hasty in securing a public hearing. It has been influenced a good deal by M. Vincent d'Indy, an eminently recommendable master, so we can hope for good things in the future from M. Samazeuilh.

Mme Raunay sang, with great feeling, the song cycle that E. Chausson composed to Maeterlinck's *Serres chaudes*. These songs are passionate metaphysical dramas on which Chausson's music comments without giving them too much weight. All the same, one wishes that he had left the inner life of the poems to speak more for itself; his musical interpretation is a very personal one.

Finally we heard the Variations on a Theme of Rameau, in which Paul Dukas once more showed his great compositional powers. There are moments when Rameau himself would not have been able to find his theme, festooned as it is with so much gilt.

But I have the impression that Dukas simply wanted to solve a few unanswered questions. Well, he solved a lot. One should look for more in these Variations than the curious play of their lines. To give my honest opinion, I prefer my Dukas without Rameau.

In so many different works, M. E. Risler showed a variety and a confidence that was simply admirable.

Richard Strauss

M. RICHARD STRAUSS, who has recently been guest conductor at the Concerts Lamoureux, was not the father of the "Blue Danube" waltz. He was born in 1864 in Munich, where his father was a musician in the royal household. He is practically the only original musician of the modern German school, leaning toward Liszt in his remarkable virtuosity in handling the orchestra, and toward our own Berlioz in his concern for music based on literary precepts. The titles of his tone poems prove this: *Don Quixote, Also Sprach Zarathustra, Till Eulenspiegel*. In the last piece we are left in no doubt that the music is concerned with telling a story, and the orchestra is used in much the same way as are the illustrations in a book. The clarinets soar like rockets into the sky; the trumpets all but choke; the horns, feeling a sneezing fit coming on, rush to put in a polite "Bless you!" and the big bass drum goes "boom-boom," as if to imitate a kick in the pants from a clown. And to cap the lot, a rattle is heard above the noise of this extravagant orgy! The art of M. Richard Strauss is not always quite so fantastic, but he definitely thinks in colored images, and he seems to draw the outline of his ideas with the orchestra. It's no mean way of doing things, but it's rarely used. What's more, M. Richard Strauss has found a highly individual way of handling the development. He no longer uses the rigorous architectural methods of a Bach or a Beethoven. Instead, he develops with rhythmic colors. He juxtaposes the strangest tonalities as if it were quite normal, for he is not concerned with what he has "abused" but only with what "new life" he has gained.

All these traits are found crystallized in *Ein Heldenleben,* a symphonic poem R. Strauss conducted for the second time in Paris. It is difficult to admire certain incongruities that are almost banal, and some worn-out Italianisms, but they soon give way to a limitless and striking variety of orchestration. One is also struck by the frenzied movement, which can carry you. One is no longer in control of one's own emotions, and one doesn't even come away with the feeling that this symphonic poem has outstayed its welcome: something which is usually the case with such exercises.

Once again, it's a book of images, even cinematography. . . . But it should be said that any man who can construct a work that hangs together so well is not far from being a genius.[2]

He began with a performance of *From Italy,* a symphonic fantasy in four parts (an early work, I think). But already his future individuality is apparent, although the developments seem conventional and a little long. However, the third part, entitled "In Sorrento Harbor," is very finely colored. Next was a love scene out of *Feuersnot,* his latest opera. This scene lost a good deal by being detached from the rest of the opera, and as the program did not tell us what it was all about, the order of events was totally incomprehensible. Such orchestral torrents seemed extraordinary for a love scene! But then they were probably justified by the text. Here is perhaps a chance for the opera houses to put on something new. I don't really think they can pretend to be doing that by performing all those operas of the young Italians. For the most part, these are just insignificant, deliberately counterfeit copies of

French music, unless it's the other way round. But then I have already spoken of this; it would be childish to press the point.

M. Richard Strauss has neither a wild lock of hair nor the gestures of an epileptic. He is a fine man, and he has the frank, confident manner of those great explorers who walk among savage tribes with a carefree smile (you perhaps need a little of this to shake the public out of their apathetic politeness). All the same, his forehead is that of a musician, but his eyes and stance are those of a "superman," in the words of Nietzsche, a man who must have had an important influence on Strauss. He must have inherited from Nietzsche a scorn for piffling sentimentalities and also the desire that music should no longer be merely a bringer of light into our darkness, but that it should replace the sun itself. I can assure you there is plenty of sun in the music of R. Strauss, but one came away convinced that the majority of the public does not like this kind of sun, for the more famous of the dilettanti made sure signs of their impatience. But that didn't prevent the rest from giving Strauss an enthusiastic ovation. . . . I repeat, there is no resisting the overwhelming domination of this man!

At the Concert Colonne

A VERY fine concert where French music found itself in the company of Polish. (Long live Poland!) Naturally, I am not going to speak to you of the French music. It was represented by Lalo, Massenet, and Bruneau. Just to quote their names means I need say no more. As for the Polish music, until now I have had only a prejudiced viewpoint. The Symphony in D minor by S. Stojowski won a prize (inaugurated by Paderewski) over all other works by Polish composers. It doesn't make one want to know the rest. We were told in advance that it had been enthusiastically received and heralded as a highly important work. If anyone asks, I will agree with this opinion as it was given to me in the program. As for the rest, I must admit that Noskowski's *The Steppe* had a certain flow, and it seemed that Cossacks were circling around giving out apache cries. Mme Bolska sings very well, and M. Mlynarski, conductor of the Polish orchestra, dampened his shirt collar with dignity.

～NOTES

1 Debussy is punning on Lamartine's line "comme le son du cor est triste au fond du bois."

2 To his original comments on Nikisch's performances of *Till Eulenspiegel* (see p. 40) Debussy adds pertinent comments on what he considers to be Strauss's most radical qualities: namely, his tendency to use color as form. Today, when we tend to regard Strauss as an extreme traditionalist, Debussy's comments may seem out of focus. But he goes to great lengths to explain himself. In fact, Strauss was allied to a French tradition of "color as form" through his revision of Berlioz's treatise on instrumentation. The common root that brought Debussy's ideas close to Strauss's was Weber, whose music Debussy considered "the finest treatise on orchestration" and who, of course, profoundly influenced Berlioz. (A more thorough study of Debussy's ideas on Strauss and the cinema will be found in R. Langham Smith's "Debussy and the Art of the Cinema," *Music and Letters,* January 1973.)

As another side of the French reaction to Richard Strauss, Colette's review is worth quoting at length:

> Richard Strauss drew a small but select audience at the Nouveau-Théâtre. I arrived early and was preceded by Mme Raunay, whose fair-complexioned neck shone out from under black crepe, and Mme Chausson, also fair and also pretty in her beautiful Louis XIII sleeves. Yes, girls, it's the latest fashion. . . .
>
> And then the Schola arrived, trooping in: Séverac, the two Castéras (since one has shaved his beard I can't tell them apart), Doire, and Guilmant—all dressed in silver gray. . . .
>
> I could go on listing them and listing them in the hope of filling my column without mentioning Richard Strauss, who embarrasses me and whom I don't like. No! Even if Debussy attacks me—or, worse, replies with a spiteful silence—I do not like that music! With Roman ruins inspiring a rowdy *allegro con brio* on Strauss's part, and the Sorrento boat slip an overripe song embroidered with the sound of the billowing sea, ingeniously twisted and deformed, I cannot accustom myself to this man, who chooses an aggressive tumult barbed

with piercing piccolos for a sticky romance—a hedgehog garlanded with forget-me-nots! After *From Italy,* which filled me with admiration for Charpentier (Gustave), Richard Strauss conducted a "love scene" from his opera *Feuersnot.* Once again my ears went *bzi-bzi!* That a love scene? My God, if I went into such tumultuous ecstasies I'd be afraid of what my neighbors downstairs might say! The program was right: a "scene" it was, not a duet. One would have thought there were fifteen of them, not just two. And Bruneau, in his box, was clapping.

Not without curiosity I awaited *Ein Heldenleben,* a piece that gave little pleasure some time ago at the Château d'Eau. Alas, my impressions have scarcely changed. I cannot muster up much enthusiasm for the hero's theme—how heroic it is! Nor do the whistling enemies sustain my interest for more than a minute, nor his companion's (perhaps he married a Hungarian gypsy?) rhapsodic violin solo. The hero's battles, the hero's peacemakings (I suppose all that thunder was for the cause of peace?), the hero's fate—he retires to the country if I understand the pastoral modification of his theme correctly— the hero's disillusionment, his dinner, even his carpet slippers. Whatever next? Well, that's enough for me.

Now I know that my article lacks any technical criticism, but what do you want me to say? Willy, shocked by my irreverent pose during this interminable Strauss festival, dryly reproached me with the words: "Nevertheless, my dear, you have to admit that the orchestral pâté has been well ground."

If only he knew I cared not a fig for his pâté! Nor for the way it's been ground! It's a kind of cuisine I detest.

Parsifal *and the Société des Grandes Auditions de France*

I NEVER have any luck! . . . The one time when I would like to have spoken to you of Wagner, the Société des Grandes Auditions de France didn't do me the honor of an invitation to hear their performance of *Parsifal,* which has just taken place at the Nouveau-Théâtre, under the direction of M. Alfred Cortot. Of all French conductors, M. Cortot is the one who has learned most from the pantomime customary among German conductors. . . . He has Nikisch's lock of hair (although he is in fact Hungarian), and we find this most attractive because it waves passionately at the least nuance in the music. See how it falls, sad and weary, at any hint of tenderness! So much so that it prevents any communication between M. Cortot and the orchestra. Then, at the warlike passages, it proudly stands on end again, and just at this moment M. Cortot bears down on the orchestra and threatens them with his menacing bâton. Just like the banderilleros tantalizing the bull! (The musicians in the orchestra take all this with the coolness of Greenlanders: they have seen it all many times before.) Like Weingartner, he leans affectionately over the first violins, whispering sweet nothings to them, and then wheels around toward the trombones, urging them on with a gesture that seems to say, "Come on, men! Put some spirit into it! Try to be even more trombone-like than usual!" Then the trombones quietly and dutifully extend their slides to the limit.

It is right to add that M. Cortot is a perfect musician. And he understands Wagner down to the last detail. He is young, and he has an open-minded love of music: good enough reasons why we shouldn't be too hard on him for using gestures that are more decorative than they are useful.

But to come back to the Société des Grandes Auditions de France: did they intend to punish me for my Wagnerian iconoclasm by not inviting me to *Parsifal?* Did they think I would carry out some subversive activity . . . a bomb perhaps? I'll never know, but I'd willingly believe that this type of private hearing was especially designed for those whose titles or standing in society authorize them to come along to these little parties with an attitude of complete indifference to what is being played. The certain fame of the name written on the program means there need not be any lighting to read by, so they can listen carefully to the latest scandal, or watch the delicious movements of the ladies' necks, without ever listening to the music. But I hope the Société des Grandes Auditions de France will watch out! They will turn Wagner's music into salon pieces, inhabiting the last salons left for conversation. All in all, it's rather annoying, this side of the Wagnerian art that requires the faithful to make costly pilgrimages, and carry out mysterious practices. I know that "Art-Religion" was one of Wagner's favorite ideas, and that he was right—this method being the best for capturing the public and for holding their attention. But it has gone rather wrong when it becomes a Luxury-Religion that excludes those with more goodwill than cash. The Société des Grandes Auditions, in continuing its exclusivist policies, seems to me to be heading for an art that is merely fashionable. A detestable idea! Wagner, when he was in a good mood, used to assert that his music would never be understood except in France.[1] Did he mean by that performances just for aristocrats? I think not. (King Ludwig II of Bavaria used to annoy him with questions about the finer points of etiquette, and in any case Wagner's proud spirit was too astute not to realize that true glory can come only from the masses and not from a gilded segment.)

One must therefore conclude that these performances, although their confessed aim is the propagation of Wagnerism, will serve only to alienate public sympathy—a cunning way to send it out of favor. I wouldn't say that they'll speed up its complete disappearance, for

I don't think it will ever die entirely. But it will inevitably decay; time leaves its mark on the most beautiful of things. All the same, wonderful ruins will remain, and our grandchildren will play in their shadow, dreaming of the former grandeur of this man who, had he been a little more human, would have been truly great.

In *Parsifal,* the final effort of a genius before whom we should bow our heads, Wagner tried to be less rigidly authoritarian toward the music, to let it breathe a little more freely. It doesn't have that nervous breathlessness that pursues Tristan's morbid passion, nor the enraged animal cries of an Isolde, nor the overblown commentary on Wotan's inhumanity. Nothing in the music of Wagner is more serenely beautiful than the Prelude to the Third Act of *Parsifal,* and the "Good Friday Spell." But Wagner's real insight into humanity comes out in the way he depicts several of the characters in this play: think of Amfortas, the sad Knight of the Grail who moans like a shop girl and whimpers like a baby. But really! When one is a king's son, a Knight of the Grail, one would plunge a spear straight into one's own body rather than parade around with a guilty wound singing melancholy cantilenas! And for three whole acts, too! As for Kundry, the old rose of hell, she has been given much material for Wagnerian literature to work on, but I must confess that I feel little affection for this sentimental old dragon. The finest character in *Parsifal* is Klingsor (former Knight of the Grail, shown to the door of the Holy Place for his rather too individual views on chastity). His hateful malice is wonderful! He knows what men are really like, and weighs up the strength of their vows to chastity on his dreadful scales. One could easily argue that this cunning magician and old offender is not only the one "human" character but also the only "moral" one in this play, in which so many wrong-headed moralistic and religious ideas are propounded—ideas of which the young Parsifal, the heroic but foolish knight, is the messenger.

All in all, nobody is willing to sacrifice himself in this Christian drama (sacrifice being one of the best of Christian doctrines), and if Parsifal recovers his magic spear, it is thanks to old Kundry, the only person who is really sacrificed in the story. She is a victim twice over—offered up both to the secret deviltries of Klingsor and to the holy world-weariness of the Knight of the Grail. The atmosphere is certainly religious, but why are the children's voices used in such strange progressions? (Just think for a moment of how much child-like freshness could have been captured if the spirit of Palestrina had been used as a means of expression?)

All this applies only to Wagner the poet, and it has nothing to do with the musical side of *Parsifal,* which is of the utmost beauty. There we hear fine orchestral sonorities that are unique and quite unexpected. It is one of the most beautiful edifices in sound ever raised to the eternal glory of music.

Despite the Société des Grandes Auditions de France, I have been able to speak about *Parsifal* at length, thanks to the memory I retain of my journey to Bayreuth in 1889. Let us hope that the vividness of my recollections compensates for my having missed this performance. . . . 1889! A marvelous year! I was full of the Wagnerian madness! Why am I no longer? Forgive me, but that is another story.

The Centenary of the Académie de France in Rome

SOON we are to commemorate the inauguration of the Prix de Rome and the centenary of the Académie de France there. We are assured of the support of their Majesties, the king and queen of Italy. Trains are being organized at reduced prices to enable the holders of the Prix de Rome and their families to congregate at this charming celebration. I'd say that we are going to see a surge of former Prix de Rome holders: nobody will recognize them anymore, and that will be a great shame for everyone concerned! One hopes that some improvement will be noted as regards the customary Prix de Rome cuisine. When I was there, we were gently being poisoned, and dyspepsia should not be an obligatory part of an artist's aesthetic. This complaint obviously is not the only one that could be made, but on such an auspicious occasion as a centenary one would not dream of being ir-reverent.

Concerts

THE interest of the last Concert Colonne was enhanced by the presence of Mme Maria Bréma. We already know her rare artistic gifts from other occasions. If one is unable to forget the splendid way she reclothed the character of Brünnhilde, with her beautiful voice and eurhythmic gestures, it should be said here that Mme Bréma showed undeniable understanding in the way she sang the finale of the third act of *Die Walküre*. And she was just as marvelous in the songs of Schubert. But why did she feel obliged to associate with her triumphs M. Webber,[2] who has usurped, although misspelled, a famous name? With his spelling, he's unworthy of a famous name. She sang a song called "La Première" by this M. Webber; it was certainly inferior to the charming "Petits Pavés" of our own Paul Delmet. Mme Bréma made a great mistake in repeating this little joke twice over, and the public clearly showed that this "première" ought to have been a "dernière."

The rest of the concert consisted of the Symphony in D Minor by César Franck. This beautiful work found in M. Colonne an interpreter sensitive to all its wonders, which, as you know, are countless. "La Toussaint," by Monsieur Joncières, and the "Nuit de Noël" by G. Pierné were received very differently: some people preferred "La Toussaint" because it was sad, and others, the "Nuit de Noël," because it was about soldiers and contains gunfire effects. Which side should I be on? I think I tend toward the "Nuit de Noël."

The last Concert Lamoureux has now taken place. M. Chevillard wanted his flock to go away with the memory of his ardent passion for *Antar,* and his scrupulous finesse in Mozart's C Major Symphony. And Mozart's delicacy went quite well with the oriental richness of *Antar.* G. Charpentier's *Impressions d'Italie* is a luxurious orgy of colors and rhythms, but he doesn't dream of Italy in the same way as Richard Strauss—who has also recorded his impressions of this country. But in his rendering of the streets of Naples, Charpentier is without equal.

ᕦᐩ*NOTES*

[1] Wagner's attitude to France was not at all as Debussy makes out; in fact, it was rather the opposite. At least as nationalistic as Debussy, Wagner insisted on the essentially German qualities of his work, on several occasions disparaging Paris as an "arrogant cultural center." Debussy may have been thinking of Nietzsche's chapter "Where Wagner Is at Home" in his *Nietzsche Contra Wagner,* for certainly he seems to have been versed in the writings of the philosopher, readily available in French editions. "The fact remains," Nietszche had written,

> that French Romanticism and Richard Wagner are closely bound together. Dominated by literary ideas that had impregnated both the eyes of the painters and the ears of the musicians, they were the first artists to have a *universal* literary culture—nearly all writers or poets themselves, passionate about several arts and several senses, interpreting each other's works. . . .

[2] Colette shared Debussy's distaste for the music of Webber, and again invoked the name of the celebrated Montmartre *chansonnier* Paul Delmet by way of comparison. She began her article of 6 April with an open admission of her love for the social tittle-tattle associated with the opera house:

> I'm without an idea in my head, for there haven't been enough people at the concerts this week. I had been counting on having a good natter about Cortot's evening and those who heard *Parsifal* minced to pieces. Zut! Sparklett [the third critic on *Gil Blas*] beat me to it, and in such a magisterial way that after him I will certainly not risk taking up the matter again. Even so, it was a temptation! Elegant pursuits, gossip, visits from box to box, bitchery, and venomous tittle-tattle, general inattention, obstinate and ill-understood enthusiasm. Were it not for the "cuts"—one might say "selection"—from the three acts, one would almost have thought oneself at Bayreuth.

Colette then turned to the songs at the Châtelet:

> After her other songs, Mme Bréma brought out a disgusting little romance that unleashed a storm: "How *vile!* What kind of music was *that!* When's the Delmet coming? Now! *Das ist zu dumm!* Call the composer!" And who was the composer? Well, the unfortunate

man was at the piano, M. Webber with two *b*s, the usual accompanist of M. Jean de Reszke. Hesitant amidst the tempest, he first went the color of overripe cheese, wanting to run away. But this German lady singer is a strong-willed woman! Bringing him back with her irrefutable biceps, she pinned him down to his instrument while one half of the audience shouted abuse and the others applauded out of sheer obstinacy. She pitched camp at the front of the stage, bowed fifty-seven times, threw kisses and menacing reprimands to the higher galleries, and . . . began again! A useless and clumsy piece of bravado. Mme Bréma is a great singer, but she is a great German singer.

At the Concerts Spirituels: César Franck's Les Béatitudes

IT is well-known that because of special sanctions granted by the Church (being to some extent her daughter), Music does not have to fast. The Good Friday concerts are positive orgies of music, and they simply call themselves *concerts spirituels* so as not to offend the ears of the pious. M. Colonne includes César Franck's *Les Béatitudes* on his program—something that can be listened to without any feelings of guilt whatsoever. But M. Chevillard replies by cold-bloodedly putting *Das Rheingold* on his; that's neither "holy" nor in any way "abstinent"![1] It is two and a half hours during which we are in the domain of the Gods, watching the "aquatic flirtation" of the Rhine maidens with Alberich, the dwarf. A passionate story, about the theft of a ring: Wotan, master of the Gods, behaves like one of those heroes in a novel by Penson du Terrail—one who must have read the *Arabian Nights!* There are flames, burning, and a great deal of noise. There are giants two and a half meters high, and dwarfs of only fifty centimeters (as usual). And it's all brought to an end by an obliging rainbow that enables the Gods to go back home. (Obviously it is nicer than having an elevator, though rather more costly!) Every corner of it all is like a modern-day fairyland: there is even one of those jolly little characters so indispensable in anything connected with magic. Here he is personified by the telltale Loge, who later (in *Die Walküre*) surrounds the virtuous Brünnhilde with a circle of fire. (Perhaps it's to destroy that scandalous legend that Jesus Christ died on the Cross . . .)

Unfortunately, at Chevillard's, all this magic took place without any scenery, and we watched a very stern-looking gentleman in evening dress brandishing the dreaded Wotan's spear beneath the cover of a tiny score! . . . Most disconcerting, and not at all pleasing to look at.

You might object that there's magic enough in the orchestra. But if one is really a Wagnerian, can that be sufficient? I would timidly put forward the suggestion of using films for animation. We have recently seen, in a play at the Ambigu, how greatly it can increase the emotional effect.[2] We should be true to our own age, and we have no right to deprive Wagner of the ingeniously expressive powers of this invention, of which the music halls make such a marvelous use— though, of course, in a far less elevated way.

Once again, *Das Rheingold* in concert is simply two and a half hours when one is bound to feel overcome by a desire to get out, or a need to go to sleep—after having politely requested your neighbor to awaken you at the penultimate bar, so that one is in time to render the applause due the masterly energy of M. Chevillard. Quite seriously, though, that is the attitude of a lot of well-brought-up people: they submit themselves, more or less willingly, to the boredom of it all, and if they don't leave, it is only because they want someone to see them, eloquent and informed, at the exit at the end. Otherwise, why would they have come?

César Franck's *Les Béatitudes* has one advantage over *Das Rheingold,* at least for a concert: it requires no scenery. It's pure music, and what's more, it's all exquisite music. . . . César Franck was a simple-hearted man; even the discovery of a beautiful new chord could fill his day with joy. If one closely examines the poem of *Les Béatitudes,* one finds a lot of images and truisms that would make the most devoted reader recoil. Only the wise, calm genius of César Franck could have passed over all this with a smile. And such a wonderful smile—that of an Apostle preaching the Gospel and saying, "Be not afraid, God will recognize his own." Nonetheless, the melodies of César Franck, so characteristic, create a very strange impression coupled with these verses, which would disgrace even a penny whistle! What is more, the genius of Franck has been much discussed without anyone ever mentioning his most personal quality—namely, naïve simplicity. This man had bad luck and he was misunderstood, yet he had the soul of a child, so thoroughly good-natured that he could look upon people's wickedness and the disorder of the world without a trace of bitterness.

It is this which caused him to write those choruses which are too facilely dramatic and those gray developments which are so boring and tedious that they sometimes seem to mar the beauty—the confidence and candor—of *Les Béatitudes,* so marvelous when Franck is really face to face with the music, whispering a prayer more full of human feeling than any other ever uttered by a mortal soul. . . . His designs are never evil or boring nor is there any trace of those sentimental orchestral pirouettes so flagrant in Wagner, designed to bring the public to attention when they are tired—as they sometimes are—of such constantly high-pitched emotions.

In Franck we find a real devotion to music. We must take it or leave it. Nothing in the world could have made him alter any part he considered right and necessary, however long it may have been— we just have to sit through it. He shows all the signs of having the kind of prejudiced imagination that checks the sincerity of every sob before it is written down.

In this, Franck is united with other great musicians, those to whom every sound had an exact meaning taken in its context: each sound is used in a precise way, and it asks nothing but to be taken for what it is. This is exactly why he is so different from Wagner, who is uniquely beautiful but impure and seductive. César Franck serves music without seeking any glory. What he takes from life, he puts back into art with a modesty that is almost selfless. When Wagner takes something from life, he conquers it, treads it under his feet, and forces it to proclaim the name of Wagner louder than the loudest trumpets of fame.

I have tried to portray Franck in his true light, so that each of my readers will have a clear picture of what he is like. Among so many other urgent matters, it is right that we should pay some attention to the great musicians—and, what is more, make others do the same. I have taken Good Friday as a chance to pay homage to one of the greatest of them, for the sacrifice remembered on this holy day throws the greatness of this man into relief.[3]

But, all in all, the music played on Good Friday was not at all well-suited to the day. Without criticizing the motives of the Concerts Spirituels it seems to me that more advantage should have been taken of the special religious significance of the day, and the concerts should have been more varied. I would hold that there are masterpieces on a smaller scale that would have been a welcome change from our usual diet—a mixture of hot spices and cooling cucumbers. The two *Passions* of Bach, and Beethoven's *Missa Solemnis* draw a large following and have inspired many studies, but among the minor masters there are things that deserve to be rescued from their unjustified neglect. Some of the dead are really much too shy and wait too long for their melancholy reward!

Careful hands are needed to lift the veil from the dead. Generally it is done by hands that are too clumsy or else too tentative; the funeral flowers are lost forever beneath a dreadful shr ud of concealed egotism. If we are truthful, the monuments erected to the glory of J. S. Bach tend to obscure Handel: his oratorios are ignored, and there are as many of them as there are grains of sand on the shore. Perhaps we would find more pebbles than pearls, but there would surely be much of interest, if only we used a little patience and good taste.

Another master—and in his case it's absolute oblivion—is Alessandro Scarlatti, founder of the Neapolitan school and remarkable for the incredible number and variety of his works. Are we dreaming when we discover that, born in 1659, he had written more than 106 operas by 1715? Not to mention other kinds of music. Lord, how he must have been gifted; how did he find any time to live? We know a *Passion According to St. John* by him, and it's a minor masterpiece, full of a primitive grace. The choruses have that light gold color that so beautifully outlines the profile of the Madonnas one sees in the frescoes of his time. Much less tiring to listen to than *Das Rheingold!* The calm that emerges from this work gives one a restful feeling of well-being. I don't know how this man found the time to have a son and to turn him into a famous harpsichordist. *He* is still appreciated these days, going under the name of Domenico Scarlatti.

There are also others . . . but don't worry, I'm not trying to add anything to the history of music! I merely want to suggest that we are perhaps wrong in playing the same old things time and time again; it makes quite innocent people believe that Music was born only yesterday. But it has a Past whose ashes should be kindled, for they contain an inextinguishable flame to which the Present inevitably must owe a part of its splendor.

We learned something from the newspaper this morning that will delight anybody who didn't have the chance to hear M. J. de Reszke at the Opéra.

De Reszke is going to open his own theater at 53 rue de la Faisanderie. He is going to put on *Fiorella,* by MM. Sardou and Gheusi, with music by M. Amherst Webber. This latter is the young composer one of whose songs Mme Bréma sang at a recent Concert Colonne. You will remember that I said, in these very columns, how it stuck in the public's throat. Perhaps M. Webber, rather ill at ease in the constricting form of the song, will make up for this in his lyrical comedy. I hope so with all my heart. Also, perhaps M. de Reszke will find for *Fiorella* the voice he lacked for *Sigurd.* We all hope so, don't we?

⤳ *NOTES*

[1] For her Holy Week article, Colette adopted her pose of an ill-brought-up, irreverent young lady, beginning with a lengthy and vivid description of the cakewalk competition at the Moulin-Rouge. "Not very 'Holy Week,' my column." She added with obvious relish, "A sad week that smells of cooking oil." For her sins she "forces herself to attend the Concerts Spirituels."

> If, like me, you had been to *Das Rheingold* at the Nouveau-Théâtre, your sins are forgiven you. Froelich sang Wotan with a German accent, Mme Grümert screamed out Fricka in American, and Mme Gay sounded like a Catalan Erda. Pure pandemonium! Except for Mme Gay, who could have been singing in Auvergnat for all one knew. Her sumptuous voice, moving in expansive waves, provoked a physical response, like the touch of deep velvet. But the others! Dreadful! . . . I will add nothing more, except that Chevillard, excited by the Lenten fast, or perhaps because he had a train to catch,

took both the water-sprite scene and the forge scene at the pace of an Irish jig.

. . . At the Châtelet, Les Béatitudes—that musical rosary—churned out before a public who soon fell into pious slumbers.

[2] The play to which Debussy refers was Eugène Sue's hackneyed melodrama Le Juif Errant. Elaborate stage machinery and cinematographic backdrops were used to heighten the effect of this play, which had previously been a favorite in the tiny shadow theater that Henri Rivière ran in the Montmartre nightclub, Le Chat Noir. Many people, including Debussy, found Rivière's early cinematographic efforts irresistible, and it was possibly the memory of the early days of the Chat Noir shadow theater that attracted Debussy to this otherwise unimportant play.

[3] For some time in the late 1870s Debussy had attended the organ class of César Franck. Little is known about this epiosode in Debussy's apprenticeship, but, according to one source, the young composer could not accept Père Franck's constant exhortations to modulate. "But why should I modulate," Debussy would retort, "when I am quite happy where I am?" Elsewhere, Debussy expressed his admiration for Franck's Symphony in D Minor: "I could do with fewer four-bar phrases. But what splendid ideas! I even prefer it to the Quintet, which I used to find thrilling."

Edvard Hagerup Grieg

M . E . G R I E G is that Scandinavian composer who had so little time for the French at the time of the Dreyfus affair. In a letter replying to an invitation by M. Colonne to come and conduct his orchestra, M. Grieg somewhat rashly declared that he had no wish ever to set foot again in a country that understood so little about liberty. . . . France has thus had to do without M. Grieg, but it seems that M. Grieg cannot do without France: he is now quite willing to pardon us for all our wrongs and cross our frontiers once again. And his business is to conduct the above-mentioned orchestra, one-time object of his scorn.

Well, the "affair" has died down, and M. Grieg is now nearly sixty—an age when the wise philosophical thinking of our later years quite naturally appeases any former grudges. An age when we sink into the role of a spectator who is content merely to weigh up and pass judgment on the trials and tribulations of the world's affairs. One is no less human for being Scandinavian, so it would be unkind to deny him the hospitable welcome that Paris usually accords foreigners. Especially those as notable as M. Grieg.

For a moment I thought I would be able to convey to you nothing of Grieg's music except an impression of color. On this occasion there were three times as many Norwegians as are usually present at the Concert Colonne. Never before have we been privileged to see so many shocks of red hair or so many outrageous hats (the fashions in Christiania are a little out of date). Then the concert began with two performances. First, a piece called "Autumn," which was accompanied by a crowd of Grieg's admirers, who were sent out by some overzealous police commissioner (evidently not a music lover) to cool themselves down on the banks of the Seine. Had someone feared a hostile reception?

It's not really my place to say so, but for a while Grieg drew some very bitter comments. As for the piece, I couldn't hear a thing, for I was too busy pacifying some of the high ranking and severe policemen.

At last I was able to catch sight of M. Grieg. From the front he looks like rather a pleasant family photograph. From behind, because of the way he wears his hair, he looks more like a sunflower of the kind so loved by parrots and planted in ornamental gardens at country railway stations. Despite his age he is lively and slender, and he conducts the orchestra with painstaking care and great vigor, underlining all the nuances and controlling the expression with unflagging attention.

After this opening (which opened the exit doors as well), came three songs sung by Mme Gulbranson who is from the opera house at Bayreuth. The first two were of little interest . . . Grieg under the influence of Schumann. The third, called "The Swan," was rather more cunning. (It is actually quite well-known as a salon piece.) It is a piece of orchestral cookery in which the aroma of the harps mingles with the lemon flavor of the oboes. All is then blended with the juice of the string section, interspersed with highly emotional silences, which cause the audience to catch its breath. Just the right tricks to secure an encore. These are songs which are very sweet, very pale—music to soothe convalescents in well-to-do neighborhoods. . . . There always seems to be one note that drags on over a chord like a water lily on a lake, tired of being watched by the moon. . . . Or a tiny balloon obscured by the clouds.[1] This music leaves one in such a quandary that one cannot resist it; it was enthusiastically encored, thanks to our good old French sensibility. One can always rely on that! Mme Gulbranson sang these three songs with a voice so light, so dreamy, that one could feel that cold sadness peculiar to the fjords, still the purest of Norway's charms.

But now the hall resounds with bravos . . . the ladies put on their best smiles. . . . What is going on? Oh, it's Pugno, the pianist with the lovely hands!

When Pugno appears on the scene you can be sure the Grieg Concerto is not far away! He plays it with tremendous effect; nobody can draw more from it. His incredible dexterity shows off the slickness of this piece to the fullest. But one is tempted to forget that the piece is really not so individual at all: it begins with an imitation of Schumann and ends with something worthy of *Excelsior*. And the way the piano is treated is really very traditional. What's more, I have never been able to understand why there are fragmentary interpolations of fanfares of warlike trumpets, which generally announce the arrival of a little cantabile section at which we are meant to swoon. (Trumpets! It's an abuse of your usual frankness.) Pugno was admirable; he never fails us. The sight of him excitedly taking an encore has to be seen to be believed: his understandably tired-out left hand waves a handkerchief, gently protesting his reluctance at being called upon to repeat the cruel ordeal.

There followed two elegiac melodies for strings: how tuneful they were! One felt the influence of Massenet, especially in the second (although it was always without that characteristically voluptuous poise that causes one to feel a perverse love for Massenet's music). With Grieg it becomes like those marshmallows they sell at fairs: they need to have been stuck to the stall holder's hands for them to be really good. These two songs repeated over again all the tricks that have made Grieg his fortune. They begin with a harmless little phrase that is to be his companion for the duration of the piece; en route it gathers a few harmonic flowers to cover up its plainness. Next it floats up on high—muted, of course—and then comes down again through a series of carefully "interrupted" cadences. It ends with a sickening ritardando and we all swoon again. We are left at the end with a strange and charming taste in our mouths—that of a rose-colored sweet coated in snow. . . .

To tell you the truth, the high spot of the afternoon was *Peer Gynt*, the orchestral suite Grieg wrote for Ibsen's play. The ideas in this are charming and the rhythms fine, and its spirit is more truly Norwegian. The handling of the orchestra is better thought out, too;

those facile effects are replaced by some ingenious discoveries. For some inexplicable reason this concert dedicated to Grieg ended with the Finale from *Götterdämmerung* sung by Mme Gulbranson. I've tried to reason it out, but I can't for the life of me see why this great German warhorse should have been chosen as an accompaniment to Grieg's Nordic melancholy. So I left before it was performed: one does not eat roast beef after petits fours.

To return to and finish with Grieg in a fitting manner: it's a pity that his visit to Paris has taught us nothing new about his art. He's a sensitive musician as long as he sticks to the folk music of his own country, although he nowhere near approaches what M. Balakirev and Rimsky-Korsakov do with Russian folk music. Apart from this he's just a clever musician more concerned about effect than genuinely artistic. Apparently his real inspiration came from a man of his own age, a born genius who was destined to become a great musician: one Richard Nordraak. But he died at twenty-four. His death was a two-fold tragedy: first because it robbed Norway of a great man, and second because it deprived Grieg of an influential friend who might have kept him on the straight and narrow. . . .

Elsewhere, Grieg's aim became like that of Solness, the master builder (in one of Ibsen's later plays, *The Master Builder*): "to build houses for the children of men where they might be happy and at home. . . ."

I found no trace of this noble ideal in the music M. Grieg played us yesterday. But then we know nothing of his later works; perhaps they are the "happy homes" of which Ibsen speaks? Whatever may be the case, M. Grieg has not given us the pleasure of entering any such homes, but then perhaps the triumphant acclaim that greeted him yesterday has made his visit worth the trouble. And let our parting wish be that he will at least consider it worthwhile in the future to make us "happy," if not "at home."

At last . . . the king of American music is in town. By that I mean that M. J. P. Sousa and his band have come for a whole week to reveal to us the beauties of American music as it is performed in the best society. One really has to be exceedingly gifted to conduct this music. M. Sousa beats time in circles or tosses an imaginary salad or sweeps away some invisible dust. Or else he catches a butterfly that has flown out of a bass tuba![2]

If American music is unique for its invention of the famous "cake-walk," and I must admit that for the moment that seems to be its single advantage over all other kinds of music, then of that M. Sousa is unquestionably its king.

↬ *NOTES*

[1] These same words were used to describe the music of Delius in Debussy's first *Revue blanche* article.

[2] Sousa's band visited Paris several times during the early years of the century. In his memoirs, *Marching Along,* Sousa proudly quotes Debussy's article. In 1901 Sousa had been awarded the Palmes d'Officier d'Académie, an honor reserved for men of literary or artistic distinction.

A Renaissance for Opera Buffa

A P R O P O S of the growing fame of Claude Terrasse, it is appropriate to recall Offenbach, a musician whose strange genius combined a transcendental irony with a decided hatred of music. . . . When Offenbach began composing, France had ears for Meyerbeer alone, but because of his gifts as an ironist, Offenbach was able to see through this kind of art and realize just how false and overblown it was. Best of all, he rediscovered hidden treasure: the high art of farce, which he understood and used to its best advantage. And we all know how successful he was. But no one saw what he was really up to, so much was it generally accepted that Meyerbeer represented the Great Art at which one was not allowed to smile. However, that dislocation of rhythms, the cosmic effect which consists of detaching one syllable from a line and repeating it ad nauseam, is found all through Meyerbeer's work. Furthermore, if one compares the entry of Paris in *La Belle Hélène* to the Calvinists' song from *Les Huguenots,* in which M. de Coligny is acclaimed for his prowess at war and the basses eagerly sing the refrain "Vive Coligny!" at the tops of their voices, you'll find there are some interesting comparisons to be made.[1]

Why is it musical farce in the first case and great music in the second? It is one of those strange classifications for which chance alone can be blamed. Also, has anyone ever noticed that in the fourth act of *Les Huguenots,* in Marcel and Valentine's duet, Valentine recognizes the sound of the "good Marcel's" voice, when in fact he has never even heard it before. An extraordinary case of stupefying telepathy!

This was the time when only things that would not be laughed at were set to music, but all the same one could quote numerous examples of laughable scenes, not only from Meyerbeer. But I won't press the point, for I would not want to put anyone off. Let us admit, however, that without such a state of affairs Offenbach would never have been able to write *Robert le Diable*: first because he was used to better texts, and second because it forced him to find an alternative to such overblown boredom. What a devil! He had a unique scorn for music, and it clearly shows when he imitates the grand solemnity of Gluck, mercilessly deforming it. But serious music, the kind that cannot take a joke, took its revenge: it made sure that the one work in which he tried to be serious met with no success. I mean, of course, *Les Contes d'Hoffmann*. (The Gods still have the means of showing how nasty they can be even though they no longer have temples, nor thunderous powers to strike them down.)

M. Claude Terrasse is more respectful. He never allows himself to stick out his tongue at great music. I sometimes find him a little bit formal. Has he not thought about the now obsolete forms of comic opera? I must say that the charming nocturne that opens the third act of *Le Sire de Vergy*, his latest work, seems to suggest so, but he has at least attempted, and often succeeds, in this revival of opera buffa.

Despite my own inexperience in the matter, I do think that these musical farces will achieve their full comic effect only if the music itself is funny. I would even dare to say that such things are as difficult to put into practice as *Parsifal* (to take an example of a piece in which there is not even the slightest hint of a laugh). This is why Offenbach is so wonderful, for if one looks at the words of the choir of "brigands," one has to admit that in themselves they don't send one into fits of laughter: "I hear the sound of boots." It is the music alone that adds the final touch. There is in Offenbach something a little "unbuttoned" (if you will excuse my saying so) and this is a part of his special effect. One must hand it to M. Claude Terrasse for knowing how to remain within the bounds of good taste during the most dreadful situations, but is this not sometimes to the detriment of the laughter produced, and of the farcical, fantastic side of things? I think he holds himself too much in check for fear of going a bit mad, like Hervé did. Offenbach's orchestration was painful, Terrasse's is very fine; in that respect, too, if I may be permitted to point it out, there could have been more unexpected timbres, for such things provide a mine of laughter. He understands them better than I, to be sure, and the car horn that announces the return of the Crusaders from the Holy Land, in *Le Sire de Vergy,* is undeniably the touch of a master. But these dreadful Crusaders sing a song that I would have preferred to be a little more halting, even a little more lame. That would have been an admirable gibe at the horrors of this war, which the joking Sire de Vergy has made into a parade of grand old dukes around Lutetia. I may seem to be critical, but I have no right to be, for on many counts *Le Sire de Vergy* is a highly amusing piece.[2]

One should go, and encourage MM. de Caillavet, R. de Flers, and C. Terrasse in their attempt at an opera buffa, even if it's only to discourage the other kind of opera. That is neither funny, nor is it really opera: it is a kind of germ that must at all costs be fought! Otherwise it will cause havoc. A race of people who no longer know how to laugh will not be capable of any enthusiasm either, and without falling back into the bad taste of the Second Empire, we should hope that this, our Third Republic, will shake off the present atmosphere of mediocrity. If we are not very careful, it will lead us toward the greatest immorality of all, namely: Ennui.

The Revival of Werther *at the Opéra-Comique*

I t is only chance that has caused the names of *Le Sire de Vergy* and *Werther* to be coupled together in this column; there is no connection at all between the two works, except that in the latter, one cries, and in the former, one laughs, and in both cases one is justified. I hardly mentioned the acclaim with which the revival of *Werther* has been greeted: it could not have been better deserved, for never before has M. Massenet, that musical historian of the female soul, shown off the high quality of his gifts to better advantage.

I must confess that for myself I prefer this feminine side of *Werther,* especially the character of Sophia, who is charming from beginning to end. From the dramatic point of view, however, Werther is most irritating. And, you know, I will never easily be persuaded that a man who has just shot himself, for his own good, would go on pouring out his grudges about life, instead of offering his soul up to God. I'd have thought that he would have no time to lose. The emotional effect gains nothing from the sad spectacle of his last moments; one is almost tempted to count the agonizing minutes going by—one just cannot believe in it.

However, what charmingly sentimental touches there are in the nocturnal return of Charlotte and Werther in the first act! But why does all this charm suddenly have to turn into barking trombones underlined with drum rolls? I can't explain it, any more than I can sufficiently deplore it. M. Massenet is sometimes guilty of snatching us away from our dreams—something he can conjure up so well. And it's merely for the sake of making a noise whose function is nothing more than to let the public know that it's time for them to clap. I daresay that he could rest assured that the public would clap without needing such a brutal invitation.

> On the other hand, it is well-known how his music is vibrant with fleeting sensations, little bursts of feeling and embraces that we wish would last forever. The harmonies are like arms, the melodies like the napes of necks. We gaze into the ladies' eyes, dying to know their thoughts. . . . The philosophical, and those in their right minds, inform us that there are none. But we don't have to believe them: M. Massenet proves that there are (at least melodically). With such preoccupations, he is bound to occupy a position in contemporary art for which, at least, he is secretly envied. And that is something which should not be scorned.[3]

Of these lines, written in 1901,[4] I see nothing that should be changed. Fortune, which is feminine, owed it to M. Massenet both to treat him well and, occasionally, to let him down. So far it has done just this. So much success has meant that for a time it was considered a good thing to copy the Massenet method of dressing up melodies, but then, all of a sudden, those who had so quietly cribbed from him began to treat him badly. It was wicked!

M. Massenet was able to see that he could do no wrong, and that, despite other people's jealousy, his beautiful lady listeners would not lose their passion for him. . . . Did they not find moments in his music where they felt all the more beautiful for having been so divinely moved? You can be sure that such a feeling isn't easily forgotten. The love of Massenet's music is a tradition that women will pass on, for many years hence, from generation to generation. That's quite enough reason for a man to achieve glory.

NOTES

[1] In his youth Debussy evidently had a strong liking for Offenbach's music for, writing from Rome to Emile Baron, he mentioned Offenbach and Manet in connection with his homesickness: "I would like to see some Manet and hear some Offenbach. This may seem something of a paradox but I can assure you that breathing the atmosphere of this spleen-factory gives you the most strange and fantastic ideas."

[2] Some years later, in 1907, Debussy wrote to Louis Laloy, not without a certain bitterness, of Ravel's *Histoires naturelles,* mentioning his attitude to "humorous" music:

> But between you and me, can you really believe in "humorous" music? Firstly, there's no such thing, *in itself*: it always depends on a "situation" or a text. Two chords with their feet in the air (or in some other preposterous position) are not bound to be funny in themselves. . . .

[3] Writing to Prince Poniatowski in 1893, Debussy had spoken frankly about his distaste for Massenet:

> We have *Werther* by Massenet, where one sees this composer as a master in the art of pandering to stupid ideas and cheap amateur standards. Everything in this work is pretty secondhand, and what is more deplorable is his habit of taking a fine subject and turning it into a facile and sentimental parody of itself.

Elsewhere, he wrote that the only work of Massenet he admired was the Overture to *Phèdre*—the work of a true musician.

[4] See pp. 56–7.

GIL BLAS
5 May 1903

London Letters

29 April 1903

My dear Editor,

Leaving home, said the poet, is like dying a little. . . . To be less poetic, it means a momentary suppression of the "self" to which one is accustomed, for nothing gives one such an acute feeling of isolation as a fleeting visit to a country whose language one does not understand. ("My metallic throat does not speak in every tongue, alas.") Despite that perfect politeness peculiar to the English policeman one somehow feels anonymous, and one begins to long for the barking of a French police sergeant.

If only we could be like those migratory birds whose homeland changes with every season! It is certainly easier for a bird to fly where he wants than it is for us to take the train: there are so many formalities! And at least those birds don't have to carry around those "morals of the house" made up of our everyday habits—something that tempts us to be rather too hard on the morals of foreign countries, quite naturally different from our own.

It's the second time I've been to London, and I'm not pretending to be unveiling the whole of English life. You must excuse me if I am sometimes prejudiced, even banal; one slips too easily from one of these pitfalls into the other. Besides, have not all the most distinguished of our men of letters written about the smoggy atmosphere of London, the efficiency of its cabs, and the pretentious bad taste of its monuments?

I would like to disagree with one point raised by no less a person than Taine himself, and oft repeated by his disciples: namely, his denial of the existence of any idling loafers in London, for the sake of affirming their hard-working natures.[1]

Quelle erreur, mylord! How often these philosophers are no more grown up than *enfants terribles.* . . . There are certainly no idlers in the City, the part reserved exclusively for business, something that is carried out with an efficiency quite unknown in Paris. One must definitely not allow oneself to idle in the City, or else one will find oneself mowed down under the wheels of one of those innumerable gaily-colored omnibuses that so tirelessly traverse the metropolis. But everywhere else, thank God, people do take it easy. Only the English do so with great seriousness: they always look as if they have just completed some noble task or other. They never have the carefree air of these who stroll our boulevards or lounge on our benches.

It's all to do with the worry about "respectability": something common to every Englishman from M. Chamberlain right down to the alcoholic newsvendors. The English feel transports of delight when they read about all the dreadful affairs of the world in the papers; their hearts are filled with a feeling of moral superiority. "Honi soit qui mal y pense"—and it is not merely a question of awakening the painful conflicts—Waterloo or the Grand Prix.

I am writing these lines to you sitting by a window that looks out on to the darker reaches of the Thames (they assure me it is more pleasant further up, but I have no time to go). In front of me is an old man reading one of those tiny English newspapers. I don't know him, and he will never know me. . . . He might even be a subscriber to *Gil Blas* (just to make up for it). It all poses so many enigmas! Even our own Paul Bourget would not be able to solve them all![2] It sometimes tempts me to forget that I'm really here as a critic, but then, tomorrow will do! Then I will tell you of the splendors of the *Ring,* given under the musical direction of Dr. Hans Richter.

30 April 1903

I don't know what it is that makes the Anglo-Saxons superior, but among other things they do have Covent Garden. Now this theater has one special peculiarity: there, music is entirely at home. One is far less struck by the sumptuous décor than by the perfect acoustics, and the orchestra is huge and unfailingly pays attention. What is more, M. André Messager looks after the artistic side of things in the best possible taste, and nobody seems to be in the least surprised. How strange all this is: they actually think a musician can usefully run an opera house! Such positions are usually reserved for fools, or at least sticks-in-the-mud. But whatever the case, I had better not make any comparisons, for it would only confirm the poverty of our way of doing things and our national pride might suffer a nasty blow. . . . And we had better not command the trumpets of fame to proclaim the glory of our own Opéra, or at least we should mute them.

I have recently been present at performances of both *Das Rheingold* and *Die Walküre*. . . . It seems to me impossible to conceive of more perfect interpretations, and if one did have certain reservations about the scenery and some of the lighting effects, one is forced to take off one's hat to the genuinely artistic care with which everything is scrupulously carried out.

Dr. Richter conducted the first performance of the *Ring* in Bayreuth in 1876. At that time both his hair and his beard were auburn; since then he has gone bald. But behind those gold-rimmed spectacles his eyes still burn bright—the eyes of a prophet. And a prophet he really is—at least, as far as the Wagnerian religion is concerned. He can only cease to be so following the decision taken by Mme Cosima Wagner: to replace him with her own worthy but mediocre son Siegfried Wagner.

It's all very well for the family business, but deplorable as far as Wagner himself is concerned. For a man like Wagner you need someone like Richter, or Lévy, or Mottl. . . . They were a part of his life, of that boundless adventure that took him into the courts of kings. . . . Not to mention Liszt, from whom he constantly cribbed, although the old Abbé merely replied with a kindly, acquiescent smile.

There was something miraculous in Wagner, and this impurity in domination almost excuses his imperturbable vanity.

If Richter seems like a prophet when he conducts the orchestra, it is because he *is* Almighty God! . . . (And you can be sure that God would not attempt to conduct an orchestra without first having consulted Richter!)

While his right hand, armed only with an unpretentious little baton, ensures that the rhythm is secure, his left seems to be in a hundred places at once, telling everyone exactly what to do. How supple they are—these undulating, constantly changing hands. Then, just when one thinks that nobody could draw any more richness and sonority from the orchestra, he raises both hands at once and the orchestra begins to move through the music in leaps and bounds—as if through fields of corn—with such fury that the most stubbornly indifferent person would be swept straight off his feet. Yet all this pantomime remains within the bounds of discretion: it is never distracting to the eye, nor does it come between the music and the audience.

I tried in vain to meet this wonderful man, but he is wise enough to be careful to avoid being interviewed. Just for a moment I was able to watch him rehearsing Fafner, the poor dragon on whom Siegfried, that heroic brute, is about to try the sharpness of his sword. You will, I am sure, understand how I felt at seeing this conscientious old man, bent over a piano, carrying out the mundane duties of an anonymous chorus master. . . . Could one really have disturbed this noble man, just for the sake of extracting a few comments from him? It would have been as ridiculous as offering to extract one of his teeth.

It would seem that they skimmed the cream off all the German opera houses to find singers who were up to such a performance. One would really have to mention them all. . . . I would like to single out M. Van Dyck, who interpreted Loge in *Das Rheingold* with a fantastic sense of irony, and Siegmund in *Die Walküre* with passionate lyricism. M. Lieban conveyed all the underhanded slyness of that incredible dwarf Mime and still managed to sing with great beauty. These two men are great artists. . . . Mlle Zimmerman almost made us forget Mme Caron with her heartrending interpretation of Sieglinde. And as for the three Rhinemaidens—I only wish you could have heard them. . . .

The English listen with great attention, as if spellbound. If they are bored they never show it, although the hall is plunged into darkness while the performance is in progress so they can even sleep safely. In accordance with the best Wagnerian tradition, they applauded only at the end of each act and Dr. Richter himself seemed pleased when he went off, quite insensible to all the ovations, perhaps impatient for a recuperative beer.

In a subsequent letter, I will tell you of all the childlike magic that emerged from the *Ring;* I have yet to hear *Siegfried* and *Götterdämmerung.*

~NOTES

[1] The reference is to Taine's influential book *Notes sur Angleterre,* written in 1872. Often reprinted, it was the first of many books to testify to the rampant Anglophilia which flourished in Paris at the end of the last century. According to Adrien Remacle, "It was Taine who buried us up to the neck in the English aesthetic and the Pre-Raphaelites."

[2] Debussy was at one time on close terms with the poet and critic Paul Bourget, some of whose poems the composer had set. As a perceptive critic of Shakespeare, he probably encouraged Debussy's taste for the English playwright. Bourget's book, to which Debussy refers here, was his "Etudes anglaises," a collection of articles entitled *Etudes et portraits,* published in 1889. It included a lengthy discussion of Pre-Raphaelite art and poetry, to which Debussy had been strongly attracted at the time of his setting of Rossetti's poem, "The Blessed Damozel," when the Pre-Raphaelites were still largely unknown in France. It seems that Bourget was one of several Anglophile writers in Debussy's close circle. Another, not mentioned here, was Gabriel Mourey, author of a book translated into English as *Across the Channel: Life and Art in London.* Although he had no English, Debussy was well-prepared for his London visits.

GIL BLAS
8 May 1903

Berlioz and M. Gunsbourg

B E R L I O Z never had any luck! He had to put up with inadequate orchestras and some of the stupidest people of his day. But now an imaginative genius by the name of M. Gunsbourg, with the support of the Société des Grandes Auditions Musicales de France, has taken it upon himself to bolster up Berlioz's fading glory with a revival of *La Damnation de Faust* in an adaptation for the stage.

Whatever one's viewpoint, one cannot deny that Berlioz died without leaving precise indications as to how the work should be performed, and its aesthetics are somewhat dubious. Besides, to step into a dead man's shoes without any specific invitation seems to me to go beyond that special feeling of respect which we usually reserve for the dead. But apparently M. Gunsbourg's unfailing confidence in Berlioz's genius authorizes him to treat Berlioz as a brother and to carry out his wishes, probably communicated to him from the tomb. . . .

In doing this, M. Gunsbourg is propagating the dreadful custom that insists that all masterpieces breed a whole host of commentators, adapters, and bowdlerizers—a vast race of people who don't really seem to know what they are doing, except to surround these aforesaid masterpieces with a haze of wordy epithets and other verbiage.

Alas, it is not only Berlioz! We also have the famous Mona Lisa's smile, which for some strange reason is always labeled "mysterious." . . . Beethoven's *Choral* Symphony has been the subject of such extraordinary interpretations that this music, so fine and strong, was for a long time unapproachable to the general public. . . . Then there are also the complete works of Wagner. Well, they needed all their solidity to counteract the eagerly industrious hands of their would-be editors!

This kind of criticism has a literature all of its own. It is even a recognized profession with limitless possibilities, provided one never leaves it, for one has only to worry about criticizing others and thus one is immune from any dangerous criticism of oneself. Sometimes it can be a praiseworthy occupation, sometimes it merely covers up inadequacy. But with a little skill one can easily become famous at it.

Until now, Berlioz has somehow escaped this invasion. Only M. Jullien, in an admirably documented book, has piously spoken of him in terms of some kind of calvary, and M. Fantin-Latour has produced some imaginative lithographs inspired by his music. Moreover, Berlioz, because of his concern for color and for literary tags, was immediately adopted by the painters. One could even say in all seriousness that Berlioz has always been the favorite musician of those who know little about music. The professionals are alarmed by the liberties he takes with harmonies (they even call them his "gaucheries") and with his rambling forms. Are these the reasons why he has exerted precious little influence on modern music, making him to some degree unique? Except for Gustave Charpentier, I can scarcely think of anyone in France in whom one recognizes any of his influence, and even there it is only a slight, almost decorative influence, for Charpentier's music is entirely his own as far as fundamentals are concerned.

This brings me to say that Berlioz was never really a theatrical composer. Despite some undeniable gems in *Les Troyens* (a lyrical tragedy in two parts), its unbalanced proportions make performances impractical. And its effects are rather monotonous, not to say boring. . . . What is more, Berlioz brings almost no inventiveness to it. It recalls Gluck, whom he adored, and Meyerbeer, whom he hated. No, it is not here that we should look for the real Berlioz. It is in the purely orchestral music and in *L'Enfance du Christ*—perhaps his greatest work—not forgetting the *Symphonie fantastique* and the music for *Roméo et Juliette.*

But M. Gunsbourg was already on the lookout: "My dear Berlioz," he said, "you really understand very little! . . . If you were not a success in the theater it is because you were unfortunately not able to benefit from the fruits of my experience. . . . But now you are dead we can put the house in order. Listen! You wrote a dramatic legend, *La Damnation de Faust*. Not bad, not bad, but there isn't much life in it! How do you expect anyone to be interested in your 'Marche hongroise' when we don't even see the soldiers parading on the stage? . . . Then there is that 'Ballet des sylphes': pleasant enough music, but you will never be able to persuade me that a mere symphony orchestra is any substitute for a real ballerina! And that 'Course à l'âbime' is nothing if not terrifying, my friend. But you wait! I'll make it even more so! I'll divert all the rivers to make real live waterfalls, I'll fetch buckets of blood from the slaughterhouses to serve as rain, and the horses of Faust and Mephistopheles will wade through real corpses! What's more, you won't be able to meddle with any of it. You were such a crank when you were alive that I'm sure you would only spoil everything!"

This said, M. Gunsbourg set to work to make his drastic adaptation. In ploughing through *La Damnation,* he decided once and for all that this confounded Berlioz really didn't know what he was up to. "Too much music," he grumbled, "and how simplistic and lacking in continuity. I must add recitatives! Oh what a pity you're dead, but never mind, we'll manage!" So M. Gunsbourg managed without the help of Berlioz, doing the recitatives himself and altering the order of the scenes. And almost all this was for the sake of ballets or mimes! The result is that the work is a cross between a conjuring act and some of the attractions of the Folies-Bergère.

In Monte Carlo it might have been all right as it was. There, people don't go to listen to the music alone; having a nice afternoon is more important than that. All those globetrotters who make the place what it is wouldn't examine the music too closely, and the cosmopolitan young ladies would see it only as a pleasant accompaniment to their own charming smiles.

But for Paris, something better had to be done. It was here that the Société des Grandes Auditions stepped in: for the sake of their openmindedness they are willing to sacrifice everything. In this case they seem to me to have sacrificed the most fundamental good taste; their desire to teach France what good music is all about has led them rather beyond the pale, and the fashionable, I think, are more likely to be led astray than anyone, on account of their lack of education in such matters. The singers were excellent. They included M. Renaud, perhaps the only singer in existence who, with his infinite tact and good taste, could have given Mephistopheles enough verve to satisfy M. Gunsbourg. M. Alvarez and Mme Calvé are too famous not to have been perfect, even in *La Damnation*. God knows, though, the roles they played were for puppets.

There were two people who would not have been very pleased at all: first of all, Faust. What do you think—he was happily joined by M. Colonne, but he was astonished at having to fill the measures with pointless pieces of pantomime by which he vainly tried to make himself understood, where before he was used to remaining silent. Second, the music seemed to balk too; it was conscious sometimes of being too much and, at the same time, completely useless. It was so far from being theater music that it was, poor thing, ashamed to be heard or even to be a maladroit part of the scenery M. Gunsbourg was trying to impose upon it.

In the future, though, Monsieur Gunsbourg may sleep peacefully. He will have his bust placed face to face with that of Berlioz in the gardens at Monte Carlo. He will be quite at home there, and Berlioz will have no cause to complain.

Saint-Saëns's Henry VIII

At the Opéra: Henry VIII, *opera in five acts;*
libretto by L. Détroyat and Armand Silvestre;
music by Camille Saint-Saëns

N o w is the time for us to pay our respects to the revival the Opéra
has just given of *Henry VIII.*

It is, perhaps, the last historical opera of all time. At least, we must
hope so. In any case, it would be difficult to outdo Meyerbeer. That is
not to suggest that M. Saint-Saëns was wrong to write *Henry VIII,*
but he does lack that grandiloquent bad taste so characteristic of
Meyerbeer's genius. He is more of a musician than a man of the
theater, and he uses those facile effects that seem to be permitted
in the opera only as a last resort. What is more, he has a sincerity
Meyerbeer never had (*he* was a born demon, although it was in Berlin
in 1791). And if Henry VIII has to sing cavatinas that are rather too
sugary, believe me, it's because Saint-Saëns wanted them to be so and
understood why. Everybody knows that the most bloodthirsty tiger is
still capable of softening a child's heart. These all too sugary cavatinas are thus scrupulously based in historical fact, for the blood-
thirstiness of Henry VIII is well-known.

Saint-Saëns has been criticized for taking liberties in his music for
the stage. Naturally this is compared with his purely symphonic music,
which takes none. But then we must conclude that the symphonic
music has not gone in the direction we would have liked.

We seem to forget that Saint-Saëns, going right against the grain, makes a point of taking no liberties; when others demolish every-thing, he sees all the more reason to conserve it. He delights in using the forms left him by those he considers his masters, and he respects them so much that he doesn't consider it worth changing a thing. What more could one wish for? He has a gift of artistic clairvoyance rare in these times, for many change merely the name of things, but nothing deeper. Such conscientious workmanship must be proof of his artistic worth. (I seem to remember a fable of La Fontaine along these lines. . . .)

The revival of *Henry VIII* has had considerable success. It was given a very good performance. Words seem insufficient to describe the personality of Mlle Bréval. To say she was "superbly beautiful" or "a marvelous singer" really says nothing. "Words, words, words," as our dear old Hamlet said. But, among other things, she does have great musicianship and an instinctively right feeling for gesture; she found just the right nuances and gestures for the last act. Mme Heglon could not have better interpreted the part of Anne Boleyn: she sang with an ardent melancholy. Nobody knows how to "die on a note" the way she does. (Generally it's some insignificant little note where we least expect it.)

As for M. Delmas, his part couldn't have been drawn in bolder lines, and his voice had its customary steely richness. Fine here, but perhaps not best suited to the sweet tones of a madrigal. But really very fine. All the rest was quite as it should have been. It is customary for first performances to be brilliant.

MUSICA

May 1903

A Consideration of the Prix de Rome
from a Musical Point of View

T H E R E are many things that can be said about the Prix de Rome.
First, one could say it was stupid—an opinion usually put in the form
of a question: "Well then, monsieur, would you kindly tell me why on
earth musicians are sent to Rome?" To which one replies that among
certain people the Prix de Rome has become something of a supersti-
tion: to have won it, or not to have won it, answers the question of
whether one has any talent or not. Even if it is not infallible, at least
it is a useful standard by which the general public can easily judge.

Unfortunately, this argument falls rather flat when we admit that
M. Camille Saint-Saëns, the official leader of the young French school,
never won the Prix de Rome. Nor did M. Vincent d'Indy, the
chief elect of a still younger school. . . . Without discussing the
relative merits of these two men, one is forced to admit that they are
"representative." To see them excluded from the honors board makes
one think that there must be something a little vindictive about the
way the prizes are distributed, for more than anyone else they would
seem to have deserved it.

To tell you the truth, I am not in the best position to criticize this
institution. I may well seem to be turning my nose up at something of
which I, among many others, have partaken. For I myself won the
Prix de Rome and have myself sat at the dining table of the Villa
Medici. If you can call it that! In the refectory there, one paid 1
franc 25 for a diet that ruined one's stomach for life! (I still shudder

when I think of a certain dish, which they rather pretentiously used to call "roba dolce" and in which the taste of gasoline went thunderously with that of soured cream—making our youthful pride at having won the Prix de Rome a bit sad!) But let us leave these purely material considerations aside! In any case, they were unworthy of us young men who were supposed to be too much in love with Art to worry about our physical well-being. . . . There are worthier reasons for discussing this institution, and although they have frequently been spoken of, even in the Chambre des Députés, until now it has had little effect.

Believe me when I say that I do consider it a good thing in that it makes it easy for young people to travel peacefully to Italy and Germany. But why restrict their voyages to these countries? And why this ridiculous diploma? It makes them seem like prize farm animals. Moreover, the cool way in which the academic gentlemen of the Institut decide which of these young people shall be artists seems to me to be strikingly naïve. What do they know about it? How can they be so confident about controlling other people's destinies—something in which there is bound to be an element of chance?

Music is a mysterious mathematical process whose elements are a part of Infinity. It is allied to the movement of the waters, to the play of curves described by the changing breezes. Nothing is more musical than a sunset! For anyone who can be moved by what they see can learn the greatest lessons in development here. That is to say, they can read them in Nature's book—a book not well enough known among musicians, who tend to read nothing but their own books about what the Masters have said, respectfully stirring the dust on their works. All very well, but perhaps Art goes deeper than this.

Let us return to the Prix de Rome. This competition is judged on the strength of a work called a "cantata," an awkward hybrid form that unfortunately shows up all the worst faults of operatic writing. Or else it is a "symphony with singers," a really institutional form; I wouldn't advise anyone to admit that he has composed one of these. With such pieces it is impossible to tell if the composers even know their craft as musicians, let alone judge between them. We all know the procedure: a few months before the competition, the entrants are led on to the course—rather like horses for the Grand Prix. Someone looks up the winning formula in all the previous prize-winning cantatas, and that's all there is to it. All to the great delight of the assembled company, the parents and so on! And one receives an embrace from M. Théo Dubois into the bargain! That's all there is to the Prix de Rome, for what it is worth.

If they really have to bestow some title upon one, could they not make do with a "certificate of higher studies"? But not this "certificate of imagination," which is worse than useless and in any case unreliable. It can even be dangerous, for it is because of the official privileges bestowed upon one for having won the Prix de Rome that we hear so much bad music. Families who are anxious about the future of their children will find comfortable words here—all the more so because the engineering profession is so crowded these days. Besides, this kind of overcultivation has the severe disadvantage of encouraging young musicians to neglect pure music; this wretched "cantata" whets their appetite for the theater rather too early. (And in many cases their later theatrical pieces are no more than frantic reworkings of their early cantatas.) Hardly are they back from Rome than they are already in search of a libretto, overtaken with a feverish desire to follow in the footsteps of their forebears. Renan said somewhere (unless it was M. Barrés) that it is merely pretentious and quite disastrous to write before one is forty. This could also be said of dramatic music, which, unless one is an exceptional genius, is really of any value only when one is approaching middle age.

When people complain about how few symphonies France has in comparison to other countries, it is perhaps the Prix de Rome that should be blamed. If I were good at statistics I could quite easily demonstrate that almost no symphonic music bears any kind of official stamp of approval whatsoever. And when it does, it often does not turn out to be quite what we expect. Take the illustrious example of M. Massenet, for example: did we not quite recently see him making his debut in symphonic music when he had his piano concerto played at the Conservatoire? One might say, a little disrespectfully, that it should return to the pages of *Manon*. But this concerto was probably no worse than any other; it's just that Massenet is not inclined toward pure music, and he will never be as surely successful in it as he has been in the theater.

As for chamber music, Mozart, Beethoven, Schumann, etc., wrote plenty. That's a good thing, too, for the modern repertoire can be counted upon the fingers of one hand! It seems to recoil before the heavy burden bequeathed by the past. Not that there are not some perfectly good modern pieces, but they are too little encouraged. Now I am speaking neither of the sonata in general nor the piano sonata in particular, for in this last case my comments are untrue. But we really have only one piano sonata representative of our time—that of Paul Dukas. Because of its grand conception it immediately takes its place next to the sonatas of Beethoven. Its first performance was an important event, and it provided a real intellectual challenge for the amateurs.

It must be confessed that this type of music demands a willingness on the part of the listener to be converted. One has to be ready to have one's peace of mind dashed to smithereens! It is difficult to listen to and seems to do nothing for you. So it's good-bye to all the privileges of a composer, good-bye to the flattering handshake of the director! Such composers must realize that they are no more than rather esoteric specialists whose companions look upon them with condescension, which, in the event of success, will turn to scorn.

But let us return again to the Prix de Rome. If for a moment we agree to this "certificate of higher studies," to be awarded only after continuing assessment of students' work, and proving that they know all about music and its forms, let these young prizewinners be sent to travel across Europe, let them choose themselves a master or, if they can find one, some brave man who will teach them that Art is not necessarily found in state-assisted institutions. Let them be told that Art must be loved for all the visions it provides, and despite the misery it creates. And let them learn that it cannot be counted upon to provide one with a "job." Let us try to recapture the old traditions of the time when artists were proud of their masters and capable of devotion to one another. If they did have to fight for the cause of Art, they did so without the bitterness that is so characteristic of these modern times.

Despite all this, one cannot but be moved when one remembers the wonderful trees surrounding the Villa Medici, fading away into the gentle violet of the Umbrian hills. The architecture of the loggia too, with its columns of purely decorative marble, brings back countless memories. It seems to me that without too much cost this setting could have been used to build one of those universities of which Oxford is so proud. This wouldn't have been a bad idea and it might have provided excellent facilities, for those at the Villa Medici leave much to be desired. They do not make one proud to be French. Such a setting would perhaps have been more beautiful than Oxford itself, and think how much of the splendor of the past it would have preserved! The Villa Medici, dominating Rome in all its imposing beauty, should have been a vibrant intellectual center for all the arts; one should have gone there full of a confident, youthful delight. Unfortunately, for many it is no more than a place where one has "done time." There, the drills are replaced by assignments which do not by any means prove that one has been working hard.

A sad conclusion, which only serves to underline the uselessness of the Prix de Rome, at least insofar as achieving a kind of art which will testify to the beauty of our age.

GIL BLAS
1 June 1903

Impressions of the Ring in London

I T is hard to imagine what mental strain four evenings of the *Ring* can cause—even to the strongest of spirits. One imagines the leit-motivs dancing quadrilles with each other after a while. (Siegfried's horn seems to be doing some very strange dances with Wotan's spear, while the curse motif appears to be dancing obsessively on its own.)

But it's much more than obsessive: its total possession! One no longer feels in control of oneself, one becomes nothing more than a moving leitmotiv marching through the *Ring*.

From now on we shall no longer be hidebound by the customary forms of address. If we want to speak to our fellow mortals we can accost them with Valkyrie cries. "Hoyotoho! . . . Hejaha! . . Hoy-ohei! . . ." How gay that is! Hoyohei! . . . And the old newspaper-man on the corner of the street would shout, "Hoiaho!"

My lord! How intolerable these men in helmets and animal skins become by the fourth evening. . . . Remember they never appear unless accompanied by their damnable leitmotiv, and there are even those who sing it! It's rather like those silly people who hand you their visiting cards and then lyrically recite key information they con-tain. Most annoying to hear everything twice!

And what are we to make of the psychological function of the orchestra? It imposes endless commentaries upon us, and all they really have to comment upon is the story of some silly ring that is lost and found again. It's like a game of hunt-the-slipper! Not to mention the way in which it is used to underline Wotan's inability to under-stand anything that is going on around him; for this king of the Gods is certainly the most stupid of them all. He spends all his time telling a story that would be immediately understood by even the silliest of those dwarfs who huddle themselves together in the factories of the Nibelung. All he can do is to brandish his spear, tend the fire, and throw everything into disarray by making irreparable gaffes. But then no doubt some people would maintain that these things are necessary in order to fill four evenings. A gigantic labor, say the hardened Wagnerites. A superhuman effort of incredible vanity trying at the same time for both quantity and quality! It is certainly an effort, which is unfortunately spoiled by that peculiarly German need to keep hammering the same point home; the fear of not being understood weighs the piece down with a lot of needless repetition.

For the most part, the characters of the *Ring* move in an unfathomable sea of pride, never considering it worthwhile to justify their actions. They all come and go, killing each other off in a way that bears no relation whatsoever to real life. In this way, in *Götterdämmerung,* Hagen takes revenge for his evil dwarf of a father by killing off Siegfried, but not one of those present at this dreadful act (all clad in their animal skins) so much as considers killing Hagen as the logical act of retribution. What brutes they all are! And in this same opera Brünnhilde, the fearless virgin, allows herself to be deceived by Hagen and Gunther as if she were some innocent little girl at her first communion. It really isn't worth being the daughter of a god! Then she falls in love with Siegfried, the military hero who is so proud of his fine suit of armor. He's something of a brother to her (Wotan's early misconduct has meant that all the characters in this opera are more or less brothers and sisters). But would she really have avenged herself as she does, betraying him in such a shameful way? Would the fact that she has fallen from a state of grace really maker her behave like a naughty little girl? And when the time comes for Siegfried's death, some divine inconsistency on the part of the gods allows her the opportunity to declare herself the only one worthy of flinging herself on his body and of making the necessary funeral arrangements. The assembled company (still clad in their animal skins) could never understand Siegfried's high-flown opinions. He lacked nothing but a little in the way of worldly education. He had previously been kept busy slaying dragons, listening to the birds singing, and so on. As if she wasn't herself responsible for his death and all its terrible consequences . . . Hoyotoho! Bravo! . . . Hoyohei! Well done!

As I told you before, the *Ring* does have a childish magical side to it. From one angle it's very serious, but we also have to contend with dragons singing, birds giving valuable advice, bears, a horse, and two crows—all intervening in a charming fashion. Oh . . . and I almost forgot the two black sheep. From another point of view this blend of savage humanity with divine savagery does cause problems: perhaps one is simply meant to wallow in all this make-believe without worrying about the occasional intrusion of human fallibility—something that weakens nearly all the heroes of the *Ring*. For heaven's sake, be gods, be magical, but spare us these conventional and useless lectures about the human condition!

This is all criticism about the dramatic side of things, though; they are not really my concern. I would prefer to assure you that there are things of great beauty in the *Ring*. Among all the hours of boredom (when one really does not know which to grasp—the music or the action), the most beautiful things appear. Passages quite beyond criticism and as irresistible as the sea. . . . Sometimes they last for scarcely a minute, often longer. I won't do you the injustice of listing them, for they might not be to your taste, but it must be admitted that there is something for every taste in the *Ring*.

In conclusion it should be said that such a huge work as the *Ring* is really beyond criticism. It is an architectural monument whose bold lines lose themselves in infinity. Its rather too sumptuous grandeur thwarts any attempt at appreciating its proportions as a whole, but one cannot help but feel that if even the slightest little stone were moved in this great edifice, the whole thing would collapse. For example, when the final catastrophe—the drowning at Valhalla—takes place at the end of *Götterdämmerung,* the gods on Mount Olympus are still smiling imperturbably down on the vain efforts of these modern-day Prometheans. (I don't much like that last phrase, but applied to Wagner it would seem to be admirable!)

In these last two operas the performances attained still greater heights of perfection. Mme Lafler Burckhard sang Brünnhilde with a fine solid tone, while her arms testified to the excellency of the

"Sandow method."[1] Mme Kirkby-Lunn made a wonderful Waltraute. Thanks to her the endless duet between Waltraute and Brünnhilde was almost tolerable, so convincing and ardent was the way she sang it.

M. Krauss is a young and superb Siegfried, freely exercising his hair-raising vocal prowess and showing off his irresistibly masculine biceps. As for M. Lieban, of whom I've already spoken, he turned the character of Mime into a creation that blended the art of the singer with that of the comedian in such unusually perfect proportions that it leaves one at a loss for words.

Richter was more Richter than ever. . . . It is he above all who ensures that the whole performance is beautiful; nobody can be anything but profoundly thankful to him. "He has taken his place among the Gods," and Wagner would have been well pleased. I will no doubt astonish many people when I tell you that they are just as enthusiastic as at Bayreuth, so we could send a bouquet of edelweiss to both Richter and Messager.

As a reward for having been so well-behaved during the *Ring,* I took an evening off to visit the Empire,[2] the London equivalent of our Folies-Bergère. It is a luxurious, comfortable place, and, what's more, very English. The musical god of this establishment is M. Léopold de Wenzel, famous in Paris for his passionate waltzes and for his development of the subtle spiritual side of dancing.

During one of this master's dances—in which "spirituality" seemed to me to be too often replaced by the close-order drilling of strictly disciplined Pomeranian regiments—I amused myself by imagining what the atmosphere of the dance should really be like. How necessary it is never to state the action in any precise way. It should be done only in the language of ballet itself, a language of mystery whose charm and symbolism is the winged grace of a dancer's leg. When her whole body is filled with rhythmic tension, this leg becomes as delicate as a flower and as tender as a woman.

The fluttering of tiny feet, whether impatient or furious, can more clearly describe love or hate than all the artificial gestures usually associated with these feelings. To this one should add a scenery composed of changing lights, rather than one composed of precise lines. Let music be the mistress, let *her* enhance the scenery! As if under a spell, she can mirror the silent rustling of gauze frocks, imitate their silken sounds. . . . But forgive me! The ballet has long since been finished, and we now have a conjurer who has produced both the English and the French flags from his top hat, the one amicably fraternizing with the other.[3] Then there is a young girl who speaks as she sings, or sings as she speaks, I'm not sure which. A charming art form of which we have an equivalent in Paris—in those people who can neither sing nor speak.

The orchestra at the Empire could have performed the *Ring* quite as well as the music of M. de Wenzel. And with this remark, in honor of the English, I end my letter to you. I am writing it on the train that takes me back to Paris, and at this moment I am in Normandy, which is clothed in blossoms of delicate white and looks like a Japanese print. . . . If you wish, I might add that this is all to the credit of the French.

ぺ*NOTES*

[1] An allusion to Eugène Sandow (1867–1925), professional strong man and exponent of physical culture.

[2] The Empire Music Hall, noted especially for its excellent orchestra.

[3] Edward VII was at this time in France to commemorate the anniversary of the Entente Cordiale.

William Chaumet's La Petite Maison

Opéra-Comique: La Petite Maison, *comic opera in three acts;
libretto by Alexandre Bisson and Georges Docquois;
music by William Chaumet*

L A S T night, the Opéra-Comique lived up to its name better than it
has done for a long time. During the evening, the smell of powdered
wigs, the malicious intrigues of the courtiers, friends of the Regent
Philippe d'Orléans, the case of Law's bankruptcy, took us back to that
time and to those worn-out styles which those people who are against
Progress continue to find charming. Others were so vexed by it that
they considered M. A. Carré to have made a grave mistake in encouraging this return to a decadent past.

It seems obvious to me that *La Petite Maison* really comes under
the heading of "grand operetta." Because of this, it is perhaps not so
well-suited to the Opéra-Comique. But then I suppose we have to put
on something for those who are fatigued by too much music, and for
those who take "symbols" as a personal insult.

Apart from a few skillful pieces of pastiche, the music of M.
Chaumet is unfortunately rather too ready to hark back to the 1840s
—a disastrous time, notorious for its glorification of Adolphe Adam
and a mediocre musician whom I like to call Clapisson!

The story is about a man named Pichon, jeweler to the Regent,
with whom he falls out. Then a certain Chevalier de Fargès falls
madly in love with the beautiful Mme Pichon, and he persuades the
honest Pichon to adopt the dissolute morals of the time—the only

way, he tells him, to get back onto good terms with the Regent. To facilitate this, he lends Pichon his own "petite maison"—with his former mistress thrown in—and organizes a *fête galante* during which his valet Jacquemin secretly dresses up as the Regent.

Naturally, he arranges for Mme Pichon to surprise her poor husband in the act, she having agreed to receive the Chevalier de Fargès's advances only on the condition that she see her husband's debauchery with her very own eyes. She sees as much as she needs; but in the third act the treachery of the Chevalier is discovered because Jacquemin, the valet, betrays him. Mme Pichon, as good-natured as she is pretty, forgives her husband, and the Regent does his jeweler the great honor of paying him a visit, which conveniently rounds off the play.

For this simple plot, M. Chaumet has written music that, as I have already said, has decided tendencies to look backwards. Despite this, one can listen to it with no fear of either fatigue or surprise, except perhaps for the unawareness of M. Chaumet, who seems to be completely ignorant of the fact that we are living in 1903. Because he does have undeniable skill as far as orchestration is concerned, and in putting scenes together, one cannot but regret that he didn't put aside his respect for M. A. Adam.

The performance was charming. M. Fugère, who played the goodhearted Pichon, is a skilled singer and a perfect comedian, and at times he gave exactly the right expression to this simple, ordinary man. He showed a rare gift for combining the musical with the dramatic. As for Mme Marguerite Carré, she made a lovable Mme Pichon, and one realized why the jeweler was so devotedly in love with her, this jewel more precious than all his gems. . . . Mlle Mastio gave all the charm of her voice and personality to the part of Florence, the forsaken but obliging girl friend of the Chevalier de Fargès. Mlle Tiphaine sang Claudine and showed herself to be as clever a comedian as she is a singer. M. Clément, whom we have not heard for some time, made us realize how pleased we were to see him again in the role of the Chevalier de Fargès; he sang as well and was as elegant as one could have wished. M. Delvoye, in the part of Dominique, Pichon's valet, threw himself into all his master's misadventures with great verve and undeniable comedy. There remains only to congratulate the rest of the performers, including the always praiseworthy M. Luigini.

All in all, if this performance tolled funeral bells for the old Opéra-Comique, it did so in a happy way, so I don't really see how one can hold anything against M. Chaumet.

Impressions of a Prix de Rome

T H E Prix de Rome is a kind of game, or rather it is a national sport. One learns the rules in particular places, the Conservatoire or the Ecole des Beaux Arts, etc.

The game is played once a year, and it is preceded by a rigorous training. The referees are members of the Institut; rather curiously, MM. W. Bouguereau and J. Massenet are always judges, whether the game is being played in music, painting, sculpture, architecture, or drawing. Nobody has yet thought of including dancing, although it would be a logical addition, for Terpsichore is not the least among the nine muses.

The happiest memory I have of the Prix de Rome is far from all this. . . . It happened on the Pont des Arts, where I was awaiting the result of the competition, watching with delight the coming and going of the *bateaux-mouches* on the Seine. I was quite relaxed, and wasn't thinking about anything to do with Rome, for the pleasant sunlight was playing upon the rippling water, with that special charm which keeps the idlers on the bridges for hours on end, making them the envy of all Europe. All at once someone tapped me on the shoulder and breathlessly said, "You have won the prize." Now I do not know if you are going to believe this, but my heart sank. I had a sudden vision of boredom, and of all the worries that inevitably go together with any form of official recognition. I felt I was no longer free.

But all this soon passed, for that halo of future glory, of which the

Prix de Rome gives one an intimation, is irresistible. So when I arrived at the Villa Medici in 1885, I pretty well thought myself the darling of the gods, as the ancient legends would have had it.

M. Cabat, a reputable landscape painter as well as a distinguished man of the world, was director of the Académie de France in Rome in those days. He was never concerned with the students except in an administrative way—a charming man. But a M. E. Hébert soon replaced him. A recent interview tells us that this eminent painter has remained a thoroughbred Roman from head to toe. His narrow-mindedness was proverbial, at least as far as anything to do with Rome or the Villa Medici was concerned, for he would allow no criticism of either. I still remember the time I complained about living in a room the walls of which were painted a green that seemed to recede as you moved toward them—a room popularly known among the students as the "Etruscan tomb." But M. Hébert would have none of it, and added that, if need be, one could sleep in the ruins of the Coliseum. The sacred privilege of breathing the "historic atmosphere" would more than compensate for the risk of catching a fever.

Hébert adored music, but he didn't like the music of Wagner at all. At this time I was Wagnerian to the point of forgetting the most fundamental good manners. I would never have thought for one moment that I would come around to where I almost agreed with this dogmatic old man! He had sifted through the emotional effects of Wagner's music very carefully, while we scarcely knew what they were, or how they might be used.

So the life of a *pensionnaire* begins, a mixture of that of a cosmopolitan hotel and an independent school, with a barracklike discipline. . . . I clearly remember the dining room, with its line of portraits of holders of the Prix de Rome, past and present. They stretch right up to the ceiling so one cannot see them very clearly, and in truth, they are never so much as mentioned. On every face the same expression: sadness and uneasiness. After several months, the vast number of these portraits, all the same size, makes the beholder feel that they are all really of the same person, repeated ad infinitum!

The conversations that go on around that dining table are very similar to those which take place at an ordinary meal. It would be vain to think that lively aesthetic discussions are held, or even deep thoughts about the Old Masters. But if the Villa Medici is rather mediocre as far as art is concerned, one soon learns about the more practical side of life there, for one becomes very self-conscious about the kind of figure one will cut when one returns to Paris. . . . Contact with the Romans themselves was almost nonexistent; their society is closed, and not very welcoming to *pensionnaires,* whose youthful and very French independence mingles poorly with that Roman chilliness.

There remains one last alternative: travel across Italy. But even that has limited possibilities, for one cannot discover as much as one would like, because of the lack of contact within the towns through which one passes. And, you know, this contact could be easily enough established if only someone would think about it. Meanwhile one makes do with buying photographs; the patience of the young ladies in the postcard trade is limitless. And so are their smiles!

Without wishing to criticize the Prix de Rome, it must be admitted that it is an institution rather lacking in foresight. What I mean by that is that we heartlessly abandon very nice young people, giving them a complete freedom that they do not know how to use. As soon as they have agreed to the terms governing the trip of "those bound for Rome," they are at once exempt from all further responsibility. When they arrive in Rome they don't know very much—and hardly anything about what they are supposed to be doing—and despite the complete change in surroundings we expect them to find out for themselves how much hard work is necessary for the artistic spirit to develop. It's impossible! And anyone who reads the annual report on the students will be surprised at its severity. But it's not the students' fault that their aesthetic sensibilities are somewhat disordered; it is more the fault of those who send them to this country, where everyone talks about Pure Art but where the students are left to interpret it as they please.

Now I am not pressing for arbitrary management, but could we not find men capable of talking about art in a broader way, who would become older and wiser friends to the students, rather than stuffy old professors of aesthetics? They could point out, in a friendly fashion, not so much the way along which these young people ought to proceed, but rather the way in which the Great Masters proceeded—the masters of a past to which those who are preparing the future are bound to be responsible. And lastly, they could perhaps give them that love of art of which nobody speaks about any longer, but of which, in a confused and interested way, they are aware. . . .

That will never be. For it is only the names of French institutions that ever change. There is much to be said for agreeing with those who want the Prix de Rome abolished, although one doesn't really know what one would put in its place. Perhaps the idea of allowing young ladies to compete is a worthwhile one. The result would be marriages from which would be born a generation of artists possessing that double soul of which Shakespeare wrote. Unless Nature, in her strange way, made them businessmen or ardent collectors. But in any case, the French sensibility could not but profit by it.

The Balance Sheet of Music in 1903

I T would be fruitless to pretend that there are not great difficulties
to be encountered, as well as things of great interest to be found,
when we take stock of the musical scene in France today. Our approach should be a learned one: we should consider these matters
with a certain objectivity, for an open-minded point of view is in-
valuable if we wish to be quietly assured, rather than authoritarian, in
our judgments.

Such an approach will certainly not come easily to me. . . . I love
music too much to speak of it in anything but an involved way. Will
I be able to prevent that little particle of subjective opinion from
getting into my arguments? Will it still tend to get in, no matter how
resolutely one tries, and can it sometimes cause one to ignore the most
straightforward, simple reason? I dare to think not, for those devoted
to Art are irretrievably in love with her, and, besides, it is impossible
to know how feminine music is. Perhaps that explains the frequent
chastity of men of genius.

Having said this to excuse myself in advance, let us proceed to examine
the Opéra without further ado. (It is not, strictly speaking, the best of
our theaters, but it is the most celebrated.) They do a lot of "reviving"
there, if I may be permitted to put it like that: revival of *La Statue,*
grand opera buffa; revival of *Henry VIII,* grand historical opera.
There was even talk of reviving *La Juive,* but the person best suited
for the title role was prevented from singing at the last moment because
of a prior engagement—in prison! I will not mention the first per-

formance of *Pagliacci* because there are some funny stories connected with it, and they are rather beyond the bounds of good manners. Nor will I mention *Bacchus,* a ballet by Mr. A. Duvernay, because I didn't hear it. In any case, these two belong to 1902.

So it appears they have done little work at the Opéra, but then perhaps they do have "off" years. I don't know. I have already criticized in this very paper what I think is bad about the way things are done at the Opéra: there is far too much division of labor, and they are too much concerned with keeping up the old traditions. I suppose it's nice for them to be more royal than the royalty, but then they should at least have a king, a real one, capable of making final decisions. However, everybody knows that the Republic of France does not care in the least. . . . If, at one of the recent performances of *Die Walküre,* the "fire scene" suddenly turned into one of those *quadrilles réalistes* that they dance at the Moulin-Rouge, do you think the Republic would put its Phrygian bonnet on back to front? . . . I'm rather afraid not. There are still people, even in Parliament, who hold the opinion that too much money is given to our opera houses.

Where is the logic in it? It is certainly not in the economic interests of the country. If the Opéra were richer, either in performers or repertoire, it would be bound to attract more foreigners to Paris. But, you see, they are generally better off at home! And you should hear the strange ways and the Anglo-Belgian irony with which they express their satisfaction with the place! It is therefore of prime importance that we not be stingy in supporting the Opéra: the minister of finance himself would assure you that it would be a sound investment.

For the end of the year, the Opéra promises us *L'Etranger* by Vincent d'Indy; *Le Fils de l'étoile* by Camille Erlanger, and even the return of M. Alvarez. That is more than enough reason for us to be patient, content that the old operas are resting in peace.

But let us move on to the Opéra-Comique. There we find a hive of industry, as methodical and organized as any factory, where hard work is going on on every floor! They revive the old comic operas: M. Albert Carré still has a weakness for Adolphe Adam's *Le Toréador* as much as he does for Verdi's *La Traviata.* That brings us no closer to the time when we can expect revivals of *Le Nozze di Figaro* and *Der Frei-*

schütz, works from which we could learn a great deal; whereas *Le Toréador* and other similar works merely remind us that French music went through some dreadful periods. Note that I am not asking that we should perform only the younger composers: that's a war cry which has been yelled far too often, and its echoes are now so tired that they refuse to echo any more! What's more, the title "young composer" is generously applied to people over sixty, and will soon fall into a justifiable disuse.

So let us put on revivals, but let us make sure that they will do good to the cause of art, and most of all to the French tradition.

M. Albert Carré can do just as he pleases at the Opéra-Comique: the public listens and the artists are on his side, two things that do not often make for a good administration. He should remember that such a state of affairs may not last very long. One composer whom I do not know how to recommend strongly enough is Rameau. He is almost a "young composer," for his century is one that has remained dormant for a long time. He wrote *Les Indes galantes;* and while one couldn't pretend it was great operetta, like *Muguette* or *La Petite Maison* (the latest works put on by Carré), it makes up for that by the elegant way in which it is written, and by its moderation in the use of the sentimental—ideals as much forgotten as the name of Rameau. He suffered much the same fate as Watteau: he died, and the years passed in silence, deliberately maintained by his colleagues, who knew very well what they were doing. Now, the name of Watteau shines with a halo of glory, and no period of painting, however self-important, will overshadow the greatest, the most moving genius of the eighteenth century; in Rameau we have his perfect musical counterpart. Isn't it about time we accorded him that place which he alone has the right to fill, instead of obliging French music to turn toward heavy cosmopolitan traditions that inhibit the natural development of her genius?

Apropos of this cosmopolitanism, I would like to point out just how weak-minded we are on this subject. We waver between Leoncavallo and Puccini and only then are we happy. And what do we find in them? An almost complete imitation of the more famous of our own masters. . . . What's more, they reach almost transalpine heights of indulgence—not without charm, but does that really suffice?

Then there's the Russian spirit. . . . Is that found only in Tol-stoy, Dostoevsky, and Gorki? Are we not forgetting musicians of the caliber of Moussorgsky, Borodin, Rimsky-Korsakov? We almost com-pletely ignore their works for the theater, and it is those which contain the aural expression of the very essence of the Russian spirit (some-thing of which we are so envious)—magnified because it's opera. I know that it is easier to publish a book than it is to put on an opera, but would it not be interesting to some people to have some friendly exchanges in this field? Despite the entente, few modern French operas are put on in Russia—a just response to our inertia.

There is also the German spirit. We are lacking as much interest in it as we are wanting in sympathy. As far as it is concerned, we are arrested at Wagner. But that in itself is enough, and we have certainly not digested it yet. Our music is played a lot in Germany, though, and it is only polite that we should reciprocate, even if the young Germans are not so very interesting. (This last remark should give some people an indulgent swell of nationalistic pride!)

I won't speak of the other "spirits" because we would never have time to finish. Perhaps we are about to discover a young musician from Greenland, whose polar operas will make the mutinous young seals tremulous with ecstasy!

All these remarks could just as well be applied, without much modification, to the Sunday concerts. For, curiously enough, these tend to turn into *"théâtres blancs"* where one hears theatrical music stripped of its natural décor, which is sadly replaced by dinner jackets and evening dress. Soon they won't be symphonic at all. All things considered, though, it is still there that one hears the music that is the least encumbered by bad taste.

To conclude, let us remain French. Let us hope that we will come to like music a little less, if only so that we might come to love it a little more. Otherwise, music will suffer the same fate as the girl who was dancing on the Pont du Nord: "She loved dancing so much that she died of it."

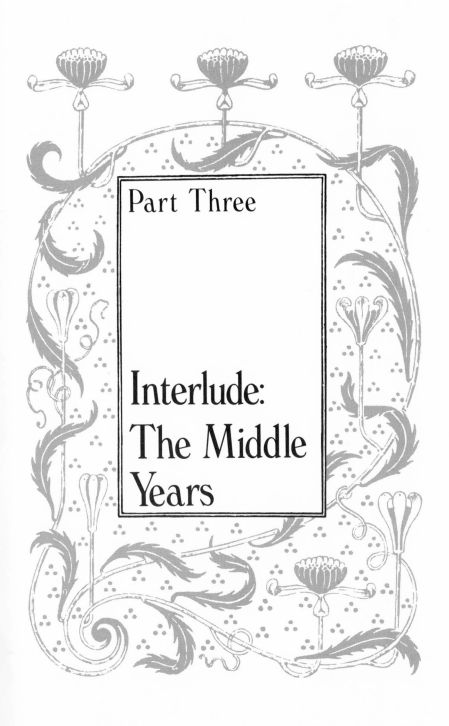

Part Three

Interlude:
The Middle
Years

It was in 1906, after some three years' rest from criticism, that Debussy announced the "death" of M. Croche to Louis Laloy, who, with Robert Godet, suggested a published collection of some of the earlier articles from *Gil Blas* and *La Revue blanche*. This interim group of articles, before the final sequence in the review *SIM*, is, on the whole, a reworking of old ideas, brief commissioned articles that contain little that has not been hinted at before. This is not to say that the articles are without interest; indeed, the two articles on Rameau are the best exposition of Debussy's enthusiasm for this composer, and the touching tribute to Mary Garden is unique in the insight it gives into the creation of *Pelléas*. One suspects journalistic intervention in the examination of music and poetry, but the composer's singling out of Henri de Régnier shows us his high opinion for the work of this poet, who was among his circle of friends. Like Laforgue, Régnier was an admired poet whom Debussy never set to music in song form, but he had indicated, in an early version of the orchestral *Nocturnes,* the influence of Régnier, whose *Scènes au crépuscule* were to have provided the title and framework of a still earlier version of these pieces.

With the exception of the two articles in Paris dailies and the final article on Rameau, all the articles appeared in the magazine *Musica*. Unlike Debussy's former journalistic territory, this was a specialist magazine, international though not yet so erudite as the bulletin of the future Société de Musique, itself the forerunner of the learned musicological magazine. From the outset it seems that Debussy had been reluctant to contribute to such journals, and writing to Laloy he admitted seeing no place for M. Croche amongst specialists. Hence the intermittence and brevity of his occasional contributions.

Three journalistic interviews of special interest have been included in this chapter. The first, from *Harper's Weekly,* is in its original English form, and has never been reprinted. The second, from *Le Figaro* of 14 February 1909, concerns the composer's appointment as member of the advisory committee to the Paris Conservatoire, a task he appears to have approached with enthusiasm, although it is difficult to assess his involvement with the institution at this stage. The third interview is from a Budapest evening paper, and was not traced in time for the Gallimard edition of this book. Thanks to the researches of François Lesure, it has recently been republished in French.[1] The latter part of the interview (where the interviewer's comments and questions are omitted) draws some interesting statements from Debussy on his two projected operas based on tales of Poe, works he obviously held in the highest esteem but that, perhaps because of their importance, he never completed. Most striking is the emphasis Debussy places on the contrasts between Maeterlinck and Poe, whom he considers to be diametrical opposites. Today we tend to view them rather as opposite sides of the same coin; certainly they inhabited overlapping spheres. Maeterlinck had been strongly influenced by the tales of Poe, and certain scenes in *Pelléas,* as well as passages in *La Princesse Maleine,* strikingly recall Poe (for example, the subterranean scenes in Debussy's opera). Reading between the lines, one realizes how the tales of Poe entered an area of Debussy's imagination close to that of *Pelléas,* demanding to be explored.

⚬➤ *NOTE*

[1] In *Cahiers Debussy,* Bulletin du Centre de Documentation Claude Debussy, no. 1 (Geneva, 1974).

MUSICA
July 1906

Apropos of Charles Gounod

MANY people with no vested interest in the matter—that is to say, not musicians—ask themselves why the Opéra persists in performing *Faust*. There are several reasons why, the best of which is that Gounod's art represents a moment in the French sensibility. Whether one likes it or not, these facts cannot be forgotten.

With regard to *Faust,* many eminent musical writers have reproached Gounod for having misrepresented Goethe's ideas. But these same people never bother to notice that Wagner also perhaps falsified the character of Tannhäuser, who in the original legend was nothing like the repentant little fellow Wagner made of him. His staff, burned in memory of Venus, would never have blossomed again. Gounod is perhaps to be forgiven because he is French, but Tannhäuser and Wagner are both German, so for them there is no excuse.

We are fond of so many things in France that music concerns us but little. There are, however, some fine people who show all the signs of being musicians, listening to music every day. But they never write music themselves; they merely encourage others. That is how a school is usually created. Do not speak of Gounod to such people, for they will only heap scorn upon you, drawing support from their present gods (who have the delightful advantage of being interchangeable). Gounod was never part of any school. It is something like that popular attitude held by the masses: when they are encouraged to raise their aesthetic sights, they merely reply by going back to what they are accustomed to. And that is not always in the best of taste, either. It wavers fearlessly between *Père la Victoire* and *Die Walküre*.

The people who so curiously make up the elite take off their hats to the famous, the accepted, and they encourage others to do the same. But nothing comes of it all, for these would-be educators soon run out of breath, and the masses will not allow their hearts to be won over: art continues to have a will of its own, and the Opéra persists in putting on *Faust*.

One should, however, take sides on the issue and admit that art is absolutely useless to the masses. But neither is it useful as a means of expression for an elite—often more stupid than the aforesaid masses. It is the power of beauty itself, which makes its voice heard when it must, with an inevitable and secret force. The masses can no more be ordered to love beauty than they can be persuaded to walk around on their hands. And in passing we should remember that Berlioz really did win the approval of the masses without anyone having prepared the way.

If Gounod's influence is questionable, Wagner's is only too apparent. He, however, influenced only the specialists, which leads one to conclude that there must have been something lacking. It must be confessed that there is nothing more deplorable than that neo-Wagnerian school in which French genius is obscured by a lot of imitation Wotans in long boots and Tristans in velvet jerkins.

Even if Gounod didn't tread the harmonious paths we would have liked him to, he must nonetheless be praised for having known how to avoid the imperious spirit of Wagner, whose utterly Germanic nature never lived up to his ideal of a fusion of the arts—an ideal that has now become scarcely more than a fashionable stock in trade among the literary.

For all his weaknesses, Gounod was a necessity. He was, what is more, cultivated: he understood Palestrina and collaborated with Bach, and he was not blinded by a respect for tradition to the extent of glorifying Gluck—another unfortunate foreign influence of ours. Rather did he recommend that young people listen to Mozart—something that is proof of his great impartiality, for Mozart never inspired him. His attitude toward Mendelssohn was somewhat clearer, for it is to him that he owed the idea of piling up melodies one on top of the other, a useful trick when one is not feeling in the best of form. (Mendelssohn's is perhaps a more direct influence than Schumann's.)

Also, Gounod took no notice of Bizet, and that's a good thing too. Unfortunately, Bizet died too soon, and although he bequeathed to us one masterpiece, the fate of French music was still left undecided. And here she is still! A beautiful widow who, having nobody strong enough to show her the way, allows herself to fall into the arms of foreigners who murder her. It cannot be denied that in art certain alliances are necessary, but they must be approached with some care: to choose those who make the most noise is not necessarily to follow the greatest. More often than not, these alliances are purposely used to conceal a need for rejuvenation when success is on the wane. But like marriages of convenience, they can only do harm. Let us welcome imported art into France, but let us not be deceived, falling into ecstasies about what are no more than penny whistles. And let us not think that our attitude will necessarily be reciprocated, for on the contrary, our friendship often provokes foreigners to be severe and impolite— something that is hardly funny. In concluding these brief notes, which have brought together a few ideas about Gounod (even if they are sometimes contradictory), let us take the opportunity of paying homage to his name, without any trace of dogmatic closed-mindedness. Let us note that there are many reasons why certain men deserve to be remembered; they don't even have to be very considerable reasons, and, in any case, to have stirred a great number of one's contemporaries is one means. Nobody could deny that Gounod employed this means abundantly.

Mary Garden

T H E scenic realization of a work of art, no matter how beautifully done, is nearly always in conflict with the interior dream whence it was born, rising in turn from alternative moods of doubt and enthusiasm. One's characters and oneself lived for some time in a delightful state of deception, from which they would sometimes seem to come alive from the silent pages of the manuscript, so that one felt one could almost touch them. Doesn't that explain one's horror when one sees them actually before you through the intervention of such-and-such a designer? One is in some way afraid of them, and one scarcely dare speak to them; they almost seem like ghosts. . . .

From this moment, one's old dreams seem to be shattered. Some being from without has interposed itself between you and your dream; a few quick gestures from the stagehands and the scenery is determined. The forest birds nest among the woodwinds in the orchestra. The chandeliers go on, and the rise and fall of the curtain cuts short or prolongs the emotional effect. The clapping, or the dissatisfied grumblings, seem to belong to some faraway festival, a feast at which one is scarcely more than a parasite on a not-always-wished-for glory. For to be successful in the theater one usually has to vow to give the public the emotions it wants.

In 1902, the year when the Opéra-Comique put on their painstakingly careful performance of *Pelléas et Mélisande,* I experienced some of the feelings described above. Perhaps it is useless to put them into words, but at least it will serve to underline the rest of what I am going to say. The character of Mélisande had always seemed to me difficult to perform. I had tried to convey her fragility and distant charm in the music, but there were still her gestures to be decided. One false movement during her long silences could have ruined the whole effect, even have made her incomprehensible. And above all, Mélisande's voice, which I had dreamed of as being so tender—how was that going to turn out? Even the most beautiful voice in the world could have been quite antipathetic to the special feelings her character requires. I am no longer able—nor would I wish to—describe the various stages we went through while working in rehearsal. Besides, these were my most precious moments in the theater; it was there that I met the boundless devotion of really great artists. Among them, one emerged as quite unique; I hardly had to speak a word to her as the character of Mélisande gradually took shape. . . . I awaited the performance in complete confidence, yet still curious. . . .

At last came the fifth act—Mélisande's death—a breathtaking event whose emotions cannot be rendered in words. There I heard the voice I had secretly imagined—full of a sinking tenderness, and sung with such artistry as I would never have believed possible. Since then, it is this artistry which has caused the public to bow in ever increasing admiration before the name of Mary Garden.

Apropos of Hippolyte et Aricie

M. DE LA POUPLINIÈRE, a rich revenue officer and lover of the arts, used to take advantage of his enviable position by reviving poor old Music when she was at a low ebb. However, he had good taste, and we are indebted to him for some part of Rameau's genius.

At least, he arrived just at the time when Rameau, showing every sign that he was going to be successful in dramatic music, could find nothing of sufficient merit to set as an opera.

La Pouplinière put him in contact with the Abbé Pellegrin, a writer of tragedies who had already bowdlerized Racine's *Phèdre*. He concocted a *Hippolyte et Aricie* for Rameau, poetically quite abominable, but having the makings of a varied and entertaining spectacle, full of shepherds' entrances, choruses of priestesses, choirs of hunters, and all kinds of musical interludes in which Rameau could show off his prodigious powers of invention.

Hippolyte et Aricie was first played at La Pouplinière's, and so great was its success that the Abbé Pellegrin gave back the fifty pieces of gold he had demanded in case of failure.

The first public performance took place on 1 October 1733. It was generally felt that there was too much music, and people took offense at this. But it could never have been otherwise, for that same force that causes genius to develop has a reflex that invariably alienates the public. In any case, it is a very old way of criticizing something, enabling people to pass judgment when they really have nothing to say. And let me hasten to add, to disperse any fears this criticism may have aroused, the times when it is justified are extremely rare.

Following this, the tumult of its initial reception subsided, and success almost became triumph.

Even if Rameau had found the necessary encouragement to continue writing for the opera, his life was lived in a state of permanent ill humor: he had a strange need for solitude, and could scarcely find rest except when listening to his own music. And God knows what torments he had to endure; he argued with the arbiters of taste, although once he had eagerly sought their approval. One of them, Rousseau, bore a real grudge against him, and he had his reasons for this, although they were not very good ones.

Each of these tastemakers had his own way of understanding harmony. In the resulting quarrel between the different systems, it was obvious that the musician would lose. At the end of his life, however, he was surrounded by recognition and honors in the form of noble titles bestowed upon him, although death prevented him from ever seeing his coat of arms.

The reason why French music forgot about Rameau for half a century is one of those mysteries so common in the history of art. It can, perhaps, be explained only by a fortuitous series of historical events. The queen, Marie Antoinette, an Austrian through and through (something for which she had to pay in the end), imposed Gluck upon the French taste; as a result our traditions were led astray, our desire for clarity drowned, and having gone through Meyerbeer, we ended up, naturally enough, with Richard Wagner. But why? Wagner was necessary for a blossoming of the art in Germany—a prodigious blossoming, although, in the end, virtually funereal—but it would not be unusual to doubt that he could ever have any success in France, and influence our way of thinking so much. If it is only the future that can put these things into perspective objectively, we must at least be certain of one hard fact: that there is no longer a French tradition.

Why do we not regret the loss of these charming ways in which music was formerly written, so lost that it is now impossible to find the least trace of Couperin's influence? His music was never super-fluous, and he had great wit—something we hardly dare show these days, considering it to lack grandeur. But grandeur is something that often stifles us without our ever achieving it.

And what has become of the subtly flowing syllables of our lan-guage? We will find them again in *Hippolyte et Aricie*, the opera of 1733 that the Opéra is going to revive, now in 1908. Despite the unfortunate reproach that lies in the juxtaposition of these two dates, we can be sure that the feeling of the opera has been preserved intact, although perhaps the setting, and something of the pomp of the music, have faded a little. It could never seem "out of place," for it is one of those beautiful things that will remain forever so, and despite the neglect of mankind, will never completely die.

Why have we not followed the advice contained in this piece: to observe nature before we try to copy it? Because we no longer have the time, I suppose. So our music blindly adopts trivialities coming from the direction of Italy, or legendary tales—crumbs fallen from the Wagnerian table d'hôte. Yet we no longer use the "sung bal-let"—something of our own of which we have marvelous examples left us by Rameau. Although it was taken up by the Russians, it is really infinitely better suited to certain traits in the French character, for it preserves something of our elegance.

We cannot foresee what the performance of *Hippolyte et Aricie* at the Opéra will be like. It is a venture that is more daring than one would readily suppose. Rameau was a musician of old-time France, and if he was obliged to concern himself with spectacle he felt no need to give up his right to compose real music. That may seem natural enough, but we don't seem to be able to do it anymore. We have adopted a frenetic way of shaking up the orchestra as if it were a salad, so that any hope of real music must be completely abandoned. The beauty of this frenzied way of doing things is so deep that it is difficult to perceive.

I fear that our ears have thus lost their power to listen with the necessary delicacy to the music of Rameau, in which all ungraceful noises are forbidden. Nevertheless, those who do know how to listen will be afforded a polite but warm welcome.

It is annoying that we should have forgotten these ways which were once our own, replacing them with our barbarous attitudes. We can be neither too respectful nor too moved. Let us listen to Rameau with our full attention, for a voice more thoroughly French has not been heard for many years at the Opéra.

Debussy Talks of His Music[1]

The first published interview with the famous composer of Pelléas et Mélisande

By Emily Frances Bauer

Paris
6 August 1908

The success in New York, last season, of Claude Debussy's remarkable music-drama *Pelléas et Mélisande* has made its composer an object of keen interest to Americans, and I consider myself privileged in having secured the first interview with the unapproachable and eccentric Mr. Debussy that has been vouchsafed.

Surrounded by luxury which bespeaks originality, this singular Frenchman spends most of his time within the four walls of his interesting workshop, a large room lined with books and hung with pictures, a close scrutiny of which further accentuates the personal tastes of a man of genius. Debussy acknowledged to the writer his aversion to meeting foreigners as due to his lack of understanding the English and German languages, and to his nervousness when the French language does not flow easily.

"It takes too much out of me, and means nothing either to me or to my visitor." I expressed surprise that during the hot months Debussy was still to be found hard at work in Paris, a fact which he explained in the following manner:

"You know, people leave their homes to get away from themselves and from their surroundings. I confess that I live only in my surroundings and in myself. I can conceive of no greater pleasure than sitting in my chair at this desk and looking at the walls around me day by day and night after night. In these pictures I do not see what you see; in the trees outside of my window I neither see nor hear what you do. I live in a world of imagination, which is set in motion by something suggested by my intimate surroundings rather than by outside influences, which distract me and give me nothing. I find an exquisite joy when I search deeply in the recesses of myself and if anything original is to come from me, it can only come that way."

I then saw Debussy differently from the way my imagination had pictured the writer of *Pelléas et Mélisande* and that vast symphony entitled *The Sea*. He is a man of intense prejudices, and one would be safe in the belief that his self-appreciation is more admiration for and devotion to his nationality than mere vanity or self-appreciation. Debussy firmly believes that his music is purely French, and he observed that that which is known as French music is quite as much German as it is French, which is to him a cause of regret as far as the purity of the French school is concerned.

"In your own early studies, Mr. Debussy, were you as antagonistic to the classics as you are in your compositions?"

Debussy answered by asking another question: "What do you call classics? Believe me that most of these are classics in spite of themselves, and that quality has been forced upon them without their knowledge, consent, or even expectation. I acknowledge one great master, but I do not know why he should be called a classic, because he lives, breathes, and pulsates today. This is Bach; but I will not say the same of Beethoven, as I consider him a man of his epoch, and with a few exceptions his works should have been allowed to rest. I can never understand why all people who study music, all countries that work to establish original schools, should be built upon a German foundation. It will take France innumerable years to work out of that influence, and when we look back upon the original French writers such as Rameau, Couperin, Daquin, and men of their period, we can but regret that the foreign spirit fastened itself upon that which would have been a great school."

It was not difficult to understand the implied word; although the name of César Franck was unspoken, it is well understood that Debussy is no admirer of the great Belgian writer, whose influence is to be found upon all of the present-day writers with the exception of Debussy himself. As may well be understood, Debussy is keenly interested in America. The appreciation manifested in *Pelléas et Mélisande* has awakened in him the feeling that there is a responsive chord in that far-away country, and in speaking of its own musical development he expressed the same regret that it should build upon a German basis. He said, "The distinction of a country like that is that it imbibes from all sources, and in that way will arrive more quickly than if it struggled into a foreign voice and then groped out of it into its own personality and individual strength—in short, they are less German-bound than are the countries who hear little or no other music through Chauvinism or antipathies." The bond between Debussy and America is now being strengthened, as he has selected as his subject for further work Edgar Allan Poe's "Fall of the House of Usher" and the same writer's "The Devil in the Belfry"—both of which appeal strongly to his tastes.

Debussy says that the work is not to be an opera though he has not as yet found the name which it shall bear. The music will be set to the prose, and he himself is writing the book. The two works will be given on the same evening in the above-mentioned order, and they are already under contract to the Metropolitan Opera Company. Debussy has long been an admirer of Poe, and thinks it quite remarkable that some American has not been moved to find an inspiration in his masterpieces. "I shall not write this in the form of an opera, because I do not want to write anything which in any way approaches *Pelléas*. I cannot understand the object of a writer who creates a second work along the same lines which made the first successful. I should no more want to repeat myself than I should want to copy someone who had written before me. Therefore when I have nothing to say I do not attempt to write. The inspiration I have through E. A. Poe is totally different in its elements from that which I felt through Maeterlinck, and I believe that it will be equally successful and when I say equally successful I mean that it will find the same number of enemies and the same number of friends."

❧ *NOTE*

[1] In *Cahiers Debussy* no. 2 (1975) Marcel Dietschy has most interestingly illuminated the background to Debussy's interview with this American journalist. Writing to his editor, Jacques Durand, on 22 September 1908, Debussy mentions Miss Bauer:

> I couldn't come to see you last Saturday as I promised, being engaged with Mlle E. F. Bauer, an American journalist, who came to ask me for advice on the best way to educate young American geniuses. . . . Don't forget that from now on all the great artistic discoveries are to come from America! And so as not to waste any time, they decide upon genius between the ages of eight and ten. Touchingly ridiculous! I assured Mlle Bauer that her compatriots would soon find a machine to deal with such youngsters, turning them into fully fledged artists in five minutes.

As the date of the interview is clearly given as 6 August, Monsieur Dietschy concludes that either Debussy gave two interviews to Miss Bauer, or else he was fabricating her visit as an excuse to avoid visiting Durand. No subsequent interview appeared in *Harper's Weekly*, so the latter explanation may be the correct one.

What Should Be Done at the Conservatoire?

(Interview by Maurice Leudet)

M. Claude Debussy has just been nominated a member of the Conseil Supérieur of teaching at the Conservatoire of speech and music, in the section of musical studies, as replacement for Monsieur Ernest Reyer. . . .

"The most surprised person at this nomination for membership of the Conseil Supérieur of the Conservatoire is, I assure you, your own obedient servant," he said to me at once. "I have never before been called to sit on such a jury, never before have the higher spheres of officialdom solicited my collaboration. So I am literally dumbfounded. And to crown it all, I am to replace poor Monsieur Ernest Reyer. While I have a profound respect for the memory of Reyer, I don't exactly conceive of music in the same way, do I?

"After all, someone has perhaps chosen me as a replacement for Monsieur Rayer because he never came to the Conservatoire. I shall come, yes, I shall come, and I'll be writing to the Under-Secretary of State for the Fine Arts to thank him for my nomination."

"But what will you do, or try to do, on the Conseil Supérieur?"

"To tell you the truth, I'm not sure. Certainly I won't be a stranger at the Conservatoire. I know the place, having been educated there myself and coming out a Prix de Rome. It wasn't the best time of my life, but it was no more disagreeable for me than for anyone else. If I can be of service somehow, I will try and find the best way."

"You do, however, have your own opinions about the teaching given at the Conservatoire, and you yourself received this teaching."

"Yes, I would say that the Conservatoire is a place where excellent things are taught, but some could benefit by modification.

"The teaching of harmony seems to me quite misguided. I can assure you I did nothing very remarkable in the harmony class. It was the custom of my time for the professors to teach their students by a useless little game that consisted of trying to discover the secrets of a particular composer's harmony. I humbly must confess that I could never discover them and it wasn't hard to console myself."

"And the instrumental classes?"

"Ah! those are perfect. No other instrumentalists in the world equal the French.

"I do not, however, have the same admiration for the singing classes. Our singers are generally badly taught. The students go to the singing classes but they never go, or rarely go, to the *sol-fa* class.

"For solfeggio is the basis of song just as of every other kind of music. How many of our singers ignore the beat! Doubtless, few are really musicians, but if they had received better teaching they would have a greater respect for the music they interpret.

"Another point is that the teaching of singing would benefit if it were always done by singers who sing, or used to sing, on the stage themselves, singers who have proved their talent. That's generally not the case. Moreover, the singing classes, as well as the others (the exceptions being more common than the rule), are not taught by the professors best suited for the task because they are not able to pay them properly."

"So the budget must be increased?"

"Yes, or it must be better allocated. But I must add that here I am only one voice among many, and apparently those who think as I do are only an insignificant minority."

At this point in our conversation I reminded Monsieur Debussy of his success at the Conservatoire, of the Prix de Rome carried off by his cantata L'Enfant prodigue *in 1883.*

"Old memories," he replied, "and ones of which I am not very proud. If there is one thing at the Conservatoire that I find useless and even damaging, it's the way in which awards are made to the students.

"The form that competitions take seems to me deplorable. Someone may work well, be a very good pupil. On the day of the competition he may be at less than his best and fail.

"There is nothing more absurd than the competition. There are pupils from the Conservatoire who have never won any prize or award and yet who have become excellent and accomplished musicians.

"For my own part, the truth is that one must escape the Conservatoire as soon as possible in order to find one's individuality.

"The state has instituted competitions everywhere, in every profession. We are creating more and more idiots through our competitions. In all professions I would say that the method is a bad one, but in art it is particularly detestable.

"That is also to say that I am against the famous tradition of the Prix de Rome. It is aimed at the least interesting thing about the competitors—their vanity. So the Prix de Rome does no good at all.

"The competitors are made to do things they will never have to do again in their career as musicians.

"But still it remains, this Prix de Rome! Let more advantages be drawn from it than have been up to the present time! Let more freedom be given the musicians in their time in Rome. Let no themes be given them!

"Now I've poured out all my ideas, without any digression. This committee on which I'm going to serve is perhaps no bad thing, but there is an atmosphere in that old place called the Conservatoire that will prevent the least wind of change from ever entering."

"But will you defend these ideas confided to me on the committee?"

"I've told you everything here, so I can assure you I couldn't repeat it all at the Conservatoire.

"One would need an authority I do not possess, powers of oration that are beyond me. Perhaps I wouldn't be able to defend my ideas: like all who have many ideas, I don't like contradiction."

Before taking leave of M. Debussy I questioned him on his own work, on his forthcoming works. He replied in a few words.

"It took me twelve years to write *Pelléas et Mélisande*, so you see I don't write quickly. One always writes too much and thinks too little."

AZEST

6 December 1910

F O R two days the most illustrious representative of French music—
her poet, apostle, and prophet—has been here in Budapest. This
illustrious visitor goes by the name of Claude Debussy. He is still a
young man but has already acquired immortality—something not
gained by passing glory, nor lasting success, but the foremost heritage
of genius. Debussy has enriched music with new impressions, sentiments and effects. And the importance of his poetic utterance is
heightened by the fact that it is perhaps more than the mere grandiose
ideas and novelties of one man alone: it shows the whole tendency of
French music in a state of renewal, advancing toward an eclipse of
the triumphant Wagnerism that resounds within it.

France herself took a long time to admit that it was Debussy who
strove to create musical impressionism, as Manet, Monet, Rodin, Verlaine, Baudelaire and Mallarmé had endeavored to create it in the
pictorial, sculptural, or poetic field. But Art triumphed over reaction-
ary prejudice, and Debussy is today the *magnus pontifex* of a new
musical credo, in his own country as well as elsewhere.

Debussy, whose acquaintance we have just had occasion to make, is
a most amiable Frenchman and full of character. He is still young,
scarcely forty-eight, but his hair and black beard make him appear
younger still. His curly hair (which, unlike the majority of artists, he
does not wear long), his swarthy complexion, and his flat nose cause
him to resemble a Negro. His profile seems to be cut by an almost
straight line, with an acute angle forming his forehead, his neck and
chin. Three lines suffice to caricature his head, by no means comic;
once having seen it, one can never forget that he is one of the greatest

composers. This man is a magisterial instrument on which play mysterious and extraordinary forces.

His face is pleasant, with soft, velvety eyes, and his speech is friendly; his voice seems caressing as it rises from the depths. His whole personality exudes a gay satisfaction and extraordinary naïveté, sometimes resembling a satisfied faun, sometimes an astonished child. While speaking he placed his hand on his buttonhole—on which was fastened his badge of officer of the Légion d'Honneur.

"You know I am most touched," said Debussy, "to see how well my works are known here in Budapest. Better than in Paris. I am ashamed to admit never having shown much interest in contemporary Hungarian music. I had not realized there was such an intense musical life here—I know few Hungarian musicians or composers—only now, since being here, have I made the acquaintance of some of them. . . . Don't think I am paying compliments, but I have been surprised to see how developed a musical center Budapest is."

"I am astonished that you have not heard our musicians spoken of. Somehow our young musicians tend to gravitate toward Paris—two of our young artists recently gave a concert there."
"Yes, I know . . . their concert caused a scandal. But one of them does not come into the category of which I was speaking . . . they were thought to be Romanian. I may even have met Hungarian artists in Paris, but they didn't tell me their nationality."

"I heard that there was a slight incident at your concert in Vienna?"
"No, one couldn't really say an incident. It was just that I would not let the Philharmonic Orchestra, which I was conducting, play my symphonic poem *La Mer,* and that was because the musicians hadn't rehearsed it sufficiently. What's more, they knew it themselves, and it was by mutual agreement that we decided to change the program."

"La Mer *was also played here last year."*
"I know. And the piece will certainly have been better performed than it would have been in Vienna. All the same I was satisfied with the performances of my other pieces; *Ibéria*—more difficult than *La Mer*—was very well played."

"What are you working on at present, cher maître?"

"For two years I have been working on two operas. The subjects are taken from the tales of Poe. One is called 'The Fall of the House of Usher,' the other 'The Devil in the Belfry.' I am pleased to have found these two subjects."

"After Pelléas et Mélisande?"

"Precisely after *Pelléas et Mélisande.* I am very pleased with these two subjects, not only because the secret atmosphere, the feelings, tensions, and the emotions contained in the tales of Poe have not previously been translated into music, but also because one could hardly find a greater contrast between Poe and Maeterlinck.

"And, you see, I believe that it ought to be the duty of every artist to depart as completely as possible from the place and subject of his previous success. I have been successful with *Pelléas et Mélisande;* that is why I will never write another piece similar in subject and atmosphere.

"I believe the principal fault of the majority of writers and artists is having neither the will nor the courage to break with their successes, failing to seek new paths and give birth to new ideas. Most of them reproduce them twice, three, even four times. They have neither the courage nor the temerity to leave what is certain for what is uncertain. There is, however, no greater pleasure than going into the depth of oneself, setting one's whole being in motion and seeking for new and hidden treasures. What a joy to find something new within oneself, something that surprises even ourselves, filling us with warmth. A person who repeats himself is like an imitator, don't you think?

"That is the great evil of today. Art has become almost an industry. But, believe me, those who are resigned to this truth are not real artists. If one day I become like that, I shall lay down my pen forever. I shall not complain but quietly go away to tune pianos. Claude Debussy: tuner."

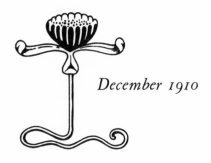

December 1910

Statement to an Austrian Journalist[1]

I AM neither revolutionizing nor demolishing anything. I am quietly forging my own way ahead, without any trace of propaganda for my ideas—as is proper for a revolutionary. I am no longer an adversary of Wagner. Wagner is a genius, but geniuses can make mistakes. Wagner pronounced himself in favor of the laws of harmony. I am for freedom. But freedom must essentially be free. All the noises we hear around ourselves can be re-created. Every sound perceived by the acute ear in the rhythm of the world about us can be represented musically. Some people wish above all to conform to the rules; for myself, I wish only to render what I can hear.

There is no Debussy school. I have no disciples; I am myself.

Berlioz, Mozart, Beethoven—they are great masters whom I venerate, the last two above all. Berlioz attached romantic buckles to fossilized old wigs. . . .

You see how mistakes are made! Some see me as a melancholy man of the North. Others would have me be a representative of the Midi or Provence—Daudet! Tirili Tirila! I am quite simply a native of Saint-Germain—half an hour from Paris.

❧ *NOTE*

[1] The publication from which this article is taken has not been traced. The extract comes from an article by Léon Vallas, *Revue musicale de Lyon,* 8 January 1911.

EXCELSIOR
18 January 1911

The Ideas of a Great Musician

(*Interview by Georges Delaquys*)
Monsieur Claude Debussy confides in us his projects and tells us of his hopes.

I interrogated him on his work in progress and at once the master interrupted:
"Don't ask me where my work lies: I never know myself. At the moment I am working on the "Saint-Sébastien" of Gabriele d'Annunzio, and this is taking up all of my time. The poem is of great beauty, and it contains real treasures in the field of imaginative lyricism. D'Annunzio, I am pleased to say, is an artist who can bring things to life. As soon as he appeared, life became energetic and fertile. Moreover, he is extremely musical. A composer could hardly have had a more valuable collaborator. Only one aspect of the work is inconvenient: it has to be finished by a stated time. I have a horror of that, and the idea of it paralyzes me. I can think of nothing else."

"Then you have abandoned the works you had in hand: 'The Devil in the Belfry' and 'The Fall of the House of Usher'?"
"Momentarily, yes. These pieces are quite advanced, but as I have no director or collaborator to hurry me to finish them, I can work on them in peace. I consider it superfluous to produce a great number of works; it is preferable to give as much as one can of oneself to a single work, in any case to a small number of them."

"It is said that Rameau's Pygmalion, *orchestrated by you, is to be presented at the Théâtre des Arts."*
"That is correct, but it is impossible to tell you when. I have no time to work on it at present. It's not a huge task, to be sure, but it is one that is very interesting to me, in that it means restoring those delicious old scores, corrupted by the intervention of copyists and conductors, so that they resume their rightful character."

"Is not Pelléas et Mélisande *shortly to be performed in several foreign cities where until now it has been ignored?"*
"I cannot say anything precise on this subject, for I know absolutely nothing about it. It is not in that sphere that, for me, the interest lies: it is more in the music itself, in what is done with it and what people love in it. I myself love music passionately, and through my love I have forced myself to break free from certain sterile traditions with which it is encumbered. It is a free art, a wellspring, an art of the open air, an art comparable to the elements—the wind, the sea, and the sky! It must not be an art that is confined, academic. Evidently, that is all very well: the writing of it, the profession—I was at one time enthusiastic for that side of things. But I have thought better of it: this *method* of writing would benefit by being simplified, the means of expression being made more direct. Now don't think that by saying that I am setting myself up as the head of a school or a reformer. I am only attempting to express, as sincerely as I can, the sentiments and sensations I feel; the rest is of little importance to me. All kinds of attitudes toward the great masters have been attributed to me, and I have been quoted as saying things about Wagner and Beethoven that I never said. I admire Beethoven and Wagner, but I refuse to admire them uncritically just because people have told me that they are masters! Never! In our day, it seems to me that we adopt poses in regard to the masters more becoming to bitter old cleaning women; I wish to have the freedom to say that a boring page of music is annoying no matter who its author. But I have no theory, no prejudices. I try to be sincere, in my art and in my opinions, that's all. Only I think that in art there is an aristocracy whom one should not compromise. That is why I have little desire to be enormously suc-

cessful or tumultuously famous. Once again, I am not the man I am reputed to be. I like only silence, peace, work, isolation, and what is said of my music is of no importance to me. Nor do I mean it to be imitated, nor that it should exert an influence on anyone. I try to remain independent, I do my work as I must, as far as I am able—that's all I can say to you."

M. *Claude Debussy and* Le Martyre de Saint-Sébastien

(*Interview by Henry Malherbe*)

I BELIEVE, in effect, in a renaissance of liturgical music. Sacred art only flourishes nobly when being persecuted. And when it appears that wrongs are being done to the Church, I think the atmosphere is ripe for the production of religious scores.

For me, religious music ceased with the sixteenth century. The fresh, childlike souls of that time alone expressed their vehement, untainted fervor in music free from worldliness. Since then we have had pious musical improvisations more or less made for show. That wonderful man Johann Sebastian Bach only escaped because of his natural genius. He built harmonic edifices as a devout architect and not as an apostle.

Parsifal is nice—it's theater, that poison of simplicity. Wagner himself called his works "spectacles." He knew only too well how to resist the temptations of humility to partake of religion. He adopted poses too dramatic for prayer, and his lofty artificial theories never left him.

For singing the praises of the divine, a quite different way of baring one's soul is necessary. One must give oneself over to one's work with a heroic generosity and a constant renunciation of self and of material things. Who can render us that pure love of the pious musicians of olden times? Who can again experience the magnificent passion of a Palestrina? Who can revive the poor but beautiful sacrifice of one of those minstrels whose tender tales have come down to us?

I myself am far from such a state of grace. I do not worship according to the established rites. I have made the mysteries of nature my religion. I do not think that a man in abbot's attire is necessarily closer to God, nor that one particular place in a town is especially favorable to meditation.

Before the passing sky, in long hours of contemplation of its magnificent and ever-changing beauty, I am seized by an incomparable emotion. The whole expanse of nature is reflected in my own sincere but feeble soul. Around me the branches of the trees reach out toward the firmament, here are the sweet-scented flowers smiling in the meadow, here the soft earth is carpeted with sweet herbs. . . . And, unconsciously, my hands are clasped in prayer. Nature invites its ephemeral and trembling travelers to experience these wonderful and disturbing spectacles—that is what I call prayer.

Now I confess that the subject of *Le Martyre de Saint-Sébastien* above all seduced me by its blend of intense life and Christian faith. Unfortunately, I am at a loss for time. Months of research would have been necessary to enable me to compose music worthy of the mysterious and refined play of d'Annunzio. And I think I am obliged only to provide music where I think the play requires it—a few choruses and incidental music. It is an anguishing constraint: I have to be finished by May, when the *Martyre* will be presented at the Châtelet. Then it will be performed in Rome, where I will go to direct a concert during which some of my works will be played.

For the rest, I think I cannot be indiscreet. Who can know the secret of musical composition? The sound of the sea, the outline of a horizon, the wind in the leaves, the cry of a bird—these set off complex impressions in us. And suddenly, without the consent of anyone on this earth, one of these memories bursts forth, expressing itself in the language of music. It carries its own harmony within itself. However much effort one makes, one could not find anything better, anything more sincere. Only thus does a soul destined for music make such beautiful discoveries.

If I speak thus to you, it is not in order to put forward an opulent display of artistic morals but rather to prove to you that I really have none. I detest doctrines together with all their impertinences.

That is why I wish to write down my musical thoughts with the greatest self-detachment. I wish to sing of my inner landscape with the naïve candor of childhood.

No doubt this innocent musical grammar cannot be put into practice without some obstacles. It always shocks those partisans of artifice and untruth; I foresee that, and it delights me! I shall do nothing, however, to create adversaries nor anything to convert my enemies into friends. One has to force oneself to be a great artist for oneself and not for others. I dare to be myself and suffer for my truth. Those who feel as I do can only love me the more for it. The others avoid me, even hate me. I will do nothing to win them over.

In all truth, that distant day—and one hopes it will be as late as possible—when I shall excite no quarrels, I shall reproach myself severely. In these last works, hypocrisy will have to have won the day—that detestable kind of hypocrisy which causes one to please everybody.

MUSICA
March 1911

What Should One Set to Music: Good Poetry or Bad Poetry, Free Verse or Prose?

(*Inquiry led by Fernand Divoire*)

CONNECTIONS between poetry and music? I have never thought about it. I am very little concerned with music. Musicians and poets who talk of nothing but music and poetry seem to me to be as intolerable as sportsmen who only talk of sport.

But seriously, one cannot put it into words. You want to know what I think? Well, it is, in effect, that musicians who don't understand anything about poetry ought not to set it to music. They can only ruin it. . . .

Schumann understood nothing about Heinrich Heine, or at least, that's my impression. He might be a great genius, but he could never capture that fine spirit of irony that Heine embodies. Look at the *Dichterliebe,* for example: he misses all the irony.

Really good poems—let us not exaggerate—are few and far between. Who writes them these days? And when one does find them, they are best left alone. Henri de Régnier, who writes pure, classic poetry, cannot be set to music, and can you imagine settings of Racine or Corneille? But then the young musicians of today merely want to see famous names beside their own. . . .

And then from music's point of view, what is the use of verse? What indeed? We have just as often put beautiful music to bad verse as we have bad music to good poetry.

Good poetry has a rhythm of its own, which makes it very difficult for us. One minute, though: recently, I set to music (I don't know why) three of Villon's ballads. But I do know why: because I have wanted to for a long time. It is very difficult to follow and to cast the rhythms in a suitable mold, still preserving one's inspiration. If one cheats and is content with a mere juxtaposition of the two arts, it is not too difficult, but is it worth the trouble? Classic poetry has a life of its own, an "interior dynamism," as the Germans would say. But then that is not our concern.

Blank verse is a little easier; we can turn to the world of the senses. But why should the musician not write his own blank verse? What is he waiting for? Wagner did it. But then his poems, like his music, are not an example that should be followed. His texts are no better than any others, but for him they are the best, and that's the main thing.

All in all, let us leave the great poets alone: they are much the happier for it. And, in any case, for the most part they are not very good-natured people.

Massenet Is No More

MASSENET was the most genuinely loved of all our contemporary
musicians. It was, moreover, this love which we had for him that
enabled him to retain his unique position in the world of music.

His colleagues never forgave him for having such a power to
please; it really was a gift. And it can be said, in all truth, that this
gift is not necessary for an artist. J. S. Bach, to take one example
from many, never had this power to please in the way that Massenet
did. Do we ever hear the young, fashionable music lovers humming
The Saint Matthew Passion? I think not. Yet it is well known that
they wake up in the morning singing *Manon* or *Werther.* Let us not
be mistaken: it is a very pleasant form of glory to have bestowed
upon one, and it is secretly envied by more than one of our great
purists—the kind whose hearts are warmed only by their somewhat
boring respect for their coteries.

He was totally successful in everything he did, and people took
revenge on him for this by saying, or rather whispering, that he was
Paul Delmet's best pupil—a joke in the worst possible taste. But he
has had many imitators, both at home and abroad.

To try and blacken the name of those they imitate is a first principle for many artists; they justify their evil designs as being a part of
the "struggle for Art." This is merely an expression used to conceal
something a little underhand, and, what is more, it makes a grave
mistake in likening art to some kind of sport.

Often, in art, the only person one has to struggle against is oneself,
and the victories thus won are, perhaps, among the most triumphant of

all. But by a strange stroke of irony one is at the same time afraid of being victorious over oneself, so one prefers quietly to copy one's colleagues or become a part of the general public—which amounts to much the same thing.

It is scarcely the right time to express regret at Massenet's fertility —something that occasionally inhibited his powers of choice. Besides, does one ever have the right to say that a man should have been the opposite of what he was?

In the time of Napoleon, many French mothers hoped that their sons would become little Napoleons. The wars that ensued shattered many of their dreams. On the other hand, there are some whose fate is unique. Massenet, in his way, was one of these.

November 1912

Jean Philippe Rameau[1]

RAMEAU was fifty years old when he began to write for the Opéra, and was ignored almost all his life. Thanks to the efforts of French scholarship, he is better known today than he was among his contemporaries, at least by reputation, although for many people he is still merely the composer of the celebrated Rigaudon from *Dardanus,* and not much more. He was tall and thin in appearance, in character at the same time both enthusiastic and complex. He hated the world. At that time, when refined manners were all that mattered, if one wasn't connected with the court, one was considered a mere nobody.

Musicians and singers at the Opéra feared and detested him, and he was always resentful of them for having forced him to suppress certain passages in his works that they could not, or would not, sing properly. His almost exclusive love of music enabled him to ignore all these troubles, inflicted on him by the elegant but indifferent times.

He was a born philosopher, although that didn't make him indifferent to fame, but it was the beauty of his works he cared about most of all. One day, toward the end of his life, someone asked him whether he found the sound of applause more pleasing to his ears than the sound of his music. He paused for a few moments in thought, and then said, "I like my own music even better."

The need to understand—so rare among artists—was innate in Rameau. Was it not to satisfy that need that he wrote his *Traité de l'harmonie,* where he claimed to rediscover the "laws of reason," and desired that the order and clarity of geometry should reign in music? One can read in the preface to that same treatise that "music is a science bound by certain rules," but that these rules must be based on a general principle that can never be known unless we enlist the aid of mathematics.

To the end, he never for a moment doubted the truth of the old Pythagorean theory that music should be reduced to a combination of numbers: it is the "arithmetic of sound" just as optics is the "geometry of light." He put it all down in words, and traced the paths along which modern harmony was going to progress, including his own. He was perhaps wrong to write down all these theories before composing his operas, for it gave his contemporaries the chance to conclude that there was a complete absence of anything emotional in the music.

His career had hardly ended when a new fashion overtook him— at first the triumph of Lully, then later the domination of Gluck, who reigned for so long over French music that it has still not fully recovered.

For a long time, and for no apparent reason, Rameau remained almost completely forgotten. His charm, his finely wrought forms— all these were replaced by a way of writing music concerned only with the dramatic effect. The discovery of harmonic "moments" to caress the ear was to give way to massive, easily understood but academic harmonies. Because of this, music split in two, ending up with Richard Wagner, another tyrannical genius.

Rameau's major contribution to music was that he knew how to find "sensibility" within the harmony itself; and that he succeeded in capturing effects of color and certain nuances that, before his time, musicians had not clearly understood.

Like Nature herself, Art changes: she moves in curved lines but always ends up exactly at the point where she began. Rameau, whatever one may think, is definitely a key figure in music, and we can follow in his footsteps without fear of sinking into any pitfalls.

That is why he deserves our attention. We should treat him with the respect he deserves as one of our ancestors. He may have been a little disagreeable, but he was a man of truth.

NOTE

[1] It was the composer André Caplet who had asked Debussy for this article on Rameau for an American magazine. Writing to Caplet while working on the article, Debussy wrote, "I have begun the article on Rameau. It's awkward having to do it without thinking, for the simple reason that in forty lines one has to summarize the life, works, and influence on art of a man who has quite escaped history, and one wonders why, except that one only knows too well."

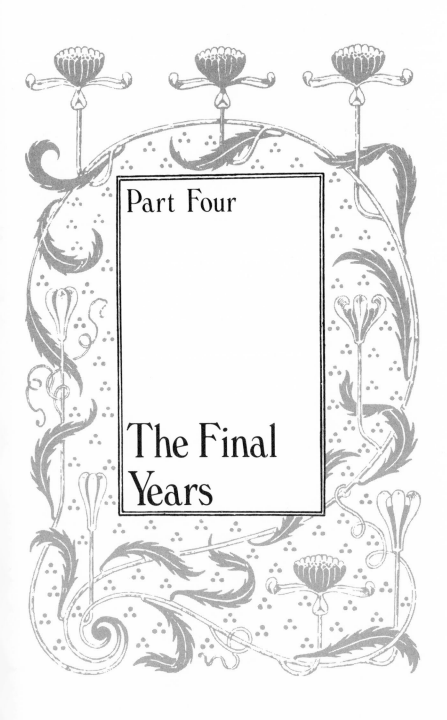

Part Four

The Final
Years

ALTHOUGH many earlier ideas recur in this last episode in Debussy's career as critic, the final sequence of articles in many ways stands apart from the more familiar ones in *La Revue blanche* and *Gil Blas*. None was included in *Monsieur Croche, antidilettante,* and M. Croche himself has passed on, making no appearance in these late essays; Debussy is now his own mouthpiece; his tone is more severe, more pessimistic than ever before—the work, one might say, of a tired and sick man, whose life had spanned an era of enormous artistic upheaval that had at last overtaken him. In addition, the magazine for which he was now writing was quite another matter from the reviews for which Debussy had first taken up the critic's pen at the turn of the century; the golden days of the all-embracing artistic *revue* were over. Debussy's last articles come mostly from the bulletin of the Société Internationale de Musique, *SIM,* a monthly magazine whose interest was limited to those whom Debussy called "hardy specialists." Despite being asked by his friend Laloy, Debussy had several times backed out of contributing to this type of paper, the forerunner of academic musicological journals, but his desire to retain a mouthpiece for his ideas on the arts seems to have triumphed in the end. Even more than before, Debussy used his column to voice his opinions on the world of music in general—broad discussions rather than mere concert reviews.

If anything, the negativism inherent throughout Debussy's writings is at its strongest in some of these later articles. Audiences, administrators, teachers, performers, and composers alike—all are seen as wheels in a factory whose production methods are at fault and whose goods are shoddy. Sometimes his pessimism allows few positive suggestions to emerge from a sea of heavy irony. And yet these final articles are perhaps the most moving documents Debussy wrote; on the threshold of a period of artistic change and a terrible war, the composer stands midway between a faded *belle époque,* of which he was formerly a part, and an unknown future in which he realizes he will play no part at all, save perhaps through his ideas, planned for publication in book form—boldly sketched pointers for the future of French music. Perhaps these ideas are best summed up in the telling lines that end his 1915 article in *L'Intransigeant*: "We have a whole intellectual province to recapture. That is why, at a time when only Fate can turn the page, Music must bide her time and take stock of herself. Only then can she break that dreadful silence that will remain after the last shell has been shot."

A glance at the first issue of *SIM,* to which Debussy contributed his column on the Concerts Colonne, clearly puts Debussy's article in perspective. Alongside, employed to review the Concerts Lamoureux, was none other than the conservative d'Indy, also using his column as a mouthpiece for broader ideas. Once again Debussy had a rival critic with whom to vie.

"In the eighteenth century," d'Indy began his column,

> Rameau had the idea of discreetly adding, under certain circumstances, a note to the perfect chord, the basis of all music. In the nineteenth century, with particular effects in mind, Russian composers used the whole-tone scale, a process that might be called *atonal* because it prevents any possibility of modulation.
>
> In the twentieth century, Claude Debussy and Maurice Ravel also used these methods, enlarging them, often applying them in most ingenious ways; but they made the mistake (one must be bold enough to speak the truth about those one admires) of forming principles from them, or at least of allowing others to form principles from them—their "muftis" and "ulemas"—until they become a sort of formulae established by fashion. From the harmonic sensation, the titillation of orchestral timbres, there is now no escape.
>
> This is a serious mistake, for far from constituting progress, a step forward, it will end up by being a step backward for our art, taking us back at least a hundred years.[1]

D'Indy's dogmatic approach to the evolution of musical impressionism was clearly diametrically opposed to Debussy's pleas for the renewal of a purely French tradition. But, to restore the balance, the same number of *SIM* also contained an article by Erik Satie, one of the series *Mémoires d'un amnésique*. Once again, as on *La Revue blanche,* the idea of employing celebrated composers as reviewers seems to have been a matter of editorial policy; thus the old pattern of complementary critics was revived and d'Indy was paired with Debussy. The main articles in the issue show the magazine to be a stepping stone between the literary *revue* of the turn of the century and the musicological magazine. Beginning with a literary fantasy, "L'homme qui improvise" by André Suarès, later to be a biographer of Debussy, the magazine also contained an article on the English virginalists by one of the founding fathers of musicology, Charles van der Borren, as well as an extended article on Asian music.

Amidst this climate of specialism, Debussy expanded upon several ideas previously mentioned. His thoughts on visual, especially cinematographic, expression were further developed in the article of November 1913. "It is musicians alone," wrote Debussy, "who have the privilege of being able to convey all the poetry of the night and the day. Painters, on the other hand, can recapture only one of her aspects at a time, preserve only one moment." He went on to recommend the cinema as a possible force of renewal, but his ideas were somewhat clouded by the irony he introduced into the subsequent passage, in which he mentioned talk of "filming the nine symphonies of Beethoven." It is probable that this was simply retaliatory, for in an article of some months earlier, d'Indy had written disparagingly of "cinematographic music." It seems that he meant exactly the same as Debussy by the term: a linked series of images, musical ideas. But whereas Debussy saw such cinematographic techniques as a renewal of form, d'Indy merely saw them as a lack of it.[2]

Also an expansion of previous ideas is the lengthy appraisal of primitive music—another force Debussy saw as regenerative. It was no doubt partly through his own interest in Javanese gamelan music and through his close association with Victor Ségalen, who was also interested in primitive music, that Debussy had developed ideas on this subject. And in his prophecy of a starker, barer kind of music, one perhaps detects a symptom of Debussy's true reaction to the music of the young Stravinsky, whose *Sacre du printemps* he had played on two pianos just at the time when he wrote his extended *SIM* article on "Taste," including a lengthy passage on primitive music. According to Louis Laloy, it was on one occasion in the spring of 1913, when Stravinsky visited Debussy at Laloy's home, that the French composer was first initiated into the primitive rites of the young Russian composer's masterpiece.[3] It seems that Debussy's feelings about this music were mixed, although reading between the lines one is left in no doubt that the piece had made a profound impression. Writing to André Caplet on the date of its first performance, Debussy describes it as an "extraordinary savage affair. . . . You might call it primitive with every modern convenience."[4] But the clue to his real feelings on the work were reserved for Stravinsky himself, after he had sent Debussy a score of the piece. Debussy wrote:

> For me, who is descending the other slope of the hill but still keeps an intense passion for music, it brings a special satisfaction to tell you how much you have enlarged the boundaries of the permissible in the empire of sound. . . . Forgive me for using these pompous words, but they exactly express my thought.[5]

Debussy already felt the undercurrents of musical change in which he would play no part. And whether his passages on primitive music grew directly out of his contact with *Le Sacre du printemps* or not, one feels in these last articles that Debussy has put his finger precisely on the pulse of these times of artistic and cultural ferment. Certainly Debussy felt the power of Stravinsky more acutely than the sensational, but now largely forgotten, escapades of the futurist musicians, who are afforded but a cursory mention.

After increasingly sporadic appearances, in one case blamed on a postal strike, a note in the issue of April 1914 informs us of Debussy's indisposition owing to influenza and promises his notice for the next number. It never appeared, and a subsequent note appeared apologizing for his "persistent indisposition." It is the postlude "Enfin, seuls! . . . ." which most appropriately concludes this final period of Debussy's career as critic. Its memorable lines ring on as the final testimony of a great composer who was also an absorbing and prophetic writer.

ᐁ*NOTES*

[1] *SIM* (November 1912).

[2] In *SIM* (February 1913), d'Indy wrote of "cinematographic music": "From the moment that all musical form is banished, as if worn out or old hat, it seems to me to be imperative that this 'sensorial' music should be accompanied by a visual representation of it."

[3] Louis Laloy, *La Musique retrouvée* (Paris, 1928).

[4] Debussy, *Lettres inédités à André Caplet* (Monaco, 1957). Letter of 29 May 1913.

[5] Quoted by Edward Lockspeiser in *Debussy*.

SIM
November 1912

> *The voices seemed to be joined as if one,*
> *so perfectly were they attuned.*
> —*Dante Alighieri*

I T appears that French music is undergoing a crisis and that the old quarrels are about to flare up again.

In all sincerity, I would say that this is desirable, for if boundless freedom is characteristic of our times, our blind acceptance of all kinds of formulae marks a laxity, an indifference that almost amounts to a scorn for art. For proof of this one has only to look at all the weather-vane souls, always ready to turn whichever way the aesthetic wind happens to be blowing. It is no longer frowned upon to adopt current opinions without flinching. Above all, one should not fear ridicule, nor even extremely long development sections. . . . When after a hundred or so bars we are completely lost, then the public (or those who control their opinions) are quite ready to call it "genius." We have many who are positive masters at throwing our minds into confusion, at least for certain periods when the orchestra completely forgets about the listeners. It has almost come to the point where the public will leave for fear of witnessing something that isn't meant for them, despite the wise precaution of forbidding them to leave during the performance. But then comes one of the old "formulae" to put things right again—a banal or heroic-sounding noise to fill the gaping void that has gone before. Everyone claps, as much to relieve the acute boredom filling the air as to thank the composer for allowing them out at last.

Some blindly continue to follow their forebears, like the Chinese who forever respect Confucius for having put life in such readily accessible formulae.

Others find a new way of serving up things which are really as old as the hills. Rather than drawing upon any instinctive ingenuity within themselves, they dig up ideals whose foundations were laid in the Stone Age, or serve up crude imitations of Javanese music. There's nothing either new or astonishing about that. M. H. Poincaré (whose excellence testifies to his great objectivity) proclaimed some years ago in his *Science et méthode* that those of the avant-gardes were not only useful but essential, even though the general public looked upon them as fools.[1] In fact, the form of a piece may be crude and out of proportion but still contain the seed of an idea from which others coming later will draw much beauty.

But people really ought to hesitate before speaking out: that's something our age is only too ready to forget. We are obsessed with "arriving," and the pieces that do nothing but pander to the latest fashion—bound to be short-lived—are piling up. And so many of those who have "arrived" never really "departed." When will someone come along and put an end to this dreadful notion, so popular at the moment, that it is as easy to be an artist as a dentist? Why don't we stop making the secrets of the art so readily available? They are as dangerous as they are useless! As so many of our learned professors testify, Beethoven felt he had to discourage quite a number of young people, for he himself knew that art means sacrifice. Today we hold him up as an example of indestructible glory. Little harm in that, but we are ignoring the games of chance. . . .

That wonderful mystery held by the forests of old, has that not come about only because of much sacrifice and death? Think how many seedlings were trampled beneath the careless tread of wild beasts, sacrificed for the sake of the blossoming of the great oak trees, which, century by century, have served as a constant reminder of beauty! Are they not an example from which we can learn, providing such a tragic contrast with the "coming into focus" that Father Time demands from the works of Man?

Without asking that anyone should make such sacrifices, let us at least try to learn a lesson from their example. Let us not keep so many people away from their true vocations at the haberdashery counters of our department stores! Let us try to rid music not of those who truly love it, but of those who take advantage of it by falsely calling themselves artists.

All this leaves us with little hope, but let this at least remain. Only then can the misunderstandings and disagreements about what music is trying to say come to an end.

Notes on the Month's Concerts

OF all the music played at the Concert Colonne the most modern—without being funny—was Ludwig van Beethoven's *Pastoral* Symphony. It remains one of the finest examples ever of expressive technique. . . . To hear an orchestra imitate the cries of animals certainly provides joy for the little ones as well as the grownups. To be seated in a comfortable seat and be subjected to a storm is pure Sybaritism! M. Gabriel Pierné conducted it really well, and by that I mean that he didn't try to encumber it with commentaries but merely allowed its charm to speak for itself. Apropos of this symphony, has anyone ever thought how much a "masterpiece" has to be a "masterpiece" to be able to survive so many different interpretations? There is the "respectful" interpretation, where the fear of disturbing the dust of centuries slows down all the movements and muffles all the nuances. . . . Then there is the "fantastic" interpretation, which is just the opposite, giving the impression that the piece has been submerged by a rainstorm. (Just because Beethoven was a little awkward doesn't mean we should try to aggravate him!)

The reason why this last performance was so pleasing? We really were in the country; the trees were not dressed in white ties, and the stream beside which these most pure, most German idylls took place was cool and fresh. We could very nearly smell the stables!

The *Symphonie fantastique* of Berlioz will always be the perfect masterpiece of romantic ardor. It astonishes us by being able to translate such excesses into music without losing breath. Moreover, it will always impress us as being as moving as a battle between the elements.

Gustave Charpentier's *Les Impressions d'Italie* pleasantly bear out the well-known saying "Les voyages forment la jeunesse" [Journeys form one's youth]. Despite the formality of some parts, one can already sense something of *Louise* with all its tumultuous crowd scenes.

The Institut, which has quite recently received M. Charpentier as one of its members, should be pleased with itself for having sent to Rome a young man who was able to set down his impressions of Italy so rapidly.

We were not able to hear *Au cimetière* by Monsieur Maurice Droeghmans. We are sincerely sorry, and we ask you to forgive us for putting off the remainder of these all too hasty notes until next month.

ᕔ*NOTE*

1 Henri Poincaré's book on the nature of scientific experiment and discovery was later translated by Bertrand Russell, who in his own preface to the book described Poincaré as "the most eminent scientific man of his generation," and *Science and Method* as "philosophical writings—not those of a professional philosopher: they are the untrammelled reflections of a broad and cultivated mind upon the procedure and postulates of scientific discovery."

On Respect in Art

T H E most unusual things sometimes remind the critic of the respect that music should command.

Apropos of a symphony by M. Théodore Dubois on which the gallery public decided to pour scorn, one has to admit that it was rather
difficult, almost to the point of inciting them to behave badly. Obviously they would have done better not to have displayed their dis-
content, for silence is the strongest criticism in cases such as these. We
should, however, ask ourselves whether the official standing of M.
Théodore Dubois necessarily means that he ought to be respected. He
has written a most distinguished treatise on harmony, and he is excellent as director of the Conservatoire. His works for voice are little
sung, but then *La Dame blanche* isn't played at all. It's a charming
comic opera in the true French tradition, admittedly just an excuse
for scores of marriages to take place and then to break up, but infinitely better than all that heavy artillery used by the Italian realists.

At the end of his very full life M. Théodore Dubois had the bright
idea of writing a symphony. The gallery public think it worthless;
they find nothing to the benefit of music in general, nor to the good
of French music in particular. But what's the harm in that? Need
everyone have taken offense? The taste for classicism in France has
already been killed off by our having forced the most dreadful people
to respect its ideals. It will be some years yet before we forget the face
of that awful school prefect who used to force us to recite Athalia's
dream! And even now we still often confuse it with Racine! In art one
shouldn't be obliged to respect anyone; it is confusions like the one

mentioned above that clutter up our minds with a whole host of names that will only become "respected" after hundreds of years.

For a long time now we have been trying to organize the most unorganizable things in the world, and, as it was bound to, this obsession has ended up by invading the art! If one wants to make music one immediately founds a society in which, for the most part, all the different and contradictory attitudes of the members eventually cancel each other out. And if one wants to learn music? One goes to the Conservatoire or to the Schola Cantorum where, whether one is a genius like Bach or gifted like Chopin, one has to undergo the same regime. How on earth did these two words, "art" and "regime," ever come to be linked? I really cannot imagine.

Without going back to the choir schools of the Renaissance— which probably wouldn't work so well these days—we could at least take a leaf out of their books by rediscovering their carefree way of teaching. It had the advantage of inducing no desire for immediate fame: the pupils became disciples, fearing their masters as much as they adored them.

Let us not confuse "respect," which is only a virtue, with "art," the most beautiful of all religions, made up of love and an acknowledgment of one's egoism.

Notes on the Month's Concerts

As regards the triptych called *De l'ombre à la lumière* by M. Paul Pierné, there is no doubt that the "darkness" is preferable to the "light"! So let us single out the second piece, for the first is scarcely more than development on the spot. There is a rhythmic figure having something of the quality of a Viennese waltz about it: it's like dragonflies learning how to fly—a most interesting spectacle. In the background a troupe of nymphs are cavorting in the latest Isadora Duncan style. The orchestral coloring of this piece is a marvelous evocation of those late hours when the intimate magic of the night sadly has to give way to the hard tones of morning. (As we had no program, it is possible that Monsieur Pierné imagined something quite different. In that case I hope he will forgive us.)

The third piece seems at first sight to begin just like the second, but in fact it merely serves to wake one up; it is not unpleasant. It is here that light attempts to take over from the dark. Unfortunately, some impudent violins begin before the trumpets, vying with each other as to which can fit most notes into a bar. So the beautiful flood of light we are led to expect by the title ends up by being somewhat diffused. M. Pierné clothes his orchestra in accordance with the latest fashions. He certainly hasn't forgotten to use a few Oriental silks, something no self-respecting orchestra is without these days. But it is always done in the best of taste and he never lets it turn into a parade. One wishes his writing were a little less deliberate here and there, so that the feelings could flow more freely. In the same concert the "Air de l'Archange de Redemption" was sung. In this case Monsieur Pierné knew just when to stop the "flow of feeling."

There are curious similarities between the art of Böcklin and that of Richard Strauss. There is a similar disregard for any kind of preconceived form, even a taste for a form derived directly from the color itself and a drawing of dramatic pictures with these very same colors. Of these two men, the first will not be changing his style, since he is deceased. But the second, very much alive, will have no scruples about changing his, since he is mainly concerned with dispensing emotions to all five continents!

In certain cookery books under the heading "Jugged Hare" one reads a very sensible piece of advice: "Take a hare. . . ." Richard Strauss proceeds quite differently. To write a symphonic poem he takes an old idea. That is why he is such an extraordinary illusionist, equaling the most highly trained of fakirs.

Tod und Verklärung, without having the sparkling clarity of *Till Eulenspiegel* or the grandeur of *Don Juan,* nonetheless contains many of the original effects so dear to Strauss's heart, although he has improved on them in the meantime.

At the beginning one senses one is in a sepulcher in which the souls of the dead move uneasily around. . . . The spirit undergoes great torments, struggling as hard as it can to break free from its fleshly chains, the body that binds it to the earth. But then an oboe comes in with a singing melody reminiscent of an Italian cantilena. At first one does not quite understand why, because one's mind is still full of all those mysteriously migrating souls. Besides, even if one is concerned about what is actually happening in a symphonic poem it is better to refrain from writing about it. It is certainly not the reading of those little guides that will prevent the frequent misunderstandings between composer and audience: each letter of the alphabet cleverly represents some symbolic phrase or other, and during the performance one tries to puzzle out which is which. Without any obvious trickery, except for some clusters of C major "transfiguration" chords, this work takes place before the public's very eyes. But then that is the key which is most certain to give people the feeling of eternity.

It has never been proved that music is any the more at home in the realms of the supernatural than in our own transitory life. That is an idea which is a little artificial and more often than not has literary roots. In this piece there is really no need for a program, although it is honey for the bees as far as any literary commentaries are concerned. Simple, bare music is quite sufficient. That is why certain parts of *Tod und Verklärung* seem a little empty and undeserving of the title. That is nobody's fault, not even Strauss's, for he is one of the most indisputable geniuses of our time.

Sunday, 1 December: The Beethoven festival . . . a necessary festival and on consideration one that is most useful, in that it puts people at their ease. One is merely called upon to admire, to exchange knowing smiles with the right people at the right places. And they are always the same old places, unchanging from one generation to the next.

On the way out people will say without hesitation, "That Beethoven—what a genius he is!" How right they are! To hold the opposite view is no more than stupid snobbery! These people thus need have no fear of having to sit through that highly charged atmosphere which is found at the Sunday concerts whenever the work of a young composer is being played. There, one has to hold an opinion, and that's not always convenient. Does one not also have to pretend to have understood, and never to seem shocked by daring harmonies?

What a problem that presents, too. If we are truthful, we often understand very little and hear even less—landscapes that are not yet celebrated know quite a lot about this pretense at appreciation.

Thus we learn that there are very well-intentioned people who are only able to hear one bar in every eight. (This arithmetic might not be infallible, for it is something that is different in every individual.) So naturally enough they are a few bars short at the end of the piece! This failure is not often admitted except by using the popular dictum that says "I need to hear that several times." Nothing could be more misguided! Putting aside any idea of training one's ears or studying the piece in advance, what one is meant to hear should be apparent at once. The rest is just a matter of environment and other extra-musical considerations. An audience is never in itself hostile to music; it often does not even care who wrote the piece, which is a lesson for the specialists! But we do have some awful dilettanti—people who only come to amuse themselves. In front of them one must not say stupid things. They are models of good behavior, and like children they feel they should choose the cake they don't really want. So then they turn sulky. Really, it is no laughing matter being the public. One begins to hope that they will save a few of their Sundays to play cup-and-ball instead. That's a game that requires an uncommon amount of skill, but at least it demands nothing special from one's auricular faculties.

SIM
15 January 1913

The End of the Year

I N order to make way for new fashions, it is perhaps necessary that the main symphony concerts be without much interest at the turn of the year. Almost no new works dare show their faces, and it is only the indestructible symphonies of Beethoven that honorably ring the old year out.

It provides rather sad food for thought when we realize what little respect we have for the past, and we have no consideration at all for our dead, though they might be of more worth than anyone.

Why are we so indifferent toward our own great Rameau? And toward Destouches, now almost forgotten? And to Couperin, the most poetic of our harpsichordists, whose tender melancholy is like that enchanting echo that emanates from the depths of a Watteau landscape, filled with plaintive figures? When we compare ourselves to other countries—so mindful of the glories of their pasts—we realize that there is no excuse for our indifference. The impression with which we are left is that we scarcely care at all for our fame, for not one of these people is ever to be seen on our programs, even at this time of year when we make a point of coming closer to our distant relatives. On the other hand, we do find *Parsifal*.

Several theaters are vying with each other for the privilege of staging this masterpiece. And they are right to do so: masterpieces are rare! To have the opportunity of putting it on in a concert becomes something worth fighting for. But does one not sense something a little out of tune, as it were, about these endeavors? Does it not rather bring *Parsifal* down to earth—something quite contrary to Wagner's own wishes, let alone something that is bound to annoy his faithful flock? It was certainly not in vain that he organized the pilgrimage to Beyreuth; he felt that *Parsifal* would never adapt itself to anything contemporary, and that to preserve its mystery intact it would have to be quite separate from all our daily cares.

Bayreuth is a suppression of the everyday. Nothing there must interfere with the religious love of the god, indeed, it is constantly forced upon one, sometimes by rather dubious means: for instance, when one is shown the table where Wagner used to drink his beer; the chubby-cheeked fräulein who used to carry the Grail; and some towels embroidered in red with the opening pages of the Prelude. An admirable if unexpected piece of propaganda! And since the public is not entirely made up of the most sensitive souls in the world, that is neither so ridiculous nor so useless as it sounds.

Because of all this patiently created atmosphere surrounding *Parsifal* one is tempted to ask oneself what would happen to all this beauty if it were transplanted, and exiled to one of the far too civilized capitals of this modern world, where people are only too ready to be skeptical and are always troubled by a whole host of unavoidable worries that gnaw away at our sensitivity.

Without a shadow of doubt, *Parsifal* would be powerful enough to override all these worries. We should honor it and bestow upon it the respect it deserves. But let us no longer ignore the memory of those who did their best for music in our own country.

Let us hope that at the side of the Société Bach, which so busily strives to preserve the memory of this forefather of all music, a Société Rameau will be born. For he is one of our own blood relations, and we owe it to him as a sign of respect.

Notes on the Month's Concerts

ERNEST Chausson, a composer deeply affected by the Flemish influence of César Franck, was one of the most sensitive artists of our time. Although the influence of this master from Liège has undoubtedly been felt by several present-day musicians, it was somewhat detrimental to Chausson, in the sense that it imposed a heavy spirit of sentimentality (something at the root of the Franckian aesthetic) on Chausson's natural gifts of elegance and lightness.

It is a great mistake to imagine that the qualities of genius peculiar to one race can be transmitted to another without something being lost in the process—a mistake that has often caused our own music to be led astray, for we have enthusiastically and unflinchingly adopted formulae into which nothing really French could penetrate. It would have been better to have used them merely for the sake of comparison with our own ways of doing things, so that we could see where we are lacking and try and make up for it. In that way the rhythm of French thought would not suffer, and it could not fail to enrich our heritage.

Franck (we are bound to come back to him) had a singular disregard for time for he completely ignored the fact that music can be boring. When he "began" well one could rest in peace, but sometimes he had difficulty in finding what he wanted to say. His natural genius was stifled amidst a curious mixture of too many complexities, interspersed with dramatic or pompous outbursts that ultimately failed, not because he was unable to handle them, but rather because they were not in keeping with his instinctive simplicity. In Chausson one finds something of the same thing, although he does break free and follows paths that are purely his own.

Le Poème pour violon et orchestre, which M. L. Capet played with warmth and conviction, contains Chausson's best qualities. Its freedom of form never inhibits a natural sense of proportion. Nothing is more touching than the gentle dreaminess at the end of this *Poème,* where, casting aside any ideas of description or narrative, the music itself is the sentiment that commands our feelings.

These are precious moments in the work of a real artist. For us they are inseparable from a sense of regret at his premature death, which prevented his genius from ever evolving to the full. Fine music this, and full of ardor.

> *À midi, quand j'entrai dans ta chaumière sombre*
> *Tu dormais, succombant à la chaleur du jour.*
> *Tes cheveux dénoués flottaient, noirs et sans nombre:*

Je te vis et sur moi planaient encor dans l'ombre
Les grandes ailes de l'Amour!
                    —À *Marie endormie*, A. Brizeaux

[At midday, when I came into your shady cottage
You slept, succumbing to the heat of day.
Your hair flowed loose, so black and endless:
And seeing you there, the wings of love began to beat
In the depths of my heart.]

To these deliciously sleepy lines, M. J. Guy Ropartz has written some rather troubled music. It would be love music, if it were not for the fact that Guy Ropartz's muse is rather severe and not very sympathetic to the games of love. . . . The orchestra surges and sighs, passionate and impulsive, before it finally dies down. The somnolence and sultriness of the poem (music being able to go even further than words) seems to have been of little concern to this eminent man, director of the Conservatoire at Nancy. At least, he only hints at these qualities in certain parts of the piece, which, truthfully speaking, is not much more than a sketch. And why are the "wings of love" in C major? That is always a fiery key, however carefully it is handled. This case is no exception, and it would have woken Marie up with a start had M. Ropartz not quickly replaced it with the gently undulating harmonies that so expertly round off this work.

The beauty of the Andante of Bach's Violin Concerto is so great that one really does not know where to begin, nor how to contain oneself so that one is able to listen to it as one ought! It haunts us long after it is ended, so that on coming out into the street one cannot but be astonished that the sky is not more blue, and that the Parthenon does not rise out of the ground before one's very eyes. But it only takes the blaring horns of the buses to bring one down to earth again.

Taste

I N these times, when we are so preoccupied with trying out various different ways of educating people, we are gradually losing our sense of the mysterious. The true meaning of the word "taste" is also bound to be lost.

In the last century, having "taste" was merely a convenient way of defending one's opinions. Today the word has come to mean much more than that: it is now used in many different ways. It generally signifies something that involves the kind of argument usually settled with knuckle-dusters; one makes one's point, but in a way somewhat lacking in elegance. The natural decline of a "taste" concerned with nuance and delicacy has given way to this "bad taste," in which colors and forms fight each other. . . . But then perhaps these reflections are rather too general, for here I am only supposed to be concerned with music—a difficult enough task in itself.

Geniuses can evidently do without taste: take the case of Beethoven, for example. But on the other hand there was Mozart, to whose genius was added a measure of the most delicate "good taste." And if we look at the works of J. S. Bach—a benevolent God to whom all musicians should offer a prayer before commencing work, to defend themselves from mediocrity—on each new page of his innumerable works we discover things we thought were born only yesterday—from delightful arabesques to an overflowing of religious feeling greater than anything we have since discovered. And in his works we will search in vain for anything the least lacking in "good taste."

Portia in *The Merchant of Venice* speaks of a music that everyone has within them: "The man that hath no music in himself . . . let no such man be trusted." Those people who are only preoccupied with the formula that will yield them the best results, without ever having listened to the still small voice of music within themselves, would do well to think on these words. And so would those who most ingeniously juggle around with bars, as if they were no more than pathetic little squares of paper. That is the kind of music that smells of the writing desk, or of carpet slippers. (I mean that in the special sense used by mechanics who, when trying out a badly assembled machine, say, "That smells of oil.") We should distrust the *writing* of music: it is an occupation for moles, and it ends up by reducing the vibrant beauty of sound itself to a dreadful system where two and two make four. Music has known for a long time what the mathematicians call "the folly of numbers."

Above all, let us beware of systems that are designed as dilettante traps.

There used to be—indeed, despite the troubles that civilization has brought, there still are—some wonderful peoples who learn music as easily as one learns to breathe. Their school consists of the eternal rhythm of the sea, the wind in the leaves, and a thousand other tiny noises, which they listen to with great care, without ever having consulted any of those dubious treatises. Their traditions are preserved only in ancient songs, sometimes involving dance, to which each individual adds his own contribution century by century. Thus Javanese music obeys laws of counterpoint that make Palestrina seem like child's play. And if one listens to it without being prejudiced by one's European ears, one will find a percussive charm that forces one to admit that our own music is not much more than a barbarous kind of noise more fit for a traveling circus.

The Indochinese have a kind of embryonic opera, influenced by the Chinese, in which we can recognize the roots of the *Ring*. Only there are rather more gods and rather less scenery! A frenetic little clarinet is in charge of the emotional effects, a tam-tam invokes terror—and that is all there is to it. No special theater is required, and no hidden orchestra. All that is needed is an instinctive desire for the artistic, a desire that is satisfied in the most ingenious ways and without the slightest hints of "bad taste." And to say that none of those concerned ever so much as dreamed of going to Munich to find their formulae—what could they have been thinking of?

Was it not the professionals who spoiled the civilized countries? And the accusation that the public likes only simple music (implying bad music)—is that not somewhat misguided?

The truth is that real music is never "difficult." That is merely an umbrella term that is used to hide the poverty of bad music. There is only one kind of music: music whose claim to existence is justified by what it actually is, whether it is just another piece in waltz time (for example, the music of the *café-concert*) or whether it takes the imposing form of the symphony. Why do we not admit that, of these two cases, it is very often the waltz that is in better taste? The symphony can often only be unraveled with great difficulty—a pompous web of mediocrity.

Let us not persist in exalting this commonplace invention, as stupid as it is famous: taste and color should be beyond mention. On the other hand, let us discuss, rediscover our own taste; it is not as if we have completely lost it, but we have stifled it beneath our northern eiderdowns. That would be a step forward in the fight against the barbarians, who have become much worse since they started parting their hair in the center. . . .

We should constantly be reminding ourselves that the beauty of a work of art is something that will always remain mysterious; that is to say one can never find out exactly "how it is done." At all costs let us preserve this element of magic peculiar to music. By its very nature music is more likely to contain something of the magical than any other art.

After the god Pan had put together the seven pipes of the syrinx, he was at first only able to imitate the long, melancholy note of the toad wailing in the moonlight. Later he was able to compete with the singing of the birds, and it was probably at this time that the birds increased their repertoire.

These are sacred enough origins, and music can be proud of them and preserve a part of their mystery. In the name of all the gods, let us not rid it of this heritage by trying to "explain" it. . . . Let it be enhanced by delicately preserving our "good taste," the guardian of all that is secret.

Notes on the Concerts Colonne

M. PABLO CASALS, the eminent virtuoso, disturbed the order of the program last Sunday by refusing to repeat the Dvořák concerto after M. Gabriel Pierné had expressed his doubts about its beauty! It seems to me he was quite within his rights. And in departing without having played it, Monsieur Casals found a new way of expressing his admiration for the work. We pay him our respects.[1]

La Damnation de Faust has been played a good deal. It usually affords much pleasure. But Goethe, looking down from the heavens (his latest abode), would not have understood a thing.

For certain extra-musical reasons, the complete performance of the Images met with a mixed reception. The performance was as exciting and vibrant as one could have wished.[2]

ᏬᎦNOTES

[1] The Courrier Musical reported this incident:

> On Saturday 25th, at the rehearsal, when M. Casals had finished his concerto, M. Pierné dared to say that he found the piece too long and in general uninteresting. Apparently he also made some fatuous comments about "music which is written only for virtuosi." Casals, furious at this remark, picked up his instrument and his hat and left, declaring that he would not be playing the following day.

[2] The music critic of Le Ménestrel noted that "the performance of these very difficult pieces brought Monsieur Pierné long and enthusiastic applause." It was at this concert on 26 January that Debussy's "Gigues"—the third of the orchestral Images—was performed.

Precursors

T H E profession of precursor dates far back into antiquity. God knows who they all are, though, for not all their names have come down to us. There are, however, a considerable number of them, although even the least important of these satellites takes several centuries to evolve.

Recent cosmological research has suggested that apes were the precursors of man. As far as music is concerned—and that is what we are supposed to be concerned with here—its precursor was simply the first savage who thought of hitting two pieces of wood together; one of them, being hollow, was resonant, and thus kept the savage amused. Another more daring savage stretched some gut across the piece of hollowed-out wood, and strummed it frenetically with his uncut fingernails. No doubt that is how the chord of the ninth originated— the *unprepared* ninth, moreover!—the very chord that was so profoundly to disturb the world of music.

The profession of precursor has undergone a development parallel to that of music; that is to say, the more music was written, the more precursors there were. If certain periods were lacking in precursors, the following period would simply have to invent some, which makes it extremely difficult to decide just how important this profession is, especially because these precursors are sometimes rather second rate. This has been proved quite recently by a most strange occurrence—a story that seems to have been ignored until now, even by our most famous musicologists. Just for the record, allow me to restate the principal facts of the case.

In Germany, in the second half of the eighteenth century, there existed a learned musician by the name of Friedrich Wilhelm Rust. A pupil of C. P. E. Bach, he later became Kapellmeister to the prince of Anhalt-Dessau and died in 1796, leaving numerous compositions that had been written to entertain his patron the prince. Some had been published during his lifetime, but they had fallen almost at once into complete oblivion. Friedrich Wilhelm Rust had a grandson who inherited the manuscripts of his forgotten grandfather and also something of his musical skill. He became Professor Wilhelm Rust, and occupied the post of choirmaster at the Saint Thomas Church, Leipzig, formerly the seat of the illustrious J. S. Bach. An international society was formed to entrust Wilhelm Rust with the task of publishing for the first time the hitherto unknown series of cantatas by the old master.

His appetite whetted by this international vote of confidence, the venerable Professor Wilhelm Rust decided in 1885 to publish a dozen of his grandfather's great sonatas. They caused a revolution in the world of music. In France the unchallenged masters of the French school lost no time in proclaiming him a precursor of Beethoven. They even went so far as to say that he was the greater genius. Recognizing the roots of Wagnerian harmonies in his sonatas, and an intelligent use of leitmotiv, they had no doubt on that score either—what a master he was!

So the Rust societies were formed. M. Ernest Neufeldt, director of one of these, envisaged the possibility of discovering new masterpieces among the manuscripts that Professor Wilhelm Rust (by now deceased) had not himself used, and that he had bequeathed to the Royal Library in Berlin. Monsieur Neufeldt dug them out only to discover that this so-called precursor of Beethoven, Wagner, and so on, was nothing of the sort! There was not a trace of the prodigious modernism of the sonatas, merely a fading perfume of a decaying past. . . . No dissolute harmonies at all, not even a trace of the ecclesiastical style that could set the latest fashion in enharmonic modulation—absolutely nothing of interest.

It is difficult to account for M. Neufeldt's subsequent distress, expressed in his article in the magazine *Die Musik*. It would surely have been sufficient compensation for him to have been able to reaffirm the glorious integrity of Beethoven, and to know that Wagner was responsible for first using the leitmotiv! It is still more difficult to see what the grandson Rust was trying to achieve—as M. Theodore de Wyzewa remarked in an article in *Le Temps* on the grievances of M. Neufeldt—particularly since Professor Wilhelm Rust had so carelessly omitted to destroy his grandfather's manuscripts and then had left the whole saga ready to be unearthed by the first person who cared to do a little probing.

It would have been better if one of our eminent musicologists had discovered this fraud. Although that wouldn't have explained this strange saga any the better, at least old Rust could have been dispensed with once and for all. And it might have served as a useful warning for future occasions: Beware of old frauds posing as precursors!

But enough of the Rust family; let us concern ourselves with more relevant questions.

For the sake of clarity, let us compare sounds to words—everyone uses the same words. From what, then, does the charm of a particular writer derive? How do certain words acquire a new charm, a new light, in the hands of certain writers? It must surely be the way they are put into context.

It is the same in music. Why else do certain chords, well known to all musicians, achieve an unexpected charm in certain hands if it is not that certain composers have the knack of putting them into exactly the right musical context? It is an activity that cannot be learned, for nowhere is this skill written down in an intelligible way. Only the initiates have an inkling of it after they have scrutinized the apparent mysteries of the masters, and often even they are mistaken: they search for the source of their emotions far from that hidden corner where—like the wild herbs and the delicate perfume of violets—the beauty of harmony can be found.

Apart from this "putting into context," there is also the difficult choice of what should come first and what should follow. . . . That is quite another story, and one with which it is better not to trouble intelligent ears. And there's another point: one architect would never dream of reproaching another for having used the same kind of stone as himself. Nonetheless, would he not be shocked to find formal similarities in the work of a colleague? It is evidently not the case in music, where a modern composer can copy the forms of some classical work without anyone turning a hair. He's even to be congratulated for it! (Respect for tradition manifests itself in some very strange ways.) But as soon as he uses a so-called forbidden chord, the public cries, "Stop, thief!" To put it another way: one chord, even if it's from a monumental piece of music, has no more importance in itself than one stone in a fine building. It's where it is placed that counts, and the way it throws into relief the flowing curves of the melodic line.

For many centuries we have been using the same sounds to express our innermost dreams, just as in writing we have been using the same words. There is very little difference. But when we realize that there are dozens of ways of writing or composing, there remain a hundred questions to be answered, and a further hundred posed by the answers themselves. . . . Whatever the answers may be, they would seem to suggest that we attach far too much importance to precursors. Are they not simply people who take advantage of the weaknesses of their age?

Notes on the Concerts Colonne

THE story of M. Ernest Fanelli is well known to everyone. He has suffered miseries for thirty years, having for luggage some of the most beautiful ideas in the world. Losing patience, he buried some of his most wonderful creations deep in the bottom of a trunk, trying to forget them and concentrating simply on being alive. When Gabriel Pierné was shown some writing by Ernest Fanelli he was bowled over, and thus Fanelli was discovered overnight. One finds a similar series of events in the early life of Poe, who, because of the beauty of his writing, won a competition when he was still quite unknown.

Having something to say often makes people shy. Fanelli, however, was not without friends to speak up for him. But these games of chance are difficult to play: there are obstacles to be overcome and a great deal of bitterness to be contended with, let alone blind indifference.

On 17 March 1912 Gabriel Pierné (to whom we should be grateful for having made such a cordial gesture) performed the first part of Fanelli's *Tableaux symphoniques,* based on *Le Roman de la Momie* by Théophile Gautier. It was an enormous success and a most moving occasion. People were surprised, and they asked each other how it could have come about that this man had been so ignored. Naturally enough, nobody could be found to take the blame: in questions of ignorance, nobody is ever to blame.

On 23 February 1913, Gabriel Pierné performed the second part of the *Tableaux symphoniques.* Its reception was noticeably different: should we see in this merely one of Fame's caprices? What is more to the point is that now Ernest Fanelli is in the happy position of being able to choose which of his works he would like performed. For the moment he is rather too concerned with obeying that familiar spirit which demands that he should pile more and more notes on top of one another without concerning himself with the overall proportions.

He is very aware of the decorative aspect of music, which sometimes leads him to concentrate too much on the description of minute details; he forgets that music can be persuasive in its own right. Let us hope that he will have time to take stock of himself: life owes him that. Meanwhile, we should afford him our generous support.[1]

Of two first performances, *La Printemps, allégresse symphonique* by G. Soudry, and "Les Deux Routes" a lyrical poem, words by René Robine, music by Marc Delmas, I heard only the latter, which was marvelously sung by Mme Jacques Isnardon. Very green music this, reminiscent of the Prix de Rome. The charming words did not deserve to be so overweighted with obvious dramatic effects. But M. Delmas is very young and has plenty of time to get rid of his present respect for what he has been taught and exchange it for a mind of his own, free of any arbitrary formulae.

❦ *NOTE*

[1] According to an article on a quintet by Fanelli (*SIM,* 15 April 1912), this neglected composer was a fellow student of Debussy in Marmontel's class and later a pupil of Delibes. He had a whole host of orchestral scores

tucked away. "As a mere triangle player in an orchestra, an obscure night-club accompanist, and a humble copyist on paltry wages, he suffered all kinds of humiliations for the cause of music" until "discovered" by Pierné.

Concerts Colonne

T H E misleadingly mild April has brought the Sunday concert season to an end. We need not therefore concern ourselves any longer
with the Concerts Colonne, and can leave them to rest upon their
laurels—not very glorious laurels this season, I think you will agree.
No need for any "shining trumpets swooning aloud on the vellums."
Rather have the famous old names blown their own trumpets once
too often this season.[1]

Let us forget for now the deplorable Rust affair, an affair that has
brought together both those who truly love music without any show
of pride or ill-temper and those whose business it is to look after the
Masters, preparing their own apologias for each one—an excellent way
to have the final say-so.

The ironic thing about this affair is that it has ended up by raising
our estimation of Beethoven. He emerges as a young revolutionary
opposed to the old professor who never makes a mistake; they were
about to reproach him for having written his last quartets. But let us
not dwell on this matter; the Rusts of this world are an innumerable
race who fulfill our eternal desire for the mediocre. We should be
silently thankful that occasionally there is a Beethoven who appears
on the scene to bring music back into its true focus.

Moreover, the further we progress the more we realize that a real
love of music is only possible in certain sophisticated quarters. Surely
loving it as well as not loving it is merely another way of making
music. Why so much hypocrisy? Isn't it about time we admitted that
music is not much cared for on this vast earth of ours? For having

misused it the way we have, will it not end up, if not by dying completely, at least by becoming as rarefied an occupation as the search for the philosopher's stone?

In a time like ours, when the genius of engineers has reached such undreamed of proportions, one can hear famous pieces of music as easily as one can buy a glass of beer. It only costs ten centimes, too, just like automatic weighing scales! Should we not fear this domestication of sound, this magic preserved in a disc that anyone can awaken at will? Will it not mean a diminution of the secret forces of art, which until now have been considered indestructible?

How much we miss those wonderful traveling minstrels, the fine-voiced ballad-singers who unwittingly held the key to the ancient legends, and whose only care in the world was winning their daily bread. Nowadays that is earned with opera, in which there is certainly more music; that is to say, it makes more noise; this inconvenience is compensated for by the use of lavish scenery.

We also have the "lyric drama," which is also based on ancient legends. . . . But are our souls adequately steeped in legend? Perhaps we have not yet found the means of expression that truly corresponds to our age?

Our fundamental mistake has been that we have considered Wagner's music to be the inspired ending of an epoch and not a pathway to the future. Making the symphonic development responsible for the dramatic action is a dead end that has only been of use to Wagner and the German school of thought. In adopting such a style our emphasis on clarity only succeeded in weakening and eventually drowning it.

That is why we are plodding along now without any idea of where we are going. There are, however, several paths open to us on which we may find, still fresh, traces of that pure but misleading French thought.

I shall only mention the so-called futurist music for the sake of recording history. It claims to reassemble all the noises of a modern capital city and bring them together in a symphony—from the sound of railway-engine pistons to the tinkling of a porcelain mender's bells. It's a very practical way of recruiting an orchestra, but can it ever really compete with that wonderful sound of a steel mill in full swing? Let us wait before we dismiss it: think what effect that final scene in

Götterdämmerung would have produced on one of those minstrels we mentioned earlier![2]

Not very optimistic reflections, these; it is strange how the fantasies of progress lead one to become conservative. We must be careful not to end up in a state of decline and to be wary of machinery, something that has already devoured many fine things. If we really have to satisfy this monster, let us feed it some of the old repertoire!

Théâtre des Champs-Elysées

A F T E R an inaugural concert that gave us the opportunity to compare all the different ways of conducting an orchestra, the concerts that M. Gabriel Astruc has organized to coincide with the performances at the Théâtre des Champs-Elysées should be welcomed with open arms. The music really seems to feel at home there; it no longer has that "invited" air which it was so often obliged to assume before. The reasons why the acoustics are perfect and the youthful verve of the orchestra and its conductor M. D. E. Inghelbrecht so admirable are questions we shall be returning to in the future. A bold gesture on the part of M. Astruc!

With charming audacity, M. Inghelbrecht has surrounded himself with the most conscientious team. Everything blends well together, and the choirs sing in tune. . . . We know only too well that, however enthusiastic the conductor, even the best-trained choir is not always capable of such miracles.

If all this continues—and continue it must—one has high hopes for this ensemble, whose most noteworthy aim seems to be unanimous love of music.

A lot could be said about these concerts; I hope we will be excused for having congratulated the promoters rather than having mentioned all the famous orchestral directors who enhanced the occasion. We will not forget them next time.

ᑫ∾NOTES

[1] "Nul besoin de 'trompettes tout au haut d'or pâme sur les vélins,' " wrote Debussy. The quotation is from a sonnet by Mallarmé, "Hommage" (à Richard Wagner).

[2] The immediate prewar years were important for Futurism. Debussy's aside on the movement reminds us of the largely forgotten musical experiments of the group, better known for its manifestations in the field of the visual arts. From Debussy's brief mention of factory noises it would seem that he was referring to Luigi Russolo's publication of a manifesto entitled *The Art of Noise,* which received considerable publicity throughout Europe. Russolo, best known as a Futurist painter, addressed his manifesto to the composer Francesco Balilla Pratella—the only musician capable of creating the "new art." After a strikingly penetrating summary of the history of Western music, Russolo claims that "Today [March 11, 1913] musical art, complicating itself still more, searches for the amalgamation of sounds more dissonant, strange, and harsh to the ear. Thus we are always getting closer to 'noise sound.' " Later, in the bold type characteristics of Futurist manifestos, Russolo stated that "It is necessary to break this restricted circle of pure sound and conquer the infinite variety of 'noise sounds.' We take greater pleasure in ideally combining the noises of trams, explosions of motors, trains, and shouting crowds than in listening again, for example, to the *Eroica* or the *Pastoral.*" As yet, the "noise orchestra" had not been formed, but it was only a week after Debussy's article that Russolo put his ideas into practice with his ensemble of *intonarumori* "noise-instruments," which played at a Futurist *serata* in Modena. In the December 1913 issue of *SIM,* an extended article entitled "Futurism, or Noise in Music" was published by J. Ecorcheville. Again this was based on Russolo's ideas; as yet Paris had not enjoyed first-hand experience of Futurist experiments with "noise sound," despite the wide publicity the manifesto had received. (See Michael Kirby's *Futurist Performance* [New York, 1971].)

Jeux

> *All the best things laugh.*
> —*Thus Spake Zarathustra,* Nietzsche

I AM no scientist and am therefore ill-equipped to talk about dancing; these days one has to be something of an anatomist to talk about this otherwise light-hearted subject. Before I wrote a ballet I had no clue what a choreographer was. Now I know: he's a man who is very good at arithmetic. I am not very learned in that subject, but I do remember one or two lessons from school. This for example: one, two, three; one, two, three; one, two, three, four, five; one, two, three, four, five, six; one-two, three; one, two-three (*a little faster*) . . . and then one adds it all up. This doesn't sound like much, but it can be very moving, especially when the problem is posed by the incomparable Nijinsky. How did a simple man like me come to be involved in a story with so many repercussions? Because one needs to eat, and because one day I dined with Sergei Diaghilev, a terrible but wonderful man who could make even the stones dance. He spoke to me of a scenario Nijinsky had written, a scenario made up of the usual "sweet nothings" that I suppose should always make up the story of a ballet: there was a park, a tennis court, and the chance meeting of two young girls with a young man in pursuit of a lost ball. A mysterious nocturnal landscape with that slightly evil *je ne sais quoi* that always accompanies twilight. And a lot of leaping and turning in the air, and nimble footwork—all the necessary ingredients for real rhythm to be born. . . .[1]

I really must confess that my ears and eyes have always been ravished by the Russian spectacles. They are always unpredictable, and the spontaneity of Nijinsky—whether it is natural or acquired—has often moved me deeply. So I found myself awaiting the première of *Jeux* (in the Maison de L'avenue Montaigne—the home of real music) with the eagerness of a precocious child who has been promised a visit to the theater.

It seems to me that in our dull schoolroom, overseen by some stern master, the Russians have opened a window looking out onto the countryside. And for anyone who loves them as I do it was simply marvelous to have had Tamara Karsavina, that subtly curving flower, for the ballerina, and Ludmilla Schollar playing so artlessly with the shades of the night.

⟞ *NOTE*

[1] According to the painter Jacques-Emile Blanche, the idea of *Jeux* was conceived during the course of a luncheon at the Savoy Hotel in London. Diaghilev, Leon Bakst, and Nijinsky instructed Blanche to propose the idea of the ballet *Jeux* to Debussy. There were to be "no ensembles, no variations, no pas de deux, only boys and girls in flannels, and rhythmic movements. A group at a certain stage was to depict a fountain and a game of tennis was to be interrupted by the crashing of an airplane." Blanche records that at first Debussy refused point blank, considering the idea "idiotic and unmusical." At the refusal, Blanche was instructed by Diaghilev to inform Debussy that the fee was doubled, and it appears that this increase was the deciding factor in Debussy's acceptance of the proposal.

His mention of the mathematical side of choreography brings to the fore an episode in the history of the Russian ballet. In 1911 Diaghilev had fallen under the spell of Emile Jaques-Dalcroze's eurhythmic ideas, and the choreography of *Jeux* reflected much of Dalcroze's influence. Debussy thought Dalcroze's ideas somewhat artificial and contrary to the spirit of true ballet, and wrote to Godet in 1913, shortly after having seen Nijinsky's choreography for *Jeux*:

Nijinsky . . . has given an odd mathematical twist to his perverse genius. He adds up demi-semiquavers with his feet, proves the result with his arms, and then, as if struck with partial paralysis, listens to the music with a look of disapproval. This, it seems, is to be called "stylization of gesture"—it is ugly! It is in fact Dalcrozian, and I consider Monsieur Dalcroze to be one of the worst enemies of music! You can imagine what havoc this method has caused in the soul of this wild young Nijinsky!

LES ANNALES POLITIQUES
ET LITTÉRAIRES
25 May 1913

Apropos of the Wagner Centenary

A N old friend of mine, M. Croche (who died recently), used to call the *Ring* the "Who's Who of the Gods." An irreverent quip! But it does underline the fact that even if Wagner no longer exerts the same influence as he used to on French music, people will still be consulting this admirable reference book for some while yet.

SIM
1 November 1913

W H E N the curtain of October fog has once more fallen on the last scenes of autumn magic, when the stagehands from Nature's theater have put away all their scenery—those rust-colored backdrops used for the Grand Finale—it is then that the concert societies start hurrying to prepare their own musical scenery, putting the symphonic shop in order ready for the annual reopening.

It must be confessed that it is not a case of the one killing off the other: the latter spectacle is hardly as impressive as the former. However, we must do something for those multitudes of good people who, on Sundays, demand their just reward for the week's labor. So, we dole them out a little piece of idealism—and we should note in passing that they are having to put up with starvation rations.

Our symphonic painters do not pay nearly enough attention to the beauty of the seasons. Their studies of Nature show her dressed in unpleasantly artificial clothes, the rocks made of cardboard and the leaves of painted gauze. Music is the art that is in fact the closest to Nature, although it is also the one that contains the most subtle pitfalls. Despite their claims to be true representationalists, the painters and sculptors can only present us with the beauty of the universe in their own free, somewhat fragmentary interpretation. They can capture only one of its aspects at a time, preserve only one moment. It is the musicians alone who have the privilege of being able to convey all the poetry of night and day, of earth and sky. Only they can re-create Nature's atmosphere and give rhythm to her heaving breast. . . . We know that it is a privilege they do not abuse. It is a rare thing when Nature wrings from them one of those sincere love cries of the kind that make certain pages of *Der Freischütz* so wonderful; usually her passion is somewhat tamed because they portray her green beauty in such a lifeless way. It comes out like pressed leaves festering in dreary old books. Berlioz made do with such an approach all his life; otherwise sweet delights were soured because he insisted on patronizing artificial flower shops.

The music of our time has learned how to free itself from the romantic fancies of this literary view of things, but other weaknesses remain. During the past few years we have seen it tending toward an indulgence in the mechanical harshness of certain combinations of landscape. We can certainly do without the naïve aesthetics of Jean Jacques Rousseau, but all the same we can learn great things from the past. We should think about the example Couperin's harpsichord pieces set us: they are marvelous models of grace and innocence long past. Nothing could ever make us forget the subtly voluptuous perfume, so delicately perverse, that so innocently hovers over the *Barricades mystérieuses.*

Let us be frank: those who really know the art of expressing themselves symphonically are those who have never learned how to do it. There is no conservatoire or music school that holds the secret. The theater offers a happy alternative, however, in its resources of gesture, dramatic cries, and movements; they come to the aid of many a perplexed musician. Pure music offers no such easy way out: one should either have a natural gift for evocation or give up the struggle. And in any case, where did the symphonic music of our country come from? Who are those ancestors who urge us toward this form of expression? . . . First of all, our musicians willingly allowed themselves to be inspired by the symphonic poems of Liszt and of Richard Strauss. And note, furthermore, that any attempts at emancipation were soon forcibly quelled. Each time anyone tried to break free from this inherited tradition he was brought to order, crushed beneath the weight of the more illustrious examples. Beethoven—who ought really be permitted to take a well-earned rest from criticism—was brought to the rescue. Those severe old critics passed judgment and threatened terrible punishments for breach of the classical rules whose construction—they should have realized—was nothing less than mechanical. Did they not realize that no one could ever go further than Bach, one of their judges, toward freedom and fantasy in both composition and form?

Why, furthermore, did they not so much as try to understand that it really would not be worthwhile having so many centuries of music behind us, having benefited from the magnificent intellectual heritage it has bequeathed us, and trying childishly to rewrite history? Is it not our duty, on the contrary, to try and find the symphonic formulae best suited to the audacious discoveries of our modern times, so committed to progress? The century of aeroplanes has a right to a music of its own. Let those who support our art not be left to waste away in the lowest ranks of our army of inventors, let them not be outdone by the genius of engineers!

Dramatic music is also directly involved in this change in symphonic ideals; its fate is governed by that of pure music. If it is suffering at the moment it is because it has wrongly interpreted the Wagnerian ideal and tried to find in it a formula. Such a formula could never be in tune with the French spirit. Wagner was not a good teacher of French.

Let us purify our music! Let us try to relieve its congestion, to find a less cluttered kind of music. And let us be careful that we do not stifle all feeling beneath a mass of superimposed designs and motives: how can we hope to preserve our finesse, our spirit, if we insist on being preoccupied with so many details of composition? We are attempting the impossible in trying to organize a braying pack of tiny themes, all pushing and jostling each other for the sake of a bite out of the poor old sentiment! If they are not careful the sentiment will depart altogether, in an attempt to save its skin. As a general rule, every time someone tries to complicate an art form or a sentiment, it is simply because they are unsure of what they want to say.

But we must first understand that our fellow countrymen have no love of music. Composers are therefore discouraged from doing battle or starting afresh. Music is simply not liked in France; if you doubt this, just listen to the tone in which the critics speak of her. How obvious it is that they feel no love for her at all! They always seem to be taking it out on the poor unfortunate creature, assuaging some nasty deep-seated hatred. Such a feeling is not peculiar to our own time. Beauty has always been taken by some as a secret insult. People instinctively feel they need to take their revenge on her, defiling the ideal that humiliates them. We should be grateful to those few critics who do not hate her: for the scrupulous severity of Sainte-Beuve, who himself cared passionately for literature, and for Baudelaire, who was not only a critic with a unique understanding but a fine artist as well.

There remains but one way of reviving the taste for symphonic music among our contemporaries: to apply to pure music the techniques of cinematography. It is the film—the Ariadne's thread—that will show us the way out of this disquieting labyrinth. M. Léon Moreau and Henry Février have just supplied the proof of this with great success.[1] Those hordes of listeners who find themselves bored stiff by a performance of a Bach *Passion,* or even Beethoven's *Missa Solemnis,* would find themselves brought to attention if the screen were to take pity on their distress. One could even provide a film of what the composer was doing while composing the piece.

How many misunderstandings would thus be avoided! The spectator is not always to be blamed for his mistakes! He cannot always prepare for each new piece he listens to as if he were engaged on a piece of research, for the normal routine of an ordinary citizen is not well suited to include matters of aesthetics. In this way the author would no longer be betrayed; we would be free from any false interpretations. At last we would know the truth with certainty—the truth, the whole truth, and nothing but the truth!

Unfortunately we are too set in our ways. We are reluctant to renounce the boring! On we go in the same old way, imitating one another.

What a pity Mozart was not French. He would have really been worth imitating!

Notes on the Concerts

WE were not able to get to the first two Concerts Colonne because it is proper at the moment to have flu. There was nothing new on the program, in any case. This honorable institution has started off like a slow train. Could we not persuade it to burn down a few stations on the way?

We were lucky enough to be able to attend the two inaugural evenings presented by the Société des Nouveaux Concerts at the Théâtre des Champs-Elysees. From the first one had the impression that it would be difficult to imagine performances closer to perfection than those offered by this young society. We have already praised the talent of its conductor, M. D. E. Inghelbrecht; his efforts have finally been rewarded—he now has the orchestra he deserves.

❧ NOTE

[1] Debussy refers to a film directed by Louis Feuillade, *L'Agonie de Byzance*.

SIM

1 December 1913

Concerts Colonne and Société des Nouveaux Concerts

Spanish Music

ON 29 October we heard some Spanish music performed by real Spaniards. For many people this occasion was something of a revelation, for in France Spanish music is little known; we merely have a few vague memories of having heard it somewhere before. So it was with a lively curiosity that we approached *La Feria;* the names of *La Macarona, La Soledad,* and so on were sufficient to whet our appetites and arouse our enthusiasm for more than the actual music. We were treated to the sound of their wonderful popular music, in which so much imagination mingles with so much rhythm, qualities that make it one of the greatest treasure-houses of musical riches in the world. The very richness of their folk music appears to be the reason for the slowness with which their "other" music has developed. The professionals were hindered by a kind of prudery that caused them to bury all those beautiful improvisations under solid racks of formulae. For a long time they were quite content with writing their popular "zarzuelas," in which the sound of the guitars was brought from the streets to the platform with little or no change. But the stark beauty of the old Moorish cantilenas remains unforgettable, and we persist in ignoring the wonderful traditions of Escobedo and Moralès, teachers of the great Victoria, all of whom illustrate the glory of the Spanish Renaissance.

There is no reason why these traditions should have changed . . . what more could one wish for in a country where the roadside stones burn one's eyes with their brilliant light, where the muleteers sing so passionately from the depths of their hearts? Why should we worry about the decadence of the last century—indeed, why treat it as decadence, for the popular music has remained as beautiful as ever. Blessed and wise are those countries who jealously guard their wild flowers, keeping them out of reach of the "classical" system-makers.

It was just about this time that this constellation of musicians was formed—a group resolved to reawaken the inestimable treasures that lay dormant in the songs of ancient Spain.

We should above all remember the name of Isaac Albéniz. An incomparable virtuoso, he later became highly skilled in the art of composition. Without in any way resembling Liszt, he recalls him because of the abundant fertility of his ideas. He was the first who knew how to make use of the rich melancholy and the special sense of humor peculiar to his country of origin (he was a Catalan). Few pieces of music are as good as *El Albaicín,* the third movement of his *Iberia* Suite, where one finds all the atmosphere of those carnation-scented Spanish evenings . . . the muffled sound of the guitar lamentingly playing to the night, with its sudden upsurges and nervous somersaults. Without using actual popular tunes he is the kind of person who has them in his blood. They have become so natural a part of his music that one barely distinguishes a demarcation line.

Eritaña, the fourth movement of *Iberia,* captures all the joy of the mornings, including that of a welcome visit to an inn where the wine flows cool. A constantly changing crowd passes by, its laughing and joking underlined with the ringing sound of the Basque tambourines. . . . Never before has music captured so many varied impressions, all of different colors. Our eyes eventually close, dazzled with having seen so many images.

There are many other things to be found within the pages of *Iberia.* It is the work where Albéniz is at his best, for he has taken pains in the writing down, commanded by an overriding desire to throw music out of the window! The other composers proceed in much the same way, although they are never as good as Albéniz himself. Whereas Albéniz's influences are clearly French, theirs, at least where form is concerned, seem to have become German.

La Procesión del Rocio, a symphonic poem by J. Turina, is as ordered as a beautiful fresco. Deliberate oppositions of light and shade make it easy to listen to despite its length. Like Albéniz, Turina is strongly impregnated with popular music. He is as yet hesitant in his treatment of the development and seems to turn to some of the famous modern suppliers for inspiration. Let us hope that he will soon see that he can do without them and instead listen to voices more familiar to him.

A mi Tierra ("To My Homeland") is a suite by Perez Casas. Its poetry has a touch of Oriental sultriness about it, and the music contains many new orchestral textures. The pursuit of color is nearly always justified by the sincerity with which the impression is rendered.

La divina Comedia by Conrado del Campo seems allied to the symphonic poems of Richard Strauss because of the solidity of its construction. It is a pity that we were able to hear only the finale.

All these pieces were played with warm conviction by the Madrid Symphony Orchestra; they were equally interesting in their performances of classical works, including Haydn's Thirteenth Symphony, full of delicate nuances. M. E. F. Arbos, their eminent conductor, justifiably merited his success as a composer in two pieces for violin and orchestra. M. A. Rivarde played them in a spirit of elegant nonchalance and with great charm. The roots of all these pieces were dug deep in popular music, although it never seemed like it. Is that not indubitable proof of its richness?

Mlle Lili Boulanger, who has just come back with the Grand Prix de Rome for her *Faust et Hélène* (a lyric cantata based on Goethe's second *Faust,* words by E. Adenis), is only nineteen. Her experience of the different ways of writing music seems older! There are little threads here and there with which one ties up the phrases in this kind of piece, but Mlle Boulanger uses still more subtle tricks. The arrival of Helen, accompanied by a high throbbing of divided strings, wavers gracefully before the eyes. But scarcely has she arrived than Helen (sung by Mme Croiza) takes on the voice that belongs to one of Zeus's daughters, oppressed by so many conflicting destinies. Meanwhile Faust was whispered in David Devriès's beautiful voice.

If the character of Mephistopheles and the inevitable trio are a little conventional, one should not forget the conditions under which one has to write a cantata. They are, in a word, unfavorable.

They demand that you should have ideas and talent at one particular time of the year; if you happen to be out of training that month, so much the worse for you! A useless tradition, and of no worth for the future! But it is no good deploring it, because all competitions are conducted in the same way. The judges of these competitions, having suffered along the same lines in their time, are very pleased to see you doing the same. Once a year, more or less, someone says that the rules set for the Prix de Rome must be changed, but nothing is done about it.

Let us indeed guard the Villa Medici as a most pleasant form of compensation, but let us do away with the Prix de Rome, which fulfills no need in our time.

Alfred Bruneau had the excellent idea of orchestrating two songs without any other intention except to "charm the ears and move the heart" (as he says in *Les Premiers Principes de la musique*). It is incredible how Bruneau's dramatic power here turns to something both tender and grave.

In Berlioz's *Roméo et Juliette*, has anybody ever asked why the theme used for the romantic "Tristesse de Roméo" is obliged to make an appearance during the quadrille in the "Fête chez Capulet"?

Surely Romeo cannot be lamenting all his woes as if shouting through a megaphone without noticing old Father Capulet, who leads him abruptly to the door? There is irony here somewhere.

We have joyfully welcomed the arrival of the Théâtre des Champs-Elysées. But after one admirable performance (in French) of *Boris Godunov*, we had to deplore its finale. It was extremely tragic and did no good to the cause of the art, for it will be a long time before we see another venture of such worth.[1]

Our sympathies to all who fought to the end.

⮑*NOTE*

[1] On the eve of a subsequent performance of *Boris*, the theater was forced to cancel it for financial reasons.

SIM

1 January 1914

(*Our eminent contributor Claude Debussy, having been called
upon to conduct two festivals of his works in Russia—they met with
a triumphant reception—has written the following note for his
readers. Let us add that the Association des Concerts Colonne has
had the good taste not to perform any new works during his absence. Awaiting his return, it has devoted its attentions to several
interesting revivals, among which we should note the Third and Fifth
Symphonies of Beethoven, an important fragment from* Parsifal, *Debussy's own three* Nocturnes, *the* Symphonie sur un thème montagnard
[Symphony on a Mountain Air] *by Vincent d'Indy, and, accompanied
on the piano, the* Dichterliebe *of Schumann. This last was enthusiastically received by the public, but devotees of the orchestra doubted
its suitability in the context of a symphony concert. This matter was
thoroughly discussed by the critics.*)

M. S. Koussevitsky[1] has invited me to come and direct two orchestral concerts, one in St. Petersburg and the other in Moscow. For this
reason I hope you will excuse me for not having been able to write
about the musical life of Paris in general and, in particular, of the
Concerts Colonne.

These [Russian] concerts were consecrated exclusively to the works
of Claude Debussy. Never before has so much been heard at the same
time. You will, I feel sure, understand why I will not be able to write
much about these pieces. . . . But let me be permitted to say above
all: how marvelous is the orchestra that Koussevitsky—entirely alone—
has assembled. It is distinguished by its disciplined exactitude and its

devotion to music, rare qualities even in some of the enlightened cities of dear old Europe!

We recall that M. Koussevitsky was an incomparable virtuoso on the double bass, an instrument that does not usually inspire much confidence. For this reason, this section of his orchestra has a quite unexpected strength. . . . It really is the foundation stone of the whole orchestra—by turns solid, tumultuous, indeed sometimes even impalpable—on which is fearlessly built a free play of all possible orchestral sonorities.

During the summer, Koussevitsky's orchestra travels up and down the Volga in one of those triple-decker boats of the kind one sees on the Swiss lakes. It stops wherever it is possible to find a room, not necessarily a concert hall, but anywhere where one can decently make music. Koussevitsky told me that he has rarely met audiences more attentive or more appreciative; they were so sincere that they forgot to clap! One should not see this as an act of stupidity, but should realize that in these places those unable to pay for their seats in money pay with a gift of some fresh fruit!

That is perhaps the greatest homage, and the most beautiful, ever rendered to music. Certainly it is at least as good as that savage noise made by clapping the hands one against the other, a habit generally adopted by even the most sensitive of our dilettanti.

Let us not be mistaken: anything that is beautiful demands many special qualities. All are united in the person of S. Koussevitsky, whose burning will to serve music admits to no obstacles.

ᕦ*NOTE*

[1] Koussevitzky, writing to Debussy in November 1913, made it clear that his visit to Russia was eagerly awaited by the musical worlds of both Moscow and St. Petersburg. Lazare Saminsky, a pupil of Rimsky-Korsakov, presented a view of Debussy which was probably widely held among young Russian musicians:

> The arrival of Debussy in Russia, at the invitation of Serge Koussevitzky, aroused enthusiasm among many music lovers but particularly

among the musicians of the young Russian school. For us, who make up the circle of young composers of Petrograd, Debussy was in some way the spiritual son of Mussorgsky and Rimsky-Korsakov, our own adored master who stood between the East (Russia) and the West (France), torchbearer and symbol of musical power in Europe, regenerated and creative. . . .

Among the most wonderful and profound impressions of that time, my memory jealously guards that of a concert conducted by Debussy in St. Petersburg. Composers have a charmingly individual way of conducting, even when the higher skills of a conductor are above them. A strange beauty is born of that curious combination of a clumsy conducting technique with a supremely convinced and personal interpretation. That was how it was when Debussy appeared on the conductor's rostrum. His thoughtful eyes, so large and piercing and betraying a measure of suffering, did not seem to see the enormous crowd that filled the vast hall. A marvelous peace affected his every movement. Never before had that marvelous music *La Mer* appeared so seductive and yet mysterious at the same time, so imbued with the enigmatic life of the Cosmos, than on that evening when her great Creator, with a gentle hand, was ruling over her waves.

Two Masterpieces

BEING a masterpiece is not always an enviable profession. For proof of this one has only to consider the unfortunate plight of the Mona Lisa's smile, which, because of too much fame and attention over the years, has become somewhat strange.

If only on seeing her for the umpteenth time those art critics had admitted that she really wasn't smiling at all! If only they had admitted that she was in fact pouting, perhaps a little voluptuously, in some private Lombardian fashion. A similar expression can be found in almost all of Leonardo's faces. Its involuntary exile might have spared us all those literary variations on "the mystery of a smile," which is simply natural shading!

Then we have also had *Parsifal,* which was deliberately mistreated! Everybody in Europe went for it! Twenty capital cities, at least, fought each other for the privilege of performing it, each one trying to be more à la mode than the next. It must have been terrible! Incredibly stupid things were said about it, and by people who were normally sensible enough. Others gravely pronounced that masterpieces belong to everybody—something that can hardly be upheld, given the way we treat them these days (see above). And more crimes will be committed, we can be sure of that. But, happily, Father Time's tarnish will tell, and he is the best of all art critics. The masterpieces will begin to be treated with greater indifference. They know they cannot rely upon secret admirers or anonymous lovers, true passion usually being more discreet.

Let us await with patience the day when a competition will be inaugurated to judge the best *Parsifal*. Let us hope that it will be an international competition and even one where the nations will be able to compete against each other without bitterness. And if, on that day, Wagner does not come tumbling down from the highest heavens onto the heads of his admirers, it is simply that miracles never seem to happen any more.

Notes on the Concerts

L'Etrangère, lyrical drama in three scenes, poem by Alphonse Métérié, music by Max d'Ollone. First scene:

Two people: Guillaume the hero, a quiet young man whose soul is troubled, given to dreaming; and l'Etrangère [the stranger], a lady who represents the desire for adventure, a need to break away to a land of bluer skies, a person full of secret desires and longings. . . .

In the orchestral prelude the individual sounds have to struggle to make themselves heard. They draw out the essential lines of a melancholy, muted landscape of the kind peculiar to those northern countries where the sun never shines save through a sooty shroud of smog.

Toward the end of the prelude, courageously gray, Guillaume and l'Etrangère stand before the gates of the town, veiled in mist, where he was born and to which he has decided to return in the hope of finding peace again—a peace that l'Etrangère has made him leave behind in order to pursue what seems like happiness, in places studded with casinos. But he prefers his former, humbler existence, sheltered from the hurly-burly of modern life—the suits and white ties, the dinners and soirées. . . . He wants to be back in his old flannel suit, a boring livery, but just right for dreaming. . . . He must bid good-bye to all those unfulfilled longings.

L'Etrangère, being faithful to what she symbolizes (for no longer is any play possible without symbols), does not want to believe that this is good-bye forever. She says, quite simply, that they will meet again. She walks away alone on the road to the sea, and Guillaume watches her disappear into the last glimmer of sunset. Night sets in. And so does boredom! Guillaume is alone now, unsure of his resolutions, so he sets out to return to his parental home. But in trying to rid himself of l'Etrangère he forgets the powers of memory. Out of the deepening darkness come forth radiant visions. . . . He breathes again the perfume of his former ways, he hears again those dances that punctuated his former joy. However, he must go back. But how will he be received? Will he not simply be told that one's youth should not be wasted in traveling, and that he should take a firmer hold on himself?

Max d'Ollone's music never plays games with our feelings, and as if out of the greatest loyalty it goes through certain developmental sections, seeming to consider it its duty to do so. Because of this some parts of it are rather boring. In the theater they will become even more boring, at least I fear they will, for these days the public seems to have lost all its patience. One has to get through things quickly nowadays, always more quickly! Thanks to which we were recently able to see Goethe's two *Fausts* performed together in one evening. A record-breaking event, but that's about all!

Not that I am recommending cinematic realism, where the characters all throw themselves one on top of the other, snatching the tunes out of each others' mouths. There you can have the whole of a lifetime in one act—birth, marriage, and murder included. . . . All so that the minimum of music may be written since, logically enough, one has no time to listen to it.

It must be confessed that major compositions for the theater will soon become redundant, a thing of the past, although they will not leave without a struggle. And talking of this, I wonder if we all know that the film makers are talking of filming the nine symphonies of Beethoven? In spite of all the spectacles and plays of this modern age! Make no mistake: it will have nothing to do with music, still less to do with Beethoven.

But to return to M. Max d'Ollone. Let us hope that he will see *L'Etrangère* given the setting he envisaged. The music is good enough to withstand the sometimes excessive psychological content. But there are hidden pitfalls in the theater: its peculiar optical tricks can be the downfall of any of its devotees who wander from the straight and narrow. . . .

Mlle Jeanne Hatto sang the part of l'Etrangère. Her voice is commanding yet gentle, like the reflection of a beautiful sky in the sea; she made us realize both the dream and the reality contained in this part. M. Lheureux, who made such a marvelous Shuisky in the altogether unique performance of *Boris Godunov* at the Théâtre des Champs-Elysées, gave the melancholy Guillaume just the right expression. Gabriel Pierné and the orchestra of the Concerts Colonne made up for the lack of scenery and lighting with an attentive understanding worthy of the highest praise.

COMEDIA

1 February 1914

Claude Debussy Tells Us of His Theatrical Projects
(*Interview by Maurice Montabré*)

Y E S , *Pelléas et Mélisande* is to be revived. I shall certainly be pleased but not as much as you might think, for its success—if there is any success—has taken a long time. The public has no taste and never will.

There is talk of putting on *La Boîte à joujoux* ["The Toy Box"] at the Opéra-Comique. That most perfect of designers Hellé has conceived the set and staging, and it is through the enthusiasm of M. Gheusi that the project has got off the ground.[1] But it will be very difficult to mount. The Opéra-Comique is only a theater, and for this work the setting and conditions for performance must be just right. You know what it is, don't you? *La Boîte à joujoux* is a pantomime to the kind of music that I have written in Christmas and New Year albums for children, a work to amuse children, nothing more. These album pieces will be brought together and made into three scenes.

The plot? Oh, very simple: a cardboard soldier falls in love with a doll, he tries to show off to her, but she betrays him with *Polichinelle.* The soldier learns of this and terrible things begin to happen: there is a battle between wooden soldiers and *Polichinelles.* In short, the soldier in love with the beautiful doll is gravely wounded in the battle, the doll nurses him and . . . they all live happily ever after.

You see how it is simplicity itself—quite childish. Only how do you put that across in the theater—the natural simplicity of it? The characters have to retain the angular movements and burlesque appearance of the cardboard originals, without which the play would lose all its significance. I cannot envisage how it could be done at the Opéra-Comique. But all things are possible, I suppose.

As for the *Fêtes galantes,* which Charles Morice and I have put together from the poems of Verlaine, that will be a ballet, an opera ballet. It's not finished—far from it. I am working on it, but I cannot say exactly on what date I will hand it over to our Académie de musique.[2]

NOTES

[1] In fact, the outbreak of war prevented the project from coming to fruition.

[2] Debussy had signed a contract for this ballet with Jacques Durand, in collaboration not with Morice, but with Louis Laloy. Since 1912 he had entertained the idea of a project based on Verlaine under the title *Crimen amoris.* Neither saw the light of day.

For the Cause of Music

L A S T month a very important event was accomplished very simply—and we now have a professional choral society. This might seem to be unimportant, because in Paris, a city that can boast so many organizations and associations, one would have thought that there was one already in existence. Well, there wasn't. We have had to make do, up till now, with admitting that they did exist . . . abroad.

Travelers had told us about the great English music festivals, where three hundred voices full-bloodedly, but respectfully, sing the praises of Handel, of Mendelssohn, and of Sir Elgar [*sic*].

They also talked about lost little villages in Thuringia where the local beer was drunk to the accompaniment of Bach chorales. It was enough to make us weep! And they didn't forget to remind us that we have nothing comparable here in France. As for Paris, we have to make do with the *café-concerts,* and it is from these and similiar establishments that our musical ability is judged. We made a few feeble attempts, but they were to no avail: Art was going through hard times, and so were her followers. . . . Lethally uncomfortable furniture was installed—chairs on which one could not possibly sit for more than three-quarters of an hour. And to crown it all, we were reproached for fearing boredom as if it were some kind of epidemic.

But at least we tried, and at least we attracted some of the most notable professors of boredom. . . .

It is perhaps difficult for us not to confuse the "boring" with the "serious." Above all it is a question of taste, and it appears that questions of taste should never be openly discussed. But is it not rather that people seldom have the courage to uphold their taste in the face of discussion?

The thousand little customs that at any one time everybody seems to observe were really only meant to serve one person; it's ridiculous! Allow me to illustrate this point with an example, albeit a trivial one. A man has a big head. After numerous consultations with his hatter in front of the mirror, he finds a kind of hat that makes his head look smaller. He takes to wearing it and it looks quite natural. But then a lot of other people—by no means all idiots—also take to wearing the same kind of hat, making themselves look ridiculous. You might say that this is really a question of fashion and not one of taste. Well, that's not true: taste and fashion are inextricably linked, or at least they ought to be. And if one agrees to make oneself look ridiculous because of one's choice of hat, that is good enough reason to suppose that one's ridiculous tastes will also extend to other areas where taste is needed, including the realms of music, the most delicate of all the arts.

Carlyle must have forgotten to include the chapter "The Links between Hats and Music" in his *Sartor Resartus*—a cruel and ironical tome. He really ought to have written such a chapter, because these links do, indisputably, exist. The hats of those with a taste for symphonies are not the same as the hats of those who appreciate *La Damnation de Faust*. And those soft felt berets that people keep rolled up in a ball, always at the ready, do not hold the same opinions as the "toppers," shining like a Negro's skin. To wear such a hat requires reserve and respectability—its wearer must not show any excesses of enthusiasm. But with a beret you have more of a free hand. You can even throw it at the orchestra as a last resort.

But to return to the Association Chorale Professionnelle. . . . It has, despite its comparatively recent formation, given some very fine performances, many of them premières. Considering that most of its members were only trained in choirs, that is quite extraordinary. And they really put their hearts into it!

I feel obliged to mention everything in their first concert. Perhaps there were simply too many beautiful things for anyone to appreciate at one sitting—we're not used to such richness. First of all came a motet for double choir by J. S. Bach. Nobody has ever surpassed his choral writing. Next came a delightful madrigal, "Mille regrets de vous abandonner" by Claude Lejeune, and then that marvelous masterpiece by Clément Jannequin, "Bataille de Marignan," which conveys all the hubbub and the rough way of life at an army camp. It is noted down shout by shout, noise by noise: the sound of the horses' hooves mingles with the fanfares of trumpets in a subtly ordered tumult. Its form is so direct that it would almost seem to be "popular music," so accurate and picturesque is the musical representation of these events.

There were children's songs—most amusing—and Norwegian dances in which one noticed something of the striking melancholy of Edvard Grieg. Then by Grieg himself, "Voyez, Jean," perhaps rather more instrumental than vocal, but all the same it won us over by its use of the men's voices alone. This music has the icy coldness of the Norwegian lakes, the transient ardor of her sharp and hurried spring.

What must be stressed is the difficulty of all these different pieces! But nothing was lacking: the ensemble was perfect and the variety of expression surprising.

It is all the work of M. D. E. Inghelbrecht—a man as thin as his bâton.[1] His enthusiastic spirit is behind this gathering together of forces, and his scrupulous authority is commanding without ever being destructive. He can pass from the sumptuous gravity of Bach to the northern fantasies of Grieg without seeming to be doing anything out of the ordinary. From all points of view this revival of our choral traditions must be encouraged. And if it suffers from being thoroughly French, let us try to forgive it.

At the Concerts Colonne

"La Vengeance des fleurs," a musical adaptation by M. G. Grovlez of a ballad by Freiligrath, here receiving its first performance at the Concerts Colonne, was composed in 1910 and was first played at the Société Nationale in 1912. It is a curious piece of symphonic pantomime.

M. Grovlez most ingeniously tries to follow Freiligrath's text, made up of tenuous images and of impressions as fleeting as the dream he is trying to evoke. But although the poetry can change the scene as it wishes, the music does not find it so easy to follow suit; it needs more time. The music is undeniably skillful, but it doesn't always succeed in covering up the disparity between so many juxtaposed spots of color; they no longer hang together.

With the artifice of the program gone, the work is rather difficult to follow. One's attention is caught now and again by a nice sonority or a fleeting line, but almost without being conscious of it, one begins to make up one's own story.

That is why Gabriel Grovlez's musical adaptation, although sensitive and often most pleasing, needs to be performed accompanied by scenery that, if light enough, would prevent such willfulness.

Gédalge's Third Symphony was in sharp contrast to "La Vengeance des fleurs." The declaration of principles that seems to underlie this symphony is plain enough: "Neither literature, nor painting." A cunning demon causes M. Gédalge to betray his principles in some parts, which are not the least pleasant of this fearless and irreproachable symphony.

❧ NOTE

[1] Inghelbrecht had some years earlier been chorus master for the first performance of Debussy's Le Martyre de Saint-Sébastien.

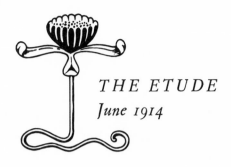

An Appreciation of Contemporary Music

From an interview secured expressly for The Etude *with the renowned French composer Claude Debussy;* by M. M. D. Calvocoressi[1]

A BEWILDERING PRESENT   What the future of music is to be, considering how bewildering the present is, has more than ever become a puzzling question. The writer, therefore, considers it a singular piece of good fortune that during a recent conversation he had the honor to hold with M. Claude Debussy this very topic should have come up for discussion.

It is quite natural to expect that M. Claude Debussy, being one of the chief innovators of today, and one whose works have been the objects of passionate criticisms, both bitterly censured and warmly upheld, which nonetheless have eventually come into their own, should take an interested and not unsympathetic view of the turmoil that surrounds us. He is also a trained critic, and has written many essays for Paris dailies and periodicals. He currently reviews concerts for a musical monthly.

M. Debussy may be briefly described as a keen, thoughtful observer and a philosopher capable of enthusiasm as well as of scepticism.

The former point is shown by his great fondness for the music of Bach, of Couperin, of Rameau, of Chopin, of Balakirev, of Moussorgsky; the latter, by pungent, irreverent comments upon certain songs of Schubert "that smell of long-closed drawers and of flowers forever faded" or upon Wagner's *Ring* with its "stilted, not very purposeful flourishes." But apart from occasional sallies such as these, he expresses himself very reticently, and when referring to his articles one should never fail to read between the lines.

"I do not profess," he said, "to supply 'criticism,' but simply and candidly to give my impressions. In criticism the individual factor plays far too great a part. And often the outcome of all that is written or said can be reduced to 'you are wrong because I happen to think differently,' or the reverse. The thing to do is to discover the many impulses that have given birth to works of art and the living principle that informs those works."[2]

A PERPLEXING CONDITION   "Interviewers have often ascribed to me surprising things which I greatly marveled to read. It is often difficult to say much on the subject of contemporary music. Events are accumulating with incredible speed, and to try to focus them is often to strive after impossibilities. At the point now reached by music, who could make a choice between the many diverging roads that composers follow? The task is distressingly puzzling. We have to deal not only with a great number of contemporary works but also with the many often contradictory teachings of the works of the past, whose influence upon our sensitivity and our culture is constantly increasing. And if even in the patrimony that came to us from the past we find food for perplexity, what is to be said of the present?

"As far as I am concerned I have little to say about it, and still less as to the future of music—all that is more or less guesswork, and tempts me little. Moreover, I do not see much of what is happening. There comes a time in life when one wishes to concentrate, and now I have made it a rule to hear as little music as possible.

"Take Arnold Schönberg, for instance. I have never heard any of his works. My interest was roused by the things that are written about him, and I decided to read one of his quartets, but I have not yet succeeded in doing so."

THE EVIL OF PREMATURE JUDGMENT   "A point that I really wish to emphasize is, that I consider it almost a crime to judge prematurely. The former policy, which consisted of allowing artists to ripen in peace and of taking no notice of them until their art had fully asserted itself I consider far sounder than the present one. It is unwise to unsettle young artists by making them the subjects of discussions that are often shallow and prejudiced. This feverish haste to dissert, dissect, and classify is the disease of our time. Hardly has a composer appeared than one begins to devote essays to him; one pounces upon his works, one burdens his attempts with ambitious definitions.

"I esteem, for instance, that, tempting as the thing may be, the moment has not yet come to judge the younger Hungarians like Bartók and Kodály. They are both extremely interesting and deserving young artists, eagerly seeking their way; no doubt about that. They are pretty sure to find it. And a noteworthy feature of their music is the obvious affinity between its spirit and that of the modern French. But further I shall not go."

MODERN RUSSIAN AND SPANISH MUSIC "Igor Stravinsky affords another excellent instance of a young artist instinct with keen and fervid curiosity. I think this attitude of mind most praiseworthy at his time of life. It is good for young artists to be alive and to look all around themselves, but I think he will sober down in due time. He is the only one of the younger Russians with whose output I am acquainted. During my recent stay in St. Petersburg and in Moscow I met several other composers but I had no occasion to hear their music."

Debussy, a keen lover of Russian music—he was one of the first in France to praise Balakirev and Moussorgsky—evinces great sympathy with the doings of contemporary Spanish composers who, like the Russians, have sought and found in national folk songs the foundation of their musical style.

"Practically the whole of modern Spanish music comes directly from folk music. And yet it never lacks variety, so that one may well judge how inexhaustibly rich the fountain is. Among the Spanish musicians of today the most typical, perhaps, is Albéniz. He has drunk at the springs of folk music deeply enough to be absolutely imbued with its style and its very spirit. The profuseness of his imagination is positively stupendous; no less so his capacity for creating atmosphere."

MODERN ITALIAN OPERA Debussy is not lavish in his praise of Italian opera: "Why talk of modern Italian opera? That would be ascribing to it an importance of which it remains totally destitute. The greater part of the public revels in the vulgar and the meretricious, and at all times has bad taste been catered for. The Italians, well aware of what the public wants, act accordingly. I do not think their influence harmful, for every artist writes the works that he was pre-ordained to write. If anyone be drawn toward the mediocre, the fact shows him to be mediocre himself, and we are to presume that under no circumstances could he prove capable of rising above mediocrity."

The vehemence of the foregoing sentences contrasts very forcibly with M. Debussy's usual reticence, a reticence in which one should acknowledge the effects not of indifference, but of the composer's innermost temperament. And it should be remembered that in M. Debussy's opinion the worst sin against works of art is indifference.

"The old quarrels are revived," he recently wrote. "So much the better! For if freedom of spirit is a characteristic trait of our time, that freedom does not go without a tendency passively to accept all kinds of styles and methods, and that inertness is almost an outrage to art."

THE ATTITUDE OF THE PUBLIC   To conclude the conversation I asked M. Debussy his impressions as to the comparative receptivity of the different publics before which he has appeared as pianist or as conductor. His answer was, "There can be, I think, no general rule. It all depends upon affinities. As I said a while ago the Hungarians are very near to us Frenchmen, and therefore, our music succeeds with them. The Russians are likewise well prepared to appreciate the output of the modern French school. From Great Britain also I have carried away an altogether favorable impression. The British public has a most remarkable capacity for attention and respect; it does not think itself compelled noisily to express dissatisfaction whenever it fails to grasp at first hearing the purport of a new work. And this of course, as far as the appreciation of modern music is concerned, is the best attitude. To believe that one can judge a work of art upon a first hearing is the strangest and most dangerous of delusions."[3]

⌇NOTES

¹ This article, kindly brought to my attention by François Lesure for last-moment inclusion, is of interest for several reasons. Calvocoressi was no mere journalist, but a respected critic and musicologist who was on fairly close terms with Debussy, close enough at least to send him a copy of his translation of Rimsky-Korsakov's *The Golden Cockerel*. Calvocoressi had also been at the center of the Debussy-Ravel rivalry in the early years of the century, publishing an article provocatively titled "Maurice Ravel et l'imitation Debussyiste." At the beginning of 1907 Debussy's opinion of professional critics such as Calvocoressi does not seem to have been high: in a letter to Louis Laloy (another eminent musicologist and critic) Debussy dismisses Calvocoressi as a "lackey," no doubt inflamed by his admiration for Ravel.

The interview naturally displays the hallmarks of an informed interviewer, and the first section has been omitted here as it contains none of Debussy's own ideas but rather Calvocoressi's own view of the current musical scene. Of particular importance is the insight the article gives on Debussy's knowledge and opinions of contemporary composers: Bartók, Kodály, and Schönberg. Though hardly illuminating, it does give us a clear indication as to the extent of Debussy's knowledge of these composers.

² Calvocoressi's free paraphrase of Debussy's well-worn paragraph on criticism is interesting in its removal of the composer's purposeful obscurity. Ironically, the Debussy who condemns the partisan nature of criticism was exceptionally susceptible to extreme partisan views in his own writings.

³ *The Etude* was a musical magazine of a popular nature published monthly in Philadelphia. The present interview is taken from vol. 32, no. 6, pp. 407–408.

Alone at last! . . .

F O R seven months now, music has been subordinated to the military regime. Although strictly confined to barracks or ordered out on charitable missions, she has in general suffered less from inactivity than from her mobilization. The public, moreover, have accepted this sacrifice with so much fervor that it is difficult to estimate whether they are really being heroic, or indeed if it has even pained them at all. It is therefore too soon, and perhaps, alas, indiscreet, to allow ourselves to be preoccupied with such trivialities as the problems of music when there are so many more urgent matters on hand.

We can only console ourselves in the knowledge that [music], the great Comforter, will soon be able to resume her magnificent, if temporarily interrupted, task. She may even emerge purer from her ordeals of fire: more brilliant, and stronger. The outcome of the war will undoubtedly have immediate repercussions in the next chapter of our history of the Art, and we should understand that victory will bring a necessary liberation to the French musical consciousness.

For many years now I have been saying the same thing: that we have been unfaithful to the musical traditions of our own race for more than a century and a half.

It is true that the public have often been misled because they have been presented with the latest fashion as if it were part of a purely French tradition. We have obscured the roots of our music's family tree: the careless observer has seen only parasitic creepers, and our indulgence toward the naturalized has been limitless!

In fact, since Rameau, we have had no purely French tradition. His death severed the thread, Ariadne's thread, that guided us through the labyrinth of the past. Since then, we have failed to cultivate our garden, but on the other hand we have given a warm welcome to any foreign salesmen who cared to come our way. We listened to their patter and bought their worthless wares, and when they laughed at our ways we became ashamed of them. We begged forgiveness of the muses of good taste for having been so light and clear, and we intoned a hymn to the praise of heaviness. We adopted ways of writing that were quite contrary to our own nature, and excesses of language far from compatible with our own ways of thinking. We tolerated overblown orchestras, tortuous forms, cheap luxury and clashing colors, and we were about to give the seal of approval to even more suspect naturalizations when the sound of gunfire put a sudden stop to it all. . . .

Let us try to understand its own rough-hewn eloquence! Today, when the virtues of our race are being exalted, the victory should give our artists a sense of purity and remind them of the nobility of the French blood. We have a whole intellectual province to recapture! That is why, at a time when only Fate can turn the page, Music must bide her time and take stock of herself before breaking that dreadful silence which will remain after the last shell has been fired.

1917

Preface in the Form of a Letter
to Pour la Musique Française: Douze Causeries

December 1916

Dear Monsieur Huvelin,

You have rather overestimated the importance of the preface that you so kindly asked me to write to your book *Douze Causeries faites à Lyon par des amis de la musique.* These "conversations" are excellent in themselves and could well enough do without my contribution! . . . So it is only with hesitation that I accept such a difficult task. . . . I will simply try to pay my sincere homage to your venture in the form of a few brief reflections, so as not to delay the pleasure that awaits your readers. . . .

For some years now, although we hardly seem to have been aware of it, French music has had to put up with a great deal of importation. Our natural hospitality has facilitated this, but we have not been enough on our guard against these often contradictory disciplines. Even at this very moment, when France is sacrificing the blood of her best children, without regard for birthright or class, one hears some strange proposals about Beethoven put forward: Flemish or German, he was a great musician. And Wagner, too—although he was more of a great artist than a musician. But that has been understood for a long time.

But it is not just that with which we are concerned. It seems that some weeds are growing, ones that should be pulled up without mercy, just as a surgeon would amputate a gangrenous leg. . . .

Without going to such extremes we must be on our guard, and above all counter that old reproach about our being too "light" . . . always made in a spirit of hypocrisy that hardly concealed a'real desire to stifle us.

Let us regain our freedom, our own style; for the most part they were our own invention, and thus they deserve to be preserved, for there are none more beautiful.

Let us no longer stifle ourselves by writing symphonies, wasting our energies, and obtaining no appreciable results. Rather let us concentrate on operetta.

Chabrier, so marvelously endowed by the comic muse, died in pursuit of the lyrical drama: a Glucko-Wagnerian importation quite opposed to our native genius.[1] "La Marche joyeuse" and certain songs are fantastic masterpieces on musical grounds alone, and thus different from Offenbach, who is often amusing simply because of the way he deforms the text; the music willingly remains in the background.

Not everyone can write "great music"—a term without any precise meaning—but everyone strives to. Thus are we weighed down with false masters and the imbecility of journalistic opinions on music.

Do not our soldiers, who trudge heroically through the mud singing songs in which sheer rhythm triumphs over good taste, have the right to shrug their shoulders at our futile preoccupations? Let us hope that they will forgive us and will realize that there are many paths to victory! Music, fertile and admirable, is one of them.

. . . but the rest will write itself!

Your devoted
Claude Debussy

 *NOTE*

[1] Chabrier's opera *Briséis* was unfinished at his death.

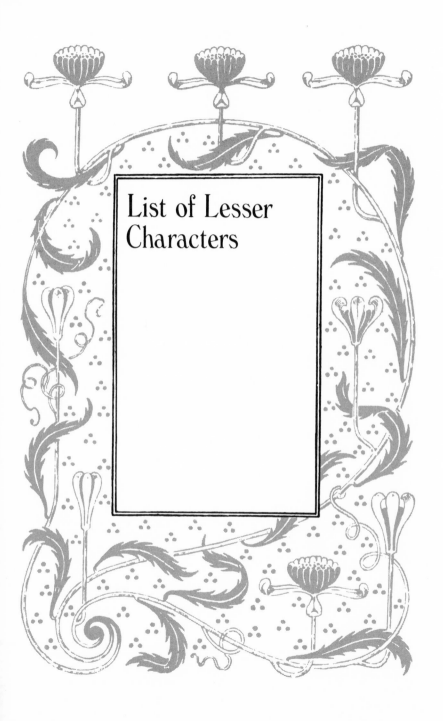

List of Lesser
Characters

ADAM, ADOLPHE (1803–56) French composer of operetta and ballet. Works include *Giselle*. Founder of the Théâtre National.

D'ANNUNZIO, GABRIELE (1863–1938) Italian poet, novelist, dramatist, and patriot, widely appreciated in France. Connected with Debussy through *Le Martyre de Saint-Sébastien*.

ASTRUC, GABRIEL (1864–1938) Impresario influential in many artistic ventures in Paris at the turn of the century. Involved in Debussy's *Martyre*, he also claimed responsibility for introducing the cakewalk into Europe.

BACHELET, ALFRED (1864–1944) French composer, mainly of operetta.

BÖCKLIN, ARNOLD (1827–1901) Swiss painter. Anticipated expressionism with introduction of fantastic elements into otherwise allegorical paintings. His works were reproduced in the luxury magazine *Pan*, to which Debussy subscribed.

BORDES, CHARLES (1863–1909) One of Franck's most prominent pupils and founder of the Schola Cantorum. Composed as well as concerning himself with the revival of Renaissance choral music. Among his associations with Debussy must be included a possible reference to Bordes's setting of Verlaine's "Streets" to the tune of "The Keel Row," published under the title *Dansons la Gigue*. The appearance of this same tune in Debussy's own *Gigues* can hardly have been fortuitous.

BOULANGER, LILI (1893–1918) Pupil of her sister Nadia at the Conservatoire. She was the first woman to win the Prix de Rome, in 1913, but suffered ill health and died young. Works include incidental music for Maeterlinck's *La Princesse Maleine*.

BOURGAULT-DUCOUDRAY, LOUIS (1840–1910) French composer and music historian. Published operas, orchestral and choral works, and collected and published folk songs.

BOURGET, PAUL (1852–1935) Poet, novelist, and man of letters. One of the first poets whose works interested Debussy and on which he was to draw as texts.

BRUNEAU, ALFRED (1857–1935) Composer celebrated during his lifetime for his naturalistic operas. Collaborated with Zola. Debussy despised both his naturalism and patriotism.

CARRÉ, ALBERT (1852–1938) Director of the Opéra-Comique, where he produced *Pelléas* in 1902.

CHARPENTIER, GUSTAVE (1860–1956) Pupil of Massenet, and composer. In 1902 founded the Conservatoire de Mimi Pinson, providing free musical instruction for working-class girls.

CHAUMET, WILLIAM (1842–1903) Composer of operetta.

CHAUSSON, ERNEST (1855–99) Pupil of Franck and father figure to Debussy for some years. A wealthy and widely cultured patron of the arts, he was probably more important in widening Debussy's knowledge of the arts in general than of music in particular, but he was also a composer of considerable talent. A rift developed between Debussy and Chausson in the years preceding his death.

CHEVILLARD, CAMILLE (1859–1923) Conductor and composer, a pupil of Chabrier. Wrote two operas and symphonic and other music, but made his reputation subsequently as conductor of the Concerts Lamoureux.

CLAPISSON, LOUIS (1808–66) French composer and violinist. Highly successful in the field of light salon music.

COLONNE, EDOUARD (1838–1910) Celebrated French conductor and founder of the Concerts Colonne in 1875. Did much to popularize Debussy's music, and by his preliminary rehearsal contributed to the outstanding success of Debussy's own conducting of *La Mer* at the Concerts Colonne in 1908. Also did much in Paris for Strauss, a composer whom he saw as complementary to Debussy. "It is strange," he confided to Rolland, "how the decadence of two races, the French and the German, is incarnate in two men who represent it, the one with his effeminate refinement, the other with his brutality."

CORTOT, ALFRED (1877–1962) Best remembered as pianist and accompanist but had also pursued a career as conductor, particularly of Wagner's music. Replaced Risler as chorus master at Bayreuth before establishing his reputation as a soloist.

DECOURCELLE, PIERRE (1856–1926) Popular author of novels in serial form and vaudevilles.

DELMET, PAUL (1862–1904) Famous Montmartre *chansonnier* associated with the Chat Noir cabaret, where Debussy, along with Satie, had at one time been a pianist.

DESTOUCHES, ANDRÉ (1672–1749) French composer of operas, ballets, etc., revived by d'Indy.

D'INDY, VINCENT (1851–1931) Originally a pupil of Franck, d'Indy became director of the Schola Cantorum. Prolific but somewhat arid composer who wrote an important *Cours de Composition*.

DUBOIS, THÉODORE (1837–1924) Organist, harmony professor, and composer. According to a memoir of Vallas, he was so impressed by the student Debussy's novel ideas that he attempted to reproduce the effect of chains of added-note chords on the organ of the Madeleine during Sunday vespers.

DUKAS, PAUL (1865–1935) Composer and fellow student of Debussy in Guiraud's class at the Conservatoire. Dukas, as well as being an ambitious composer, was a critic and published some interesting memoirs about Debussy.

DUPARC, HENRI (1848–1933) Pupil of Franck who composed very little. Best remembered for his *Mélodies*. Also secretary to the Société Nationale.

ERLANGER, CAMILLE (1863–1919) Conservatoire-trained French composer and winner of the Prix de Rome. Mahler was responsible for introducing his operas in Vienna.

FANELLI, ERNEST (1860–1917) French composer who studied with Alkan and Delibes. Too poor to pursue his career, he resigned himself to musical hackwork. Several orchestral and chamber works were eventually produced.

FÉNÉON, FÉLIX (1861–1944) French literary critic at first associated with post-impressionism and symbolism. Mainly published in reviews. Editor of *La Revue blanche*.

FÉVRIER, HENRI (1875–1957) French composer, pupil of Massenet and Fauré. Mainly wrote operas and songs.

FLERS, ROBERT DE (1872–1927) French playwright, also literary critic. Wrote several libretti in association with Terrasse.

FRANCK, CÉSAR (1822–90) Belgian composer, organist, and pianist, Franck had been a child prodigy. Settled in Paris in 1844, later becoming organ professor at the Conservatoire. His classes had a considerable influence on many French composers. Although Debussy was for a short time a member of his class, resisting his celebrated exhortations to modulate, he seems to have retained a surprising degree of respect for "Père" Franck.

GAILHARD, PIERRE (1848–1918) Originally establishing a singing career, Gailhard was at various times joint and sole manager of the Paris Opéra.

GARDEN, MARY (1877–1967) Scottish soprano most celebrated for her creation of the role of Mélisande in the première of Debussy's opera.

GODET, ROBERT (1866–1950) Swiss man of letters and also a composer. Lifelong close friend and correspondent of Debussy. Works include an important early study of *Boris Godunov*.

GOUNOD, CHARLES (1818–93) Composer best known for his *Faust*. From 1852–60 he conducted the massed choirs of Paris, known as the Orphéon. In Debussy's student years Gounod helped him both in recommending him for acceptance at the Conservatoire and in finding him some bread-and-butter employment.

GUNSBOURG, RAOUL (1859–1955) Romanian-French impresario. Directed the Monte Carlo opera for fifty years. His first production was his version of Berlioz's *Faust*, first staged in 1893.

HERVÉ (pseudonym of Florimond Ronger) (1825–92) Organist, composer, librettist, and administrator who wrote many operettas and much light music.

HOLMÈS, AUGUSTA (1847–1903) Irish pupil of Franck, also singer and poetess. Mostly wrote operas and nationalistic cantatas.

Franck, Saint-Saëns, and others were all supposed to have been in love with her.

HÜE, GEORGES (1858–1948) French composer and winner of the Prix de Rome in 1879. Succeeded Saint-Saëns as member of the Académie des Beaux-Arts.

KOUSSEVITSKY, SERGE (1874–1951) Russian conductor and double-bass player. Promoted Debussy's orchestral music in Russia.

LAFORGUE, JULES (1860–87) Short-lived but important poet connected with the symbolist movement. Debussy never set his work to music, but his ideas underlie an extraordinary number of Debussy's imaginative conceptions.

LALO, EDOUARD (1823–92) Composer and viola player. Best known for the ballet *Namouna* and the opera *Le Roi d'Ys*.

LALO, PIERRE (1886–1943) Important French music critic closely associated with Ravel and Debussy. It was to Lalo that Ravel wrote to protest after Lalo had ascribed the invention of a new kind of piano writing to Debussy. Ravel claimed that his own *Jeux d'eau* had predated Debussy's innovations. Lalo defended *Pelléas* but disapproved of *La Mer*.

LALOY, LOUIS (1874–1944) French critic and writer on music, author of a biography of Debussy authorized by the composer himself. Debussy at one time frequently held bridge parties with Laloy, and a considerable amount of correspondence between the two men has been preserved.

LENORMAND, RENÉ (1846–1932) Composer and founder of an international society for the collection of popular songs. Author of a treatise on harmony.

LEONCAVALLO, RUGGIERO (1858–1919) Italian composer, principally of opera. *Pagliacci* was his greatest success.

LOUŸS, PIERRE (1870–1925) French poet and novelist, intimate friend of Debussy. His *Chansons de Bilitis* were twice the basis for music by Debussy.

LUIGINI, ALEXANDRE (1850–1906) French violinist, conductor, and composer. In 1897 became conductor of the Opéra-Comique.

MAETERLINCK, MAURICE (1862–1949) Belgian poet, dramatist, and essayist. Perhaps Debussy's attraction to his work stemmed particularly from their mutual interest in Poe and the Pre-Raphaelites.

MARIVAUX, PIERRE (1688–1763) Dramatist and novelist celebrated for amorous and affected comedies.

MASSENET, JULES (1842–1912) Popular and highly successful composer, mainly of operas. Works include *Manon, Werther,* and *Thaïs.* Became a senior professor at the Conservatoire.

MESSAGER, ANDRÉ (1853–1929) French composer and conductor, one-time pupil of Saint-Saëns. Associated with both the Opéra and the Opéra-Comique, he was also on the staff of Covent Garden for some time and helped to encourage the first performance of *Pelléas.*

MENDÈS, CATULLE (1841–1909) French writer who produced prolifically, and married Judith, daughter of Théophile Gautier. Author of the libretto of Debussy's unpublished *Rodrigue et Chimène.*

MEYERBEER, GIACOMO (1791–1864) German opera composer who was the leader of grand opera in France. Influential on Franck.

MISSA, EDMOND (1861–1910) Pupil of Massenet at the Paris Conservatoire. Composer of operas, orchestral and choral works, etc. Winner of the Prix de Rome in 1881.

MOTTL, FELIX (1856–1911) Austrian conductor, who traveled extensively and was particularly associated with Wagner's music.

NIKISCH, ARTUR (1855–1922) Widely celebrated Hungarian-German conductor.

NORDRAAK, RIKARD (1842–66) Norwegian composer and friend of Grieg. Nationalist composer whose works include the Norwegian national anthem.

NOSKOWSKI, ZYGMUNT (1846–1909) Polish composer who studied in Berlin and became professor of composition at the Warsaw Conservatory. Works include operas, ballets, and variations on a Chopin prelude for orchestra.

OFFENBACH, JACQUES (1819–80) German-French composer and conductor. Debussy's teacher Guiraud was responsible for the completion of his *Tales of Hoffmann.* Wrote eighty-nine operettas.

PIERNÉ, GABRIEL (1863–1937) French composer and conductor and pupil of Franck and Massenet. Became conductor of the Concerts Colonne at which in 1910 he conducted the first performance of Debussy's *Ibéria*.

PUGNO, RAOUL (1852–1914) French pianist and composer in Debussy's circle for some time. Became a professor at the Paris Conservatoire.

REYER, ERNEST (1823–1909) French composer strongly influenced by Wagner. Mainly remembered for his opera *Sigurd*.

RICHTER, HANS (1843–1916) Celebrated conductor, especially of Wagner. An assistant at Bayreuth, he conducted the first *Ring* there.

RISLER, EDOUARD (1873–1929) French pianist of German descent. Professor at the Conservatoire, he established a special reputation for his performances of Beethoven.

ROPARTZ, GUY (1864–1955) Pupil of Franck who became director of the Strasbourg and Nancy conservatoires. Composed five symphonies and was especially renowned for his orchestration.

SAINT-SAËNS, CAMILLE (1835–1921) Child-prodigy pianist and composer. The biblical opera *Samson and Delilah,* symphonies, and piano concertos are among his more famous works. Founded the Société Nationale de Musique in 1871.

SAMAZEUILH, GUSTAVE (1877–1967) French composer and critic, pupil of Chausson, d'Indy, and Dukas. His works include a study of Rameau and a collection of memoirs, *Musiciens de mon temps*.

SARDOU, VICTORIEN (1831–1908) French playwright and librettist. Wrote for Offenbach and Saint-Saëns (*Les Barbares*).

SAVARD, AUGUSTIN (1861–1943) A pupil of Massenet and winner of the Prix de Rome in 1886. He was chorus master of the Opéra and subsequently director of the Conservatoire at Lyon. Not to be confused with his father, also Augustin.

SOUSA, JOHN PHILIP (1854–1932) American composer of marches, a bandleader, and a novelist, who published a memoir of his life with the band.

STOJOWSKI, SIGISMOND (1869–1946) Polish pianist and composer.

Teachers included Delibes, Massenet, and Paderewski. Eventually became a professor of piano in New York.

TAINE, HIPPOLYTE (1828–93) Philosopher, critic, and man of letters, extremely important in French nineteenth-century thought. Also an avid Anglophile.

THALBERG, SIGISMOND (1812–71) Austrian pianist and composer, a pupil of Hummel. His piano works achieved great popularity.

VALÉRY, PAUL-AMBROISE (1871–1945) Poet, critic, and essayist, early friend of Gide and Louÿs. *La Soirée avec Monsieur Teste* was one of his earliest successes, and one to which he returned after his fifteen years of "silence" as a civil servant.

VERLAINE, PAUL (1844–96) French poet, bohemian associated with the Parnassians and later the symbolists. Most important from Debussy's point of view were his *Fêtes galantes,* poems whose subject matter was directly drawn from paintings by Watteau and his contemporaries.

VIERNE, LOUIS (1870–1937) Blind French organist and composer, a pupil of Franck and Widor. Became organist of Saint-Sulpice and later of Notre-Dame.

WAGNER, SIEGFRIED (1869–1930) Richard Wagner's son, wrote a dozen or so operas. Gave up a career as an architect to become an assistant at Bayreuth. Established a reputation as a conductor throughout Europe.

WEBBER, AMHERST (1867–1946) Composer, like Debussy a pupil of Guiraud, who later became a conductor at Covent Garden and the Metropolitan Opera in New York.

WEINGARTNER, FELIX (1863–1942) Austrian conductor and composer who studied under Liszt. Composed prolifically and conducted internationally.

WILLY (pseudonym of Henri Gauthier-Villars) (1859–1931) Amussing and often caustic critic, championing several young French composers. Wrote in *L'Echo de Paris* under the pseudonym *L'Ouvreuse* ("the usherette"). First husband of the writer Colette.

WITKOWSKI, GEORGES (1867–1943) A pupil of d'Indy who became the director of the Conservatoire at Lyon. Compositions include operas and several large works for chorus and orchestra.

YSAŸE, EUGÈNE (1858–1931) Violinist, composer, and conductor from celebrated Belgian family of musicians, who toured widely.

Index

A Note About the Editor

François Lesure was born in Paris in 1923. A leading Debussy scholar, he is Chief Music Librarian at the Bibliothèque nationale and President of the Centre de documentation Claude Debussy (Saint-Germain-en-Laye) and is a professor at the University of Brussels. He is also a member of the American Academy of Arts and Sciences and of the Académie Royale de Belgique. M. Lesure is the author of *Musicians and Poets of the French Renaissance* (1956) and *Music and Society* (1968).

A Note About the Translator

Born in London in 1947, Richard Langham Smith was educated at the University of York and the Amsterdam Conservatorium of Music. Since 1972 he has been a Lecturer in Music at the University of Lancaster.

A Note on the Type

The text of this book was set in Intertype Garamond, a modern rendering of the type first cut by Claude Garamond (1510–1561). Garamond was a pupil of Geoffroy Tory and is believed to have based his letters on the Venetian models, although he introduced a number of important differences, and it is to him we owe the letter which we know as old-style. He gave to his letters a certain elegance and a feeling of movement that won for their creator an immediate reputation and the patronage of Francis I of France.

Composed by American Book–Stratford Press, Inc., Brattleboro, Vermont; printed and bound by The Haddon Craftsmen, Inc., Scranton, Pennsylvania.

Designed by Earl Tidwell.